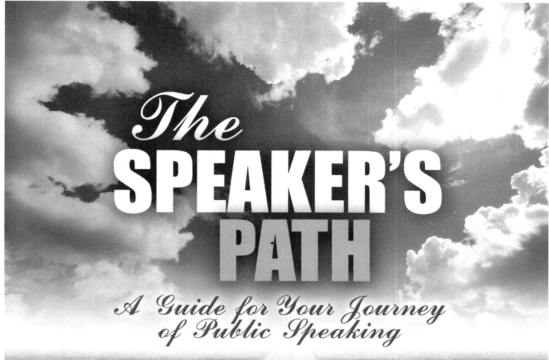

The SPEAKER'S PATH

A Guide for Your Journey of Public Speaking

Meg Laxier Farrell

SECOND EDITION

Kendall Hunt
publishing company

Cover image © Shutterstock, Inc.

Kendall Hunt
publishing company

www.kendallhunt.com
Send all inquiries to:
4050 Westmark Drive
Dubuque, IA 52004-1840

Copyright © 2009, 2012 by Meg Laxier Farrell

ISBN 978-1-4652-0218-5

Printed in the United States of America
10 9 8 7 6 5 4 3 2 1

To Tim

Contents

Acknowledgments

I wish to thank my husband Tim and daughter Mairin above all others, as their love and patience made this work possible. My gratitude also goes to Tim Farrell and Timothy Farrell Sr. for their comprehensive copy-editing, Bill Laxier and Kevin Troxell for their constructive feedback, Marge Laxier and Lynne Farrell for taking care of my daughter so that I could write this work, and my past and present Communication Studies Department colleagues at West Valley College for their support, especially Dr. John Hannigan, Paul Sanders, Randy Fujishin, and Dr. Monica Flores Pactol.

Thank you also to all of my former students and corporate training clients for teaching me about what effective public speakers need in order to succeed.

Last, a special thank you to my mentors over the years, particularly Hedy Fraedrich, who recently passed away.

WALKING THE SPEAKER'S PATH:
The Benefits of Public Speaking

Above all, do not lose your desire to walk. Every day I walk myself into a state of well-being. I have walked myself into my best thoughts . . . if one just keeps on walking, everything will be all right.

—Soren Kierkegaard

Kierkegaard emphasizes not losing a desire to walk, but what about walking a path that leads to public speaking? Let's be honest, desire is not what comes to mind for most people when they think of giving a speech in front of a large group of people. Instead, many people associate public speaking with anxiety, or even outright dread. According to one Gallup Poll, some people even fear public speaking more than death.

The Speaker's Path will help anyone conquer his or her insecurities and anxieties to be able to access the many benefits of being an effective public speaker. Perhaps you aren't so fearful of speech giving, but instead simply want to sharpen your presentation skills. Either way, come take a walk along *The Speaker's Path*.

The metaphor of walking is woven throughout this text. Walking is defined as moving at a moderate rate with at least one foot always on the ground, and that is figuratively what you will be doing as you work toward becoming more skilled at the art of public speaking. You will progress through the many steps of developing, organizing, and delivering informative and persuasive extemporaneous speeches, one step at a time. The methodology of *The Speaker's Path* is designed to keep you grounded and balanced.

Your first step in Chapter One of *The Speaker's Path* is identifying the myriad benefits of public speaking in order to create your desire for public speaking success. Once you recognize why you desire to be a more confident and capable public speaker, your next step is to do all that you can to maintain that desire, even when there are bumps on the trail, precipitous uphill switchbacks to manage, and seemingly insurmountable mountains to climb. Without some desire to succeed on *The Speaker's Path*, you may be facing a windy, steep, solo expedition into unknown territory.

Desire to Succeed

Desire is the natural longing to possess any seeming good, or an eager wish to obtain or enjoy something. It is the burning internal quality that pushes you to be successful. Desire empowers you to meet the challenges of this text, and compels you to fulfill your purpose as a speaker.

In the article *Increase Your Desire to Succeed,* Paul Meyer of *SUCCESS Magazine* highlighted at least three factors that fuel desire for success: anticipating rewards, creating goals, and observing others (Meyer, 2008).

> **Factors That Fuel Desire**
>
> The ability to anticipate rewards, the willingness to set goals, and the capacity to thoughtfully observe others

1. **Anticipating rewards.** Focus on the intrinsic and extrinsic rewards of success, instead of on the sacrifices. Allow these rewards to motivate you to do your best.
2. **Creating Goals**. Set conceivable, achievable and measurable public speaking goals for yourself, write your goals down, and remind yourself of your goals often.
3. **Observing Others.** Take advantage of every opportunity to observe, model, and imitate effective public speakers in your workplace and in your community.

Anticipating Rewards

> *Extrinsic motivations* are external motivations that come from outside the individual.

> *Incentive Theory* is the influence of rewards on behavior.

Successful speakers continually nurture and maintain the kind of desire that will make them effective. This desire becomes a habit, a deliberative course of action. Some people find the rewards that motivate their behaviors to succeed in public speaking are driven by extrinsic motivations or incentives, such as the desire to achieve a high grade in a course, satisfying a university general education requirement, or moving up the ladder within your organization.

Extrinsic motivations are rewards that come from outside a person, such as a raise or an A grade. Common extrinsic motivations are rewards and incentives. A social-psychological theory known as *Incentive Theory* first conceptualized by Sigmund Freud in the early 1900s and later researched by behavioralist B.F. Skinner and others, highlights the influence of rewards on behavior. This theory suggests that people are motivated by a positive reward or goal that is presented or achieved after the occurrence of a behavior, with the intent to cause the behavior to occur again. Thus, positive meaning is associated with the behavior and the behavior is reinforced. For example, a person who receives heartfelt applause for a well-rehearsed speech may want to rehearse his or her second speech equally, if not more. Although Incentive Theory explains how some behaviors are shaped by external stimuli, not all of our behavior is motivated by wanting a reward.

For other people, desire is not about external rewards. Instead, desire is fueled by *intrinsic motivations*, which means for them, the reward of a job well done is satisfying within itself. The person is driven by an interest or enjoyment in the task, or by how a behavior makes them feel. Intrinsic motivation does not mean that a person will not look for external incentive, it simply indicates that extrinsic benefits are not always sufficient to maintain motivation. These people are motivated internally by something less tangible. The rewards are within.

> *Intrinsic motivations* are less tangible as the rewards come from within the individual.

We have reviewed two different types of anticipated rewards that may motivate your success in public speaking, intrinsic and extrinsic. Are you focusing on developing your public speaking skills in order to get a good grade, to meet a graduation requirement, to enhance your career opportunities, to improve your confidence when communicating up in front of large groups of people, or the satisfaction of being able to do a difficult job well?

YOUR VIEW

Consider what factors motivated you to do well in the past. Are you more motivated by intrinsic or extrinsic rewards, or a combination of the two? Give an example.

_____

_____

_____

Creating Goals

Part of your growth and your movement through the steps of public speaking competency will be due to your peers, your textbook, or your manager, coach, consultant, or instructor. Most of your success, however, will be a result of honest evaluation of yourself as a communicator. *Self-reflection* is the capacity that we have to exercise introspection and the willingness to learn more about ourselves. One method of self-reflection is creating goals. You are successful to the extent that the goals that you set are achieved.

To begin, identify your goals about how you plan to evolve as a communicator throughout this text. The following ideas will help you define and establish realistic goals for your public speaking. Setting and achieving worthwhile short and long-term goals will enable you to find the success you desire. Three goal setting guidelines according to renown sales training consultant Bruce Wares who specializes in conducting workshops on achieving measurable results are that goals must be: conceivable, achievable, and measurable (Wares, 1998).

> **Three Goal Setting Guidelines**
>
> Conceivable, Achievable, Measurable

Conceivable

Your goals must be realistic and must be capable of being conceived. You have to be able to imagine, visualize, and comprehend the particulars of the goals you set. By visualizing your success in great detail, you are conditioning your mind and preparing yourself to achieve your desired success in public speaking.

Achievable

You must have the skills and ability to be able to attain your public speaking goals. It is necessary to possess the mental, emotional, and physical capacity to achieve the goals you set. While it is important for your goal to cause you to stretch beyond normal self-imposed limits, if your goals are too challenging to realistically be achieved, unnecessary disappointment may result.

Measurable

You should have clear standards by which you can measure your progress, otherwise, how will you know if your goals have been realized? These standards could include being more confident, having clear structure, being able to support your arguments, and using valid evidence.

YOUR VIEW

What are three conceivable and achievable goals you have for yourself? How will you measure your success at the end of this text?

Goal One:

_____

_____

Goal Two:

_____

_____

Goal Three:

_____

_____

Having short-range and long-range goals when it comes to your public speaking will help you to take a more direct route to success. Remember to reflect back on your goals often, so that your goals are in the forefront of your mind. Moreover, do not forget to revisit your three goals at the completion of this text to see how well you accomplished them

Observing Others

In addition to anticipating rewards and goal-setting, the last factor that *SUCCESS Magazine* believes is paramount to success is observing others who are already experts in the field (Meyer, 2008). This would consist of speech givers that you have watched online, on television, or in person. Some people learn best by observing those who already know what to do. This is an aspect of social learning theory that emphasizes the importance of observing, modeling, and imitating the behaviors, attitudes, and emotional reactions of others as a means of understanding exactly what it takes to be successful.

Social learning theory is a theory proposed by psychologist Albert Bandura that focuses on the learning that occurs within a social context (Bandura, 1977). While rooted in many of the basic concepts of traditional learning theory, social learning theory asserts that learning has a social element, known as observational learning or modeling. In this case, the context or social element would listening to someone give a speech in public.

Bandura (1977) said, "Learning would be exceedingly laborious, not to mention hazardous, if people had to rely solely on the effects of their own actions to inform them what to do. Fortunately, most human behavior is learned observationally through modeling: from observing others one forms an idea of how new behaviors are performed."

According to life coach Andrew Leigh in his article "The Power of Observation", building your observation habit can be surprisingly simple (Leigh, 2007). He advises that you simply make it more like a hobby than an assignment or chore. Take every opportunity possible to observe what

Social learning theory is a theory proposed by psychologist Albert Bandura that focuses on the learning that occurs within a social context.

effective public speakers do and say. Listen to the speaker's words and observe the speaker's actions. Make note of which behaviors and words worked well and which hampered the speaker's success. Last, one of the general principles of social learning theory is that people also learn by witnessing the outcomes of behaviors. One outcome of speech giving, for example, is how the audience responds to the speech and the speaker. Thus, you should also take note of the audience's reactions to the speaker in addition to observing the speaker.

If you want to get the most out of what Leigh calls "enhanced vision," and remember the oral presentations that you see and hear, he also suggests that you utilize a speech observation journal as a tool. You can sharpen your speech spectator skills by noting the positive and negative behaviors of each speaker you witness on your tablet, computer, or in a paper journal. Then review your findings and look for themes to apply to your own speech giving "Once you get into the swing of being more observant you'll probably find an interesting by-product—it's actually great fun" (Leigh, 2007).

YOUR VIEW

To hone your public speaking observation skills, watch a video clip of a recent political debate or public address, such as the State of the Union address. Or, go online and find a famous speech to watch, such as Martin Luther King's "I Have a Dream." Or, observe an outstanding teacher, trainer, professor, or religious leader give a presentation to a large audience. After you observe the speech and the audience, answer the following questions:

Do you think the speaker was highly motivated to do the best job possible? Why or why not? How did the audience react to the speaker? What did the speaker say or do that particularly impressed you? Explain.

_____

_____

_____

_____

Benefits of Public Speaking

In addition to cultivating the three factors of success just discussed, another way to boost desire and your success is to become conversant about the benefits of a course of action. In this case, the course of action is your choice to learn how to be a more proficient public speaker. There are numerous personal, academic, community, cultural, and professional benefits that you can obtain by improving your public speaking skills. Let these advantages fuel your desire to embark on this interesting journey. We will begin with the personal benefits of increased confidence, higher self-esteem and relational satisfaction.

Personal Benefits

One of the most profound benefits of becoming a more effective public speaker is increased confidence—not only in speech giving, but also in all social situations, from dating experiences to selling yourself in job interviews. This public speaking text will help you with different skill sets, build upon your inherent strengths, and develop new aptitudes. You will learn to look inside and explore what matters most to you, and discover how to share this new found knowledge in a way that listeners can appreciate. As a result, you will grow to be a more empowered person. After walking *The Speaker's Path*, you will know what it means to have found your "voice."

> **Benefits of Public Speaking**
>
> Personal, Academic, Professional, Cultural, Community

Self-Esteem

Once you have found your voice, your self-esteem will blossom as you find that you have the ability to influence and enhance the lives of others. *Self-esteem* is defined as having a favorable opinion of yourself. This favorable opinion may enable you to be a more successful public speaker. While it is certainly not always the case, people who think they are effective public speakers often are more likely to be.

Your potential to achieve what you most desire as a public speaker is directly related to your self-esteem; that is, your perception of your own worth and your belief in your abilities. More confidence and the resulting higher self-esteem can positively influence your life as well. Self-acceptance, self-love, a positive self-image, and the freedom to be ourselves, are all crucial aspects of self-esteem.

Nathaniel Braden wrote in *The Six Pillars of Self Esteem* (1994) that the level of our self-esteem has profound consequences on every aspect of our existence—how we operate in the workplace, how we deal with people, how high we are likely to rise, how much we are likely to achieve. He says "healthy self-esteem correlates with rationality, realism, intuitiveness, creativity, independence, flexibility, ability to manage change, willingness to admit (and correct) mistakes, benevolence and cooperation (Braden, 1994)."

Relational Satisfaction

Another personal benefit that may help fuel your desire to become a more effective public speaker is *relational satisfaction*, which describes how content you are in your relationships. Public speaking is a form of

> *Relational satisfaction* is how content you are in your relationships.

communication. Your quest to improve your public speaking skills will also impart you with valuable communication skills that you can apply to your personal relationships.

Levels of Communication

Good communication is key to a healthy and fulfilling marriage, life partnership and lifelong friendship. Learning how to communicate more effectively in the public speaking realm can also increase your relational satisfaction. One way to improve relational satisfaction is to learn how to communicate on a deeper level.

> **Levels of Communication in Relationships**
>
> Superficial, Personal, Validation

In *The Path to Love,* Deepak Chopra asserted that the path to healthy relationships begins with you (Chopra, 1998). This means that you have the power to influence and impact others with your communications According to marriage counselor Diana French in her 2010 article "Essential Skills: Communication, 7 Barriers to Communication that can Cause Divorce", there are three levels of communication in relationships (French, 2010). *Level One: Superficial communication* is on the surface. This simplistic type of communication sounds like "How was your day?" or "What are we doing this weekend?" Level One encompasses between 80 to 90 percent of all communication in relationships. Level Two communication is more personal. *Level Two: Personal communication* involves questions such as, "How are you feeling about your parents?" or "What do you value most?" and makes up about 10 to 20 percent of our communication in relationships. People seldom communicate at the most sincere and heartfelt Level Three, doing so only about 1 to 2 percent of the time. Two examples of affirming and loving *Level Three: Validation* communication are "I appreciate it when you listen to me" and "You are so lovely tonight."

When people who are in a relationship feel less connected and less satisfied, chances are they are communicating at Level One (French, 2010). This text may help you be more comfortable communicating with Levels Two and Three, as you may feel yourself open up more to deeper levels of communication. The deeper your communication with your partner or dear friend, the more relational satisfaction you may feel.

YOUR VIEW

What personal relationship are you currently involved in, perhaps a family member, close friend, or romantic partner, that you think could be made stronger by more effective communication? Explain.

_____

_____

_____

The Languages of Love

The walk on *The Speaker's Path* is an audience-centered approach, which has the premise that the best speeches are those that target the needs and wishes of audience. Communication in personal relationships is similar in that to be effective at it, you need to target your message to the needs and wishes of the other person. Thus, if you boost your desire to be a more effective speaker and become successful at it, you may also be able to transfer the audience analysis skills you learned to your own love relationships.

Each person has his or her own love language, which is a primary way of expressing or interpreting love. Many of us who love another person intensely are not effective communicators of that love because we fail to understand or appreciate the significance of our partner's love language. The more we target our messages to our partner, family member, or friend's love language, the fewer misunderstandings will occur and the more that person will feel appreciated.

According to Gary Chapman in his 1995 book *The Five Languages of Love*, writes that there are *five love languages* that people speak (Chapman, 1995). *Words of affirmation* are verbal compliments or words of appreciation. *Quality time* is giving someone your undivided attention. *Receiving gifts* is a symbol, something you can hold in your hand, that does not necessarily cost money. *Acts of service* are doing things for other people, or serving others. *Physical touch* is a power vehicle of nonverbal expression and includes hugs, holding hands, massages, or sex.

> **Five Love Languages**
>
> Words of Affirmation, Quality Time, Receiving Gifts, Acts of Service, Touch

Chapman says that if you want to express heartfelt commitment to your life partner or genuine love for a dear friend or family member, you must speak in his or her language, or else your message might be misunderstood (Chapman, 1995). In other words, if you express love in a way your partner, family member, or friend does not emphasize, he or she won't fully realize the love you have expressed. Maybe your mother needs to hear encouraging words, but you feel cooking dinner for her will make her feel loved. When she still doesn't feel appreciated, you are puzzled. Or, perhaps you feel under appreciated by a friend who buys you expensive birthday presents, because your love language is quality time, not gifts.

The Five Love Languages model asserts that each of us has a dominant love language. Unfortunately, we often mistakenly assume the people in our lives speak the same language as we do. This text will teach you the audience-centered approach to public speaking, which means you will learn how to read the people you love more accurately and as a result will effectively express your love, and maybe even feel more loved in return.

What is your dominant love language? What are the dominant love languages of the people you cherish? How can you use the awareness of love languages to enhance your relationship with you loved ones?

_____

_____

_____

_____

Academic Benefits

Stimulating your desire to be a more effective public speaker might earn you academic benefits as well. As part of the general education requirements for your Associates or Bachelor's degree, you may be required to take a communication course. While public speaking is not universally mandated due to academic freedom, it may be challenging to find an accredited higher-level institution that does not require you to pass a public speaking/speech/oral communication course in order to get a college degree. Perhaps you have wondered why learning how to speak in public is a requirement for graduation at many colleges and universities.

Oral Communication Requirement

Oral communication skills are a set of abilities enabling individuals to become confident and competent speakers by the time they graduate.

California State University's website *CSU Mentor* asserts that one of the highest priority classes in terms of general education requirements is oral communication. *Oral communication skills* are a set of abilities enabling individuals to become confident and competent speakers by the time they graduate. Oral communication skills equip students to effectively comprehend, critique, and analyze information, to communicate clearly and persuasively, and to express ideas. Oral communication is an essential learning outcome for graduation. After all, what is the value of gaining academic knowledge if you cannot communicate what it is you know?

YOUR VIEW

Why do you think that many universities require students to take a course in public speaking?

_____

_____

_____

Public Speaking for All Majors

Researcher Richard Emanual in a 2005 *The Community College Journal of Research and Practice* article entitled "The Case for Fundamentals of Oral Communication", states "dozens of studies support the fact that communication skills are essential for success in a number of academic areas. Few would argue with the overwhelming amount of research and testimonials that all point to the importance of effective communication (Emanual, 2005)." This article goes on to explain that when 1,000 faculty members from a cross section of disciplines identified basic competences for every college graduate, communication skills topped the list.

Even majors such as accounting require effective communication skills. An article in *Global Perspectives on Accounting Education Journal* in 2007 called "Student Perceptions of Oral Communications Requirements in the Accounting Profession", found that most entry-level students studying accounting perceived the profession as one that requires little oral communication, so they did not understand why this course was mandated. The authors of the study concluded that students' perceptions were mistaken, and that without communication skills, the graduates would be under prepared for an important aspects of the job. They stated in their conclusions, "It appears that the profession needs to focus on accounting as the communication of financial information. Accounting educators in introductory classes should be encouraged to emphasize the importance of oral communication in the accounting profession (Ameen, Jackson, & Malgwi, 2007)."

During a college career, preparing and delivering speeches for individual and team presentations will be common. No matter what your major, chances are that you will be standing in front of an audience many times again after graduation. *The Speaker's Path* will assist you in being more effective when giving those speeches. This text will help you improve your organizational, writing, and research skills in your other classes, in your major, and in your profession.

Critical Listening

Because a component of communication involves listening to speeches that other people give, encouraging your desire to be an effective speaker will also assist you in honing your academic critical listening skills.

Critical listening is an active form of listening that involves analysis, critical thinking, and judgments. It is a rational process of evaluating arguments and statements put forward by others. The ability to listen critically is essential to academic and professional success. When you are listening critically, you are not just thinking passively and accepting everything you hear from your parents, professors, politicians, peers, or managers. Instead, you are asking questions about what you are hearing, by evaluating, categorizing, analyzing assumptions and biases, avoiding emotional reasoning and oversimplification, considering other interpretations, tolerating ambiguity and finding relationships.

Critical listening is a rational process of evaluating arguments and statements put forward by others.

Critical Thinking

A by-product of critical listening is critical thinking, which is making reasoned judgments through metacognition. The *Center for Critical Thinking* defines critical thinking as "thinking that assesses itself". *Critical thinking* is also defined as higher order thinking that questions assumptions.

In the book *Critical Thinking,* B.K. Beyer describes five essential aspects of critical thinking, most if not all of which will be cultivated by researching and developing your own speeches and by attentively analyzing the speeches of others. Beyer identifies the five facets of critical thinking as dispositions, criteria, argument, reasoning, and point of view (Beyer, 1995).

Critical thinking is higher order thinking that questions assumptions, or thinking about thinking.

According to Beyer, *dispositions* means having healthy skepticism, being open-minded, and respecting evidence. *Criteria* are defined as being able to apply different criteria based on credible sources that are free from logical fallacies in reasoning. *Argument* is identifying, evaluating and constructing logical arguments. *Reasoning* is the ability to infer a conclusion by examining relationships among data. *Point of View* is the ability to view phenomena by different points of view in the search for understanding (Beyer, 1995).

Five Facets of Critical Thinking

Dispositions, Criteria, Argument, Reasoning, Point of View

You will be expected to apply these critical listening and critical thinking skills as a university student, member of society, or as a working professional. This text will teach you how to develop and apply critical thinking skills to academic studies and problem solving at work and at home. Let these numerous benefits influence your desire to succeed in public speaking. Remember, the more comprehensively you understand the various factors that will fuel your desire for speech-giving success, the more motivated you will be to accomplish your public speaking goals.

Which of the five facets of critical thinking do you think is most important in public speaking situations? Why?

_____

_____

_____

Professional Benefits

Along with personal and academic benefits already identified, there are professional benefits to becoming a more competent public speaker. Many employers specifically identify communication skills as a job requirement in their job position listings, or they have a strong assumption that the requirement is implicit to doing the job. Skills like conflict management, negotiation, and public speaking are essential to many professions. Yet many people still enter the workforce without much experience in public speaking.

> **Top Personal Qualities Employers Look For**
>
> Oral and written communication skills, strong work ethic, teamwork skills, initiative, analytical skills

Marilyn Macke, executive director of the National Association of Colleges and Employers (NACE), said, "for more than ten years, we've asked employers about key skills, and they have consistently named communications skills as critical, yet have also said that this is something many candidates lack (Macke, 2009)." *NACE's Job Outlook 2009 Survey,* which asked "What are the top personal qualities employers look for in college graduates?", reported the following results as the top five skills:

1. Oral and written communication skills
2. Strong work ethic
3. Teamwork skills
4. Initiative
5. Analytical skills

In addition, How contributor Curt Fletcher said in his article "Skills Needed in a Business," "Attitude, communication and leadership are essential. . . . When you learn to master these three skills, success becomes more attainable and learning new abilities becomes an easy proposition (Fletcher, 2012)." Fletcher's emphasis on communication is not surprising given that roughly 75 percent of all managerial time is spent in a verbal one-to-one exchange. Communication is the common thread throughout every working day.

In the *Journal of Employment Counseling*, a study by Betsy Stevens in 2005 entitled "What Communication Skills Do Employers Want" revealed that a large percentage of the 104 Silicon Valley California employers surveyed stated they were less satisfied with overall communication skills of their new hires and recommended that students receive more training in both oral and written communication skills (Stevens, 2005). This text will provide you with applicable training in these much needed career communication skills.

Securing and Retaining Employment

Effective communication skills can also help you secure and retain your employment. Reports from the Department of Labor's *Secretary's Commission on Achieving the Necessary Skills* show that employers rate communication skills as a top priority for both obtaining and maintaining employment. An analysis of the Department of Labor data regarding future workplace skills determined that communications skills are essential workplace tools and have been correlated with career success and increased pay. It has been long established that college alumni consistently rank communications courses as the most important courses that lead to their advancement and promotions. In almost every profession, the power to communicate in public in an effective manner is the most important skill necessary for securing, retaining and advancing in today's job market.

Motivational speaker Jeff Vankooten echoes this perception in his article "The Importance of Communication in Success." He argues that for people who are already highly effective in their jobs and desire to get promoted to higher positions of leadership within their companies, "it is even all the more important for them to fine tune their communication skills (Vankooten, 2010)." He explains that this is because being able to communicate effectively enables them to connect with other people in various teams within the organization.

YOUR VIEW

Have you or anyone you have known been penalized on the job for communicating ineffectively in meetings or at events, or to co-workers, management, work teams, or clients? What did you learn from this experience about how important effective communication is on the job?

_____

_____

_____

Career Success

Effective oral communication in meetings, email, texting, face-to-face, tele-conferences, video conferences, phone conferences, etc., are always one of the top skills demanded by employers. *The Speaker's Path* will teach you how to think on your feet during your next job interview or salary negotiation session and will help you accurately assess what persuasive strategy to use with your boss the next time you ask her or him for a raise. You can make a major stride in developing your career by fueling your desire to become a more effectual public speaker.

Cultural Benefits

Intercultural benefits may also boost your desire for walking *The Speaker's Path*. Most of us are not as proficient in intercultural communication as we wish we could be, because we are challenged by communicating effectively with people from different cultures. Your choice to improve your public speaking skills may also have the residual effect of improving how you communicate with people from dissimilar cultural backgrounds.

Culture is a term that has many different meanings. However, one aspect that most anthropologists and behavioral scientists seem to agree on is that while culture can include genetic variables such as race and ethnicity, it is not necessarily inherited. Culture is learned. It is the behaviors and beliefs that are characteristic of a particular group. Researchers Larry Samovar and Richard Porter offer a comprehensive definition of *culture* in their text *Communication Between Cultures.* They write that "culture refers to the cumulative deposit of knowledge, experience, beliefs, values, attitudes, meanings hierarchies, religion, notions of time, roles, spatial relationships, concepts of the universe and material objects and possessions acquired by a group of people in the course of generation through individual and group striving (Samovar & Porter, 2003)."

Culture has a major influence on our communication. The two concepts of culture and communication are inextricably linked. As anthropologist and cross cultural researcher Edward T. Hall so clearly summarizes in his renown book *Beyond Culture*: "culture is communication, and communication is culture (Hall, 1976)." Therefore, it is not possible to study communication and public speaking without first recognizing the effects that culture has on our communication with others.

Cultural Competence

Cultural competence refers to an ability to interact effectively with people from different cultures. This text will assist you in honing three important communication characteristics of cultural competence called cultural

> *Culture*
> is the behaviors and beliefs that are characteristic of a particular group

> *Cultural competence*
> is the ability to effectively communicate in different cultural contexts.

knowledge, cultural awareness, and cultural sensitivity, all which lead to cultural competence.

Diane L. Adams, M.D., whose advocacy and innovation has been responsible for numerous research and service programs for minorities, defines *cultural knowledge* as familiarization with selected cultural characteristics, history, values, beliefs systems and behaviors (Adams, 1995). *Cultural awareness* is developing an understanding of a cultural group that is different than your own. *Cultural sensitivity* is being aware that differences as well as similarities exist, without assigning judgments on the similarities and differences.

Because public speaking involves talking with and listening to many types of people who come from different races, belief systems, and cultures, you should become skilled at being more knowledgeable, aware, and sensitive to each of them, making you more culturally competent communicator. As your cultural competence level increases, you will discover how to steer clear of four barriers to effective communication: ethnocentrism, stereotyping, prejudice and discrimination. This will be the case even if you disagree with the values, norms, or rituals of given cultural groups.

> Characteristics of cultural competence: cultural knowledge, cultural awareness, and cultural sensitivity

Barriers to Effective Cultural Communication

> **Barriers**
>
> ethnocentrism, stereotypes, prejudice and discrimination

Ethnocentrism is when a person has the belief that his or other own cultural group is superior to all other groups. Believing that your culture is superior is not bad in and of itself, and indeed most of us have ethnocentric tendencies because we take pride and solace in our own way of viewing the world. But ethnocentrism taken to the extreme becomes a barrier to communication because it prevents people from even trying to see another's point of view. In *Experiencing Intercultural Communication*, Martin and Nakayama argue, "it can be very difficult to see our own ethnocentrism (Martin & Nakayma, 2011)." This is because ethnocentrism often operates below our conscious level.

Speaking and listening to diverse audience members will help you become aware of your ethnocentric tendencies if you have them. You will have the opportunity to learn from other cultures and be more receptive to differing cultural identities. *Cultural identity* is the identity of a group or culture, or of an individual that has been influenced by belonging to a group or culture. Cultural identities serve as a bridge between culture and communication. You have multiple cultural identities, based in part on your gender, age, ethnicity, sexual orientation, politics, physical ability, and even occupational or academic interests.

Oftentimes we judge one another based on cultural identities or cultural affiliation, and this can limit our communication effectiveness if we stereotype others by assuming that all people who share the same cultural identity are in fact the same in all areas. *Stereotypes* are "widely held beliefs about a group of people and are a form of generalization" (Martin & Nakayama, 2011), which is a way that our brains categorize and process information. Like ethnocentrism, stereotypes are not inherently bad, and they often develop out of both negative and positive experiences with other people and other groups.

When these mental shortcuts develop out of negative experiences, such as when we have unpleasant communications with certain people in a cultural group, we may generalize the same disagreeable traits to all people in that particular group. For example, one could stereotype all people of a specific religious identity as being malicious, based on an experience with one small extremist group that operates under the umbrella of that religion. This can result in *prejudice,* which is a negative attitude toward a cultural group or a pre-judgement based on little experience. Or worse, it can result in discrimination, a behavior that stems from prejudicial attitudes and stereotypes. *Discrimination* is the overt action to exclude or avoid all people within the group or culture. Discrimination may range from subtle forms of exclusion like avoiding eye contact, to verbal insults or overt physical violence. It can be interpersonal, collective, or institutional in nature. Prejudice, ethnocentrism, stereotypes, and discrimination can be attitudinal or behavioral barriers to communication (Martin & Nakayama, 2011).

YOUR VIEW

Have you ever been in a situation where ethnocentrism, stereotypes, prejudice, or discrimination made communication more challenging or perhaps prevented effective communication entirely? What communication skills were missing or lacking?

_____

_____

_____

The Speaker's Path will assist you in recognizing and removing these barriers to effective communication so that you become a more competent intercultural communicator. This text will be your guide on how to increase your cultural competence and better comprehend each of the many audiences whom you encounter, regardless of whether you agree with their beliefs, values, culture, or perspectives. As a result, you will be able to exchange more meaningful information across cultural boundaries, in a way that preserves mutual respect.

Community Benefits

Increasing your desire to become more skilled at speaking in public has tangible community benefits for you as well. When you learn to be more effective in communicating in front of large groups, you may also in the process learn to become a more skilled advocate for your community. Beyond work or school, you likely wear many different hats in your community and as such, belong to several different groups. You might be active in religious groups, athletic leagues, parent-teacher associations, student groups, or political groups. Group membership will often make you aware of issues that need addressing. This text will assist you in advocating for your groups and your community as a student, parent, citizen, customer, or taxpayer.

Advocates and Advocacy

advocate
An advocate is someone who speaks on behalf of a person or cause.

Advocacy
is speaking up, pleading the case of another, or fighting a cause.

An *advocate* is defined as someone who speaks on behalf of a person or cause, seeking to influence policy and/or resource allocation within political, economic, or social systems or institutions. *Advocacy* means to speak up and plead the case of another, or to fight a cause. The term is derived from the Latin word advocare, which means coming to the aid of someone.

For centuries, people around the world have studied the art of public speaking as advocacy and used public addresses to inform, influence and persuade others. For example, as far back as fifth century B.C.E., all adult male citizens in Athens had the right to speak out at public assemblies and advocate for proposals relating to civic matters. These large communal assemblies sometimes had thousands of people in attendance.

In *On Rhetoric*, Aristotle argued that public speaking was a special form of reasoning, with the goal of persuading listeners what is best for the civic good (Aristotle & Kennedy, 1991). Armed with strong public speaking skills, anyone can be an advocate. The skills highlighted in this text will provide you with the tools to effectively voice your opinion so that your cause will be heard. Speaking out at town meetings, public events, or religious or organizational meetings can support your advocacy efforts by better informing and educating members of your group or community, attracting attention to an issue or problem, or gaining press coverage. Let these community benefits fuel your desire for public speaking success.

YOUR VIEW

Have you ever felt wronged by, or wanted to promote change in your government, city, town, or your neighborhood? Did you choose to advocate for yourself or your community? If so, what communication skills did you use to influence the outcome?

_____

_____

_____

CHAPTER SUMMARY

This chapter was written to inspire you to develop your competency in public speaking. It began with an identification of desire, arising from extrinsic and intrinsic motivations, as a key component to success in public speaking. Next, the varied academic, personal, professional, cultural, and community benefits of cultivating effective communication skills were emphasized. Along the way, various schema of communication such as the five love languages and cultural competence were introduced. You should now be aware of the countless benefits to creating your desire to become a more effective public speaker.

THE LAY OF THE LAND:
An Introduction to Communication

2

The true charm of pedestrianism does not lie in the walking, or the scenery, but in that talking. The walking is good to time the movement of the tongue by, and to keep the blood stirred and active; the scenery and the woodsy smells are good to bear in upon a man an unconscious and unobtrusive charm and solace to eye and soul and sense, but the supreme pleasure comes from the talk.

—Mark Twain

As Mark Twain wrote, the ultimate satisfaction when enjoying a scenic walk in nature comes from being able to talk to others as you make your way along the path. This chapter will delve into what "talking" means in terms of the field of communication and public speaking, along with other relevant terminology. This chapter will also overview "the lay of the land," the topography of the public speaking landscape, by comparing three communication models and describing the components of the communication process.

Many people interchange the words talking, speech, language, dialect and communication, but these terms are not synonymous. *Talking* is delivering or expressing in speech to exchange ideas via the spoken word. *Speech* is defined as the faculty or act of expressing or describing thoughts, feelings, and perceptions by the articulation of words. Speech refers to the actual grammar, the spoken utterance, the pronunciation of sounds. *Language* is the communication of messages through a system of arbitrary verbal and nonverbal symbols. Such a system is used by a nation, people, or other distinct community. Language can encompass the actual words and grammar like speech, or it can encompass nonverbal behaviors such as eye contact, posture, clothing, and vocal pitch. Languages, as in American Sign Language, do not always involve talking. A regional or social variety of language distinguished by pronunciation, grammar, or vocabulary, is considered a *dialect*.

Communication encompasses talking, speech, language, and dialect, but it is more than even that. The term has several different definitions. In fact, if you were to interview ten scholars in the field of Communication, it is likely that you will learn a different definition from each of the ten. For the purposes of this text, we will use the most basic definition.

Communication is the ability to share thoughts and experiences, while at the same time taking in, processing, and responding to the person(s) you are communicating with. This means we can send and receive messages synchronously. In public speaking, we are communicating as a speaker, and we are also communicating as a listener. We play the role of speaker and listener at the same time, interchangeably.

> *Communication* is the sending and receiving of messages.

Models of Communication

> **The Three Models of Communication**
>
> Linear, Interaction, and Transaction

In the early days of studying communication, social science researchers created models to illustrate the communication process. The first attempt resulted in the Linear Communication model, which depicts communication as something the sender does to the receiver. This research was followed by the Interaction Model, and finally, the Transaction Model, which updates and expands the previous models to better capture communication as a human process.

Some of these models are still taught today, despite some identified weaknesses. This can be regarded as an indicator of the value of these models in highlighting key elements of the communication process.

Linear Model

> *Linear Model*
> The linear model views the transfer of information as an act being done to the receiver by the sender.

Claude Shannon, an engineer for the Bell Telephone Company, first created the linear model, which was the most influential of all early communication models. His goal was to formulate a theory to guide engineers in finding the most efficient way of transmitting electrical signals from one location to another (Shannon and Weaver, 1949). Later, Shannon added the receiver or listener mechanism to this linear model.

The linear model visualizes the transfer of information as an act being done to the receiver by the sender. It is also known as the Action Model. In the linear model of communication, communication is a one-way static event whereby a sender sends a message to the listener, and the listener receives it. This model assumes that each audience member receives the exact same message from the speaker despite various backgrounds, culture, frame of reference, etc. A metaphor for the linear model is the syringe, as in when each patient receives the same flu vaccine shot (Supple, Gruber, & Reid, 2010).

The linear model works well for electronic media like television or the Internet because of its one way nature, but it does not make sense for human communication because our conversations with others are rarely one way. The entire nature of a conversation is to exchange observations, feelings, opinions, and ideas, at the same time. The linear model fails to address the possibility that we can speak and listen synchronously, and that listener and speaker both play an active role in the process of communication.

Interaction Model

The *Interaction Model* takes the linear model a step further, by acknowledging that both speaker and listener affect the communication process. Wilbur Schramm (1954) was the first to truly alter the mathematical model of Shannon and Weaver. He made provisions for a two-way interchange of messages, not just a one way. He indicated that the linear model should also examine the impact that a message has, both the desired and undesired, on the receiver. The interaction model is still linear in nature, however. This model focuses on the back-and-forth nature of communication, much like how players alternate turns in the game of chess. First we play the role of speaker, and then we play the role of listener, one role at a time, but never both roles at the same time. One person speaks and rests, and then the other person speaks and rests. This model does not address the concept that participants can be both speaker and listener simultaneously.

Interaction Model

The interaction model is a linear model that focuses on the back-and-forth nature of communication.

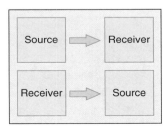

Transaction Model

While most scholars today still rely on these previous linear models for context, the majority of today's researchers and communications professors no longer view communication as a linear, one-way transmission of messages as in the linear model, or the back-and-forth, one role at a time, interaction model; because these models fail to see communication as a dynamic transaction.

In light of the weaknesses of the aforementioned linear models, Barnlund (2008) moved away from the linear view in its entirety and proposed a transactional model of communication. A *transaction* is a communication exchange in which all participants continuously send and receive messages simultaneously.

In the transaction model, the elements of communication are seen an interdependent, like the ingredients in a marinara sauce. The herbs, meat, tomatoes, and olive oil simmered together form the sauce's unique flavor. Any change in one element—garlic for basil, for example—changes the flavor of recipe. In communication, any change in a component of the model might change the outcome or event. For example, if you are talking with friends after work, and your manager comes up to your group and listens to your conversation, this change in audience will lead to changes in overall communication. Perhaps you will change what you say or how you say it when your manager is in earshot.

The *Transaction Model* acknowledges that public speakers both create and consume messages concurrently, or at the same time. This model posits that while a listener is receiving, the listener is also sending.

Transaction Model is a nonlinear model that views communication as dynamic and continuous.

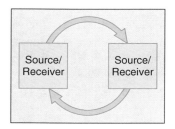

Communication Is Dynamic

In the transactional model, every behavior or word is a kind of communication. Even if someone tries not to communicate, there is always some element of communication going on. Sitting quietly in silence is a form of communication, just as powerful oftentimes as a loud, verbal, outburst. This means that we are communicating even when we do not intend to send a message to someone or when the message is misunderstood.

Communication is a dynamic, continuous process. The old axiom first theorized by Austrian American psychologist and communication theorist Paul Walzlawick states that "one cannot not communicate (Watzlawick, Beavin-Bavelas, & Jackson, 1967)." Human beings constantly communicate. Walzlawick asserted that since behavior does not have a counterpart (there is no such thing as anti-behavior), it is not possible to cease behaving, or to stop communicating. His perceptions about the process of communication are still echoed by modern researchers today.

Communication Process

There are seven components of the process of communication.

Seven Components of the Communication Process

Sender, Receiver, Message, Channel, Context, Feedback, and Noise

Sender

The *sender* is the speaker, the originator or creator of the message. In other views of communication, the sender might also be called the source of communication. The communication process begins with the source or sender. The sender encodes meaning, which can be sent intentionally or unintentionally to the receiver. This means that sometimes a sender encodes a message they do not mean to transmit. *Encoding* is defined as converting ideas or emotions into a code, a verbal or nonverbal language pattern, so as to transmit meaning to the receiver.

sender
is the speaker, the originator or creator of the message.

Encoding
is converting ideas or emotions into a verbal or nonverbal language pattern or code.

Communication Style

The sender's communication style impacts how messages are encoded and sent, thus the transactional nature of the communication process. *Communication style* is defined as the method by which you communicate, largely based on your culture, personality, gender, and experiences. Communication style combines verbal and nonverbal elements. It refers to the way people use verbal and nonverbal language to send messages. The four distinct dimensions of communication style are indirect/direct, doing/being, high context/low context, and elaborate/understated.

Direct/Indirect Styles

A speaker who employs a *direct style* views being indirect as being dishonest and passive and instead will speak directly and honestly, even if what is being spoken is offensive or hurtful. For this person, it is more important to state the truth clearly than to keep harmony (Martin & Nakayama, 2011). The direct style communicator emphasizes specific words and the spoken word when communicating. Most English speakers in the United States view the direct style as most appropriate in most contexts. Although white lies may be permitted in some situations, the preference for honesty and forthrightness, especially in business, is valued.

Four Communication Styles

Direct/Indirect, Doing/Being, Elaborate/Understated, and High/Low Context

Communication style
is the method by which you communicate, largely based on your culture, personality, gender, and experiences.

direct style
will speak directly and honestly, even if what is being spoken is offensive or hurtful.

indirect style
emphasizes politeness and maintaining harmony above being truthful.

Doing-style
speakers pay closer attention to deadlines and the timing of the speech.

Being style
is more flexible and relationship focused, and is less worried about time constraints.

Low-context style
places the most emphasis on the explicit written or spoken word rather than in the more implicit nonverbal.

By contrast, some cultural groups in the United States and around the world prefer a more indirect style. A speaker who communicates with the *indirect style* emphasizes politeness and maintaining harmony above being truthful (Martin & Nakayama, 2011). For this speaker, it is more important to "save face," make people feel good, and not hurt feelings. This person will forgo being brutally honest in order to not offend. This person is sensitive to the well-being of others and looks for a "softer" way to communicate. Indirect style communicators often choose to leave it up to the listener to fill in the blanks and decode the meaning of the message by reading contextual cues.

Doing/Being

Doing-style senders believe people are supposed to have personal opinions, but are not expected to necessarily verbalize them. Doing style is eager to get to the point. These senders are concerned about deadlines, and due to their hectic schedules, only the details directly related to the topic will make it into the conversation. They believe in "less is more." Since great emphasis in the doing style is placed on deadlines, doing-style speakers pay closer attention to the timing of the speech. Many English speakers in the United States favor the doing-style approach.

However, there are still millions of people in the world who favor the opposite approach. *Being-style* communicators would rather spend some time getting to know the listener or audience and will talk about personal things before getting to the point. They need more details in order to fully understand an issue enough to be comfortable talking about it. Being-style speakers spend much time on details, introductions, and conclusions. Being style values relationship. This style is more flexible and less worried about time constraints.

High/Low Context

The terms high and low context were originally presented by anthropologist Edward T. Hall in his book *Beyond Culture* (Hall, 1976). These terms refer to a person or culture's tendency to encode messages in different ways. *Low-context style* places the most emphasis on the explicit written or spoken word rather than in the more implicit nonverbal. Things are rarely left unsaid in this type of communication. A low-context sender places the majority of the meaning encoded into the verbal message, or into the explicit words. For example, if a low-context communicator was negotiating for a new car loan from a car dealer, he or she would most likely ask for all of the details for the loan in writing. Many people in the United States consider themselves to be low-context in communications.

The straightforward and verbal low-context style can be disagreeable to communicators who prefer a high-context style. A high-context sender, according to Hall (1976), is one in which "most of the information is either in the physical context or internalized in the person." *High-context style* is when contextual and nonverbal cues are attended to and highly valued and people read between the lines instead of concentrating primarily on the spoken word. High-context communicators are observant and pick up on conversation cues and subtly implied meanings that other people miss. A high-context communicator might seal a new car negotiation session with a handshake or a meal.

Elaborate/Understated

This dimension refers to the quantity of talk that people value and attitudes toward speaking and silence. People who communicate with the *elaborate style* use rich, expressive, emotive language to communicate messages (Martin & Nakayama, 2011). For elaborate-style senders, simple, assertive, pithy, statements mean little and are perhaps even considered insincere. This style believes it is best to expose emotions authentically and in opulent detail so that no misunderstandings occur. For this person, emotion cannot be separated from logic. He believes that communicating emotion means communicating respect.

By contrast, the *understated style* discourages emotional displays and values restraint and simplicity. For this person, staying logical, emotionally calm, and focused on factual evidence communicates respect. This person may remove herself from a conflict if emotions get too high, perhaps by taking a walk to cool off. The understated-style sender does not value free self-expression and believes that "if you can't say anything nice, then don't say anything at all." This style believes that sometimes it is best to not over-disclose. These emotionally reserved senders are comfortable with silence and believe it to be especially appropriate in ambiguous situations.

High-context style is when contextual and nonverbal cues are attended to and highly valued.

elaborate style use rich, expressive, emotive language to communicate messages.

understated style discourages emotional displays and values restraint and simplicity.

YOUR VIEW

Are you more direct or indirect, doing or being, high- or low-context, elaborate or understated? What feedback have you received that enabled you to make such an assessment? How does your style influence how you send and encode messages?

Receiver

Expressing our wants, feelings, thoughts, and opinions clearly and effectively is only part of the communication process. The other half is listening to what others communicate to us. The listener or the audience is also known as the *receiver*. The receiver is the recipient of the message. The receiver decodes the message the sender sends. *Decoding* is when the receiver assigns meaning to a message by translating or reconstructing ideas or emotions received from the sender from one format into another so that understanding can occur. Understanding is when you learn what a speaker means.

Decoding or listening is an important component of the communication process, yet many people are not skilled at listening. Listening is difficult for many of us in part because of inevitable differences in values between speakers and listeners. Because each person has a unique set of experiences, each person's meaning system is going to be different. When speakers or listeners come from different cultures or are of different genders, these differences are often magnified.

Frame of Reference

Our culture, gender, personality, and previous experiences influence how we translate and reconstruct messages, even though we are often not aware of these influences. To use the analogy of an iceberg, our observation of overt sender behaviors such as the sender's nodding or smiling, is the 20 percent that is visible above the surface. The criteria that determine how we process the information we listen to in our minds is the other 80 percent of the iceberg that is hidden below the surface. We translate what we listen to in part based on our frame of reference. *Frame of reference* is your individual world view based on your culture, gender, beliefs, experiences, and values. Your frame of reference is your listening lens; it is how you see the world, and how you interpret messages that you receive.

This value statement self-quiz is designed to help you explore the possible influence of your frame of reference on your communication.

---

receiver
is the listener, the recipient of the message.

Decoding
is when the receiver assigns meaning to a message that was transmitted.

Frame of reference
is your individual worldview based on your culture, gender, beliefs, experiences, and values.

Frame of Reference Self-Quiz

Directions: Below are seven values that may form part of your frame of reference. For each value, indicate your own values on a scale of 1 to 3. The overall value is in the center. A "1" means you agree most with the statement about the value on the left, a "3" means you most agree with the statement about the value on the right, and a "2" means that you weigh in somewhere between the two value statements. What do you value?

	Competition	
It does not matter if you win or lose, it is how you play the game.	1 2 3	It is important to win at all costs. Winning is everything.

	Capitalism	
People should be free to operate or manage their property for profit.	1 2 3	The community or collective should distribute profit evenly.

	Equal Access	
We are all treated equally; there is no such thing as privilege.	1 2 3	Some people receive more privileges than other people.

	Theism	
God's existence can never be proven or confirmed.	1 2 3	God exists. God will guide and intervene when called to.

	Obligation	
Your first obligation is to your family and dear friends.	1 2 3	Your first obligation should always be to yourself.

	Time	
Learn from the past and work hard now to create a better future.	1 2 3	Live in the present. Do not worry about the past or future.

	Gender Roles	
Men and women are equal and should be treated as such.	1 2 3	Men and women have clear gender roles to which to adhere.

	Government	
Government in which one person possesses unlimited power.	1 2 3	Government by the people or their elected representatives.

Review the list of value statements above and identify one specific way that your values and frame of reference may influence how you receive messages.

_____

_____

_____

Message

Message
is meaning or
content; can
be verbal or
nonverbal.

The *message* is meaning or content and includes ideas and feelings, expressed verbally or nonverbally through signs and symbols. There are two different types of messages, verbal and nonverbal.

**Two
Different Types
of Messages**

Verbal and
Nonverbal

Verbal Messages

The term *verbal communication* is often misunderstood. Verbal communication is not a synonym for oral or spoken communication. Just because it comes out of your mouth does not make it verbal. For example, vocal sounds like a grunts or "ums" are not considered to be verbal, because they are not actual words, even those these sounds originate in the mouth. Vocal pitch and volume are also not verbal messages. *Verbal messages* are spoken and written words. Sign languages and types of written communication such as texting or emailing are generally understood as forms of verbal communication, as both make use of words.

Verbal messages
are spoken and/or
written words.

While many animals communicate, verbal language differentiates humans and makes us unique from all creatures. By talking to another person, you are sending verbal messages. Verbal messages are based on formal rules for word and grammar use and more subtle informal rules such as knowing which words are appropriate in certain situations or with certain cultural groups. There are over 6,000 languages currently being spoken in the world today (Martin and Nakayama, 2011), and each language has its own set of rules. With so many rules, many of them unspoken, it is easy to see how miscommunication can occur.

Linguistics

linguistics
is the study of
verbal messages.

The study of verbal messages is called *linguistics* Linguistics usually divides this study into four parts: phonology, syntactics, semantics, and pragmatics.

Phonology is the study of the sound system of language, including how words are pronounced (Martin & Nakayama, 2011). Because different languages often use different sounds, it is typically quite challenging for non-native speakers to learn how to pronounce different words. For example, the Vietnamese language has six tonal differences. This means that one word could have six different meanings based on how the word is tonally pronounced.

Semantics is the study of the meaning of specific words and phrases and how words and phrases communicate the meaning we are trying to get across. For example, in Great Britain, a sweater is a jersey, pants are trousers, and pumps are tennis shoes.

Syntactics is the study of the structure of language, the rules for combining words into meaningful sentences (Martin & Nakayama, 2011). Each language has particular rules concerning the structure and expression of subject-verb-object arrangement, gender forms, and possessives. For example, in Spanish, the subject is placed at the end of the sentence instead of at the beginning.

Last, *pragmatics* is the study of the practical use of language. Pragmatics goes beyond structure, grammar, and punctuation to what it means when groups of words are strung together. For example, if someone says "that other shirt looks much better on you" you might interpret it in different ways depending on how the speaker said it, your relationship with the speaker, or how you are feeling that day.

> **Four Components of Linguistics**
>
> Phonology, Semantics, Syntactics, and Pragatics

Nonverbal Messages

Both verbal and nonverbal messages and language patterns are symbolic, both communicate meaning, and both are patterned and rule governed. Just as different cultures and groups have different verbal languages, so do they also have different nonverbal communication patterns. Researcher Paul Ekman in his book *Handbook of Cognition and Emotion* (1999) has posited that while there are six universal nonverbal facial expressions (happiness, sadness, surprise, disgust, fear, and anger), there is no universal nonverbal gesture (Ekman, 1999). Gestures and other nonverbal messages mean different things to different people in different places. For example, in Brazil the OK sign is considered obscene, in Kenya pointing with your index finger is also considered very insulting, and in Samoa it is rude for a person standing to sway while having a conversation.

Nonverbal messages are defined as everything but the words and are said to encompass more than 80 percent of the meaning behind a message (Mehrabian, 1981). Nonverbal communication is comprised of facial expressions, body movements and posture, gestures, eye contact, touch, space, voice, scent, and other realms of wordless expression. Nonverbal communication is generally understood as the process of communicating

Nonverbal messages are everything but the words.

wordless messages. Nonverbal communication, oftentimes called body language, is a vital form of communication. When we interact with others, we constantly give and receive countless wordless signs and symbols. All of our nonverbal behaviors—the gestures we make, the way we sit, how walk, how loud we talk, the smell we emit, how close we stand, the eye contact we give, the clothes we wear, the tone of our voice—send strong messages, even if we do not intend to send them.

According to Albert Mehrabian in his often quoted study from *Silent Message: Implicit Communication of Emotions and Attitudes* (1981), we spend a considerable amount of time in nonverbal communication. He found that as much as 93 percent of the meaning transmitted in a message is nonverbal. His research indicated the following: 38 percent of the meaning of the message is vocal, based on voice; 55 percent of the meaning of the message is expressed via facial expression; and only 7 percent is expressed verbally (Mehrabian, 1981).

Further, Anthropologist Ray Birdwhistell's study (1975) found that 60 to 70 percent of what we communicate to one another is nonverbal. While most researchers looking at the impact of nonverbal communication suggest that his figures are rather high, at the same time it is accepted in the field that nonverbal communication has a high impact on the meaning of a message.

Types of Nonverbal Messages

Nonverbal communication is communication through means other than verbal language. There is usually a nonverbal element to verbal messages, but not necessarily a verbal element to nonverbal messages. If you email someone a message in all capital letters, while all the words you type in are verbal, the all caps, signifying yelling, is considered to be nonverbal.

Nonverbal communication cues can play three major roles: complementing, contradiction, and substitution according to various researchers in the field of communication.

> **Roles of Nonverbal Communication**
>
> Complement, Contradict, or Substitute

Nonverbal messages *complement* or amplify verbal messages. They can repeat the message a person is sending verbally or add to or complement the verbal message. This repetition usually gives the verbal message more emphasis. For example, frantically waving goodbye and blowing a kiss will give a simple statement of "goodbye" more meaning.

Nonverbal messages can *contradict* a verbal message a person is trying to convey. That is, someone's words may say one thing, but his body something entirely different. Generally, if there is a discrepancy between the verbal and the nonverbal message and a contradiction occurs, what a speaker says versus what a speakers does, the receiver of the message will tend to pay more attention to, and believe, the nonverbal component of the message.

The receiver may not know consciously why they do, and perhaps attribute it to a "hunch," intuition, or a feeling that something just isn't right.

Nonverbal messages can *substitute* or take the place of verbal messages, sometimes with a more pronounced effect. For example, a person's eyes can often convey a far more vivid message that words do. If you have ever been at a social event, found a romantic interest, and tried to get this person's attention from across the room with your eyes, you know what this is referring to.

YOUR VIEW

Become aware of your own communication by concentrating on your verbal and nonverbal communication with someone close to you. Think about the messages you are sending and receiving. Are you sending the messages you wish to send?

_____

_____

_____

Sender Phenomenon and Recipient Phenomenon

The curious philosophical debate over what constitutes communication relates back to the old riddle, if a tree falls down in the forest and no one hears it fall or observes it falling, did the tree really fall down? Does someone need to have received the message of the tree falling by witnessing the actual fall for the fall to have occurred?

Some researchers would say that the tree fell even if no one witnessed the falling, and that communication takes place regardless of whether the message was received. These researchers believe that communication has occurred once a verbal or nonverbal message has been encoded by a sender. This is called the *sender phenomenon*. Whether the sender's message was ever received is beside the point. If the sender attempted to send the message, it is communication. For the sender, it is all about intention.

Other researchers believe that in order for communication to have occurred, the message must be received and decoded. For example, if someone sent an email and it got stuck in the recipient's spam filter and no one ever read it, they would assert that communication did not occur. This view is called the *recipient phenomenon*. These researchers believe that communication is two-way, that a message must be transmitted and decoded in order for communication to have transpired.

Channel

The *channel* is the bridge that connects the sender and receiver. It is also known as the medium or venue. The channel is how ideas are transferred from sender to receiver. The channel is also considered the medium of communication. Channels include PowerPoint, your smartphone, the whiteboard, and video clips.

Learning Styles and Multiple Intelligences

Effective public speakers should use multiple channels for delivering speeches to accommodate the differing learning styles and types of multiple intelligences of audience members. *Learning styles* are various approaches to ways of learning. *Multiple intelligences* are, according to developmental psychologist Howard Gardner's Multiple Intelligence Theory (1993), different ways to demonstrate intellectual ability.

Gardner asserts in his text "*Intelligence Reframed: Multiple Intelligences for the 21ˢᵗ Century*" that all human beings possess all intelligences in different amounts, and we can improve our communication with others if we address the multiple intelligences of our audience members (Gardener, 1993 and Gardener, 1999). Some of these styles and intelligences include visual, auditory, kinesthetic, logical, musical, and relational. Speakers should use a wide variety of media to communicate a message during a speech because audience members have different learning styles and various types of intelligences (Armstrong, 1994). These learners are said to therefore learn most effectively through distinctive channels. This next section will review six various types of channels as conceptualized by Gardener (1999), Armstrong (1994), and others.

Visual/Spatial channel audience members learn through seeing. These listeners need to directly observe the speaker's body language and facial expressions in order to fully understand the content of the message. Visual learners tend to think in pictures and need to observe in order to understand. They tend to score high on visual/spatial intelligence spectrums. Their skills include having a good sense of direction, drawing, manipulating images, and interpreting visual images. The most effective way to communicate with a visual learner is to include visual displays in your message to include diagrams, PowerPoint slides, multimedia presentations, and videos, because they think in pictures.

Auditory/Linguistic channel audience members learn through listening to words and how the words are spoken. They interpret the underlying meaning of messages through listening to tone of voice, vocal pitch, and rate of speaking. For them, written information may have less meaning until it is heard. They absorb the most content from messages by listening to what a speaker says and then talking it through. Because auditory learners have highly developed auditory skills and tend to think in words rather than pictures, their skills include storytelling, understanding syntax and meaning, and analyzing use of language. The best way to reach an auditory audience member is by using effective and descriptive language.

Tactile/Kinesthetic channel audience members learn by doing, moving, and touching. These learners favor the hands-on approach and prefer to actively explore the world around them. People who favor this channel express themselves through movement. They learn by doing. Their skills include using and reading body language, acting, and expressing emotions through the body. They are able to process the message and remember the content of what was transmitted by getting involved in the process. The most effective way to transmit a message to a kinesthetic listener is to use appropriate body language or get them moving around.

Logical/Mathematic channel audience members learn through reason, logic, and numbers. These learners think linearly in logical and numerical patterns. They enjoy statistics, charts, graphs, and geometrical patterns, because they like to draw connections between pieces of information. Their skills include classifying and categorizing information, performing mathematical calculations, working with abstract concepts to figure out relationships, and working with geometric shapes. The best channel to reach a logical listener is through the medium of numbers and logic by providing statistics and sound reasoning in the message.

Musical/Rhythmic channel audience members learn by listening to sounds, rhythms, and patterns. These learners are sensitive to environmental sounds and music. Their skills include playing musical instruments, remembering melodies, and understanding the structure of music. The best way to communicate with a musical or rhythmic listener is to through the medium of sound by adding video or sounds clips into your message.

Relational channel audience members learn by relating to and understanding self and others. These interpersonal- and intrapersonal-based learners see things from their own and others perspectives. *Interpersonal* is defined as communication between people. *Intrapersonal* is defined as communication with ourselves, in our minds.

Relational listeners are sensitive to how others feel and are highly capable of detecting overt and hidden emotions. They also have the ability to be self-reflective, which is the ability to reflect of their own inner feelings, dreams, relationships with others, strengths, and weaknesses. Their skills include noticing people's moods, establishing positive relationships with others, understanding their role in relationships with others, and peacefully resolving conflicts. Since they use both verbal and nonverbal channels to communicate with others, the best channel for a relational listener is to appeal to emotions and communicate authentic feeling.

Preferred Channel Self-Quiz

Your View

What is your preferred channel for communication? This quiz, adapted from Statewide Parent Advocacy Network "Multiple Intelligences Worksheets", will tell you where you stand. Read each statement. If it expresses some characteristic of yours and sounds true for the most part, write a "T" for "True." If it doesn't, mark an "F" for "False." If the statement is sometimes true, sometimes false, leave it blank.

1. _____ I would rather draw a map than give someone verbal directions.
2. _____ I can play (or used to play) a musical instrument.
3. _____ I can associate music with my moods.
4. _____ I can add or multiply in my head.
5. _____ I like to work with calculators and computers.
6. _____ I pick up new dance steps fast.
7. _____ It is easy for me to say what I think in an argument or debate.
8. _____ I enjoy a good lecture, speech or sermon.
9. _____ I always know north from south no matter where I am.
10. _____ Life seems empty without music.
11. _____ I always understand the directions that come with new technology or appliances.
12. _____ I like to work puzzles and play games.
13. _____ Learning to ride a bike (or snowboard or roller blade) was easy.
14. _____ I am irritated when I hear an argument or statement that sounds illogical.
15. _____ My sense of balance and coordination is good.
16. _____ I often see patterns and relationships between numbers faster and easier than others.
17. _____ I enjoy building models or sculpting.
18. _____ I'm good at finding the fine points of word meanings.
19. _____ I can look at an object one way and see it sideways or backwards just as easily.
20. _____ I often connect a piece of music with some event in my life.
21. _____ I like to work with numbers and figures.
22. _____ Just looking at shapes of buildings and structures is pleasurable to me.
23. _____ I like to hum, whistle and sing in the shower or when I'm alone.
24. _____ I'm good at athletics.
25. _____ I'd like to study the structure and logic of languages.
26. _____ I'm usually aware of the expression on my face.

27. _____ I'm sensitive to the expressions on other people's faces.
28. _____ I stay "in touch" with my moods. I have no trouble identifying them.
29. _____ I am sensitive to the moods of others.
30. _____ I have a good sense of what others think of me.

Next, place a check mark by each item you marked as "true." Add your totals. A total of four in any of the categories indicates strong ability

Auditory	Logical	Musical	Visual	Kinesthetic	Relational
7 ____	4 ____	2 ____	1 ____	6 ____	26 ____
8 ____	5 ____	3 ____	9 ____	13 ____	27 ____
14 ____	12 ____	10 ____	11 ____	15 ____	28 ____
18 ____	16 ____	20 ____	19 ____	17 ____	28 ____
25 ____	21 ____	23 ____	22 ____	24 ____	30 ____

Totals: ____ ____ ____ ____ ____ ____

YOUR VIEW

How does your preferred channel influence how you send and receive messages?

_____

_____

_____

Context

Context
is the situation,
climate,
environment, or
the place where
communication
occurs.

Context is the situation, climate, environment or the place where communication occurs, including how that space is used, valued, and perceived. The context affects how speakers create messages, and how listeners create meaning. A more subtle aspect of context is the concept of place. *Place* is defined as an area with definite or indefinite boundaries, or a portion of space. The physical context or space that communication occurs in can impact the process of communication. Lawrence Durrell of Importanceofplace.com, a website devoted to exploring why physical environment is so vital to humans, writes in his article "We Are the Children of Our Landscape" (2009), "We are the children of our landscape; it dictates behavior and even thought in the measure to which we are responsive to it."

Context Dimensions

The concept of context and place in speech-giving has at least five dimensions according to communication scholar Joseph Devito (2005) and other researchers: physical, cultural, social-psychological, temporal, and situational.

Five Dimensions of Climate:

Physical, Cultural, Social-Psychological, Temporal, and Situational

The room, workplace, or outdoor space that communication occurs in is called the *physical dimension*. The physical dimension includes the lighting, temperature, and arrangement of chairs, decor, and the degree of natural light in the room.

The *cultural dimension* consists of the rules, norms, and beliefs of a group of people that is passed along from one generation to another. It is not possible to communicate without the cultural dimension.

The *social-psychological dimension* can include personality characteristics and social factors like status, relationships, power, formality, friendliness, or competitiveness.

The *temporal dimension* has to do with where a particular message fits into a time sequence, for example, whether the message was delivered before or after a conflicting message. This dimension also encompasses the time the message is given, be it early morning or late in the afternoon.

The *situational dimension* deals with audience size, audience demographics, or the occasion of your speech. All of these dimensions need to be taken into consideration when communicating.

Communication Climate

While context and place in speech-giving are often invisible or inperceptible, sometimes a more observable change in climate can affect the process and outcome of communication between individuals and groups and within organizations. For example, in many organizations, an open, transparent communication climate tends to increase productivity, allow for higher profit margins, and foster job satisfaction. This is primarily because employees, customers, and stakeholders know what is expected of them. When people know what is expected of them, they feel more empowered and will often rise to the occasion. Transparent procedures include open meetings, financial disclosure statements, and budgetary review. When an organization implements these types of procedures, it will change the climate of the organization and as such, can produce a profound shift within a group. Effective public speakers do not underestimate how a change in climate, context, and place can alter relationships, perception, and the outcome of communication.

YOUR VIEW ───

Consider communication context, climate, and/or place. What is an example of when context, climate and/or place influenced a recent communication had with someone?

_____

_____

_____

Feedback

Feedback is a response to a message. It is letting the speaker know that she has been heard and understood. Feedback is an excellent source of learning for both the speaker and the listener because it helps us become more aware of what we do when we are communicating, how we are communicating, and the consequences that result from communicating effectively or ineffectively. Feedback makes communication both meaningful and continuous.

Feedback is an immediate or delayed response to a message.

In the process of communication, the sender first communicates the message and encodes thoughts, ideas, and feelings to the received. Once the receiver decodes the message, the immediate or delayed verbal or nonverbal response the receiver gives to the speaker is called immediate or delayed feedback.

Giving Feedback

There is a Chinese proverb that says, "to know the road ahead, ask those coming back." Providing speakers with valuable feedback is how we complete the journey on *The Speaker's Path* and come full circle. We begin our walk in Chapter One with creating a desire to be successful, and we end our walk with Chapter Ten, which focuses on helping others be successful. Giving feedback completes the cycle.

If you want to provide valuable peer feedback to others, you must listen with your heart and mind, decode the meaning the speaker is trying to communicate, and offer authentic and constructive responses, which will take energy and focus. Actively listening to speeches and then giving appropriate positive or constructive feedback to your peers will take as much, if not more, energy than speaking.

Categories of Feedback

Psychologist and author of several psychotherapy books Carl Rogers described categories of feedback. The three we will focus on are probing, evaluative, and supportive feedback (Rogers & Freiberg, 1994).

Categories of Feedback

Probing, Evaluative, Supportive

Probing feedback is attempting to gain additional information or clarify a point the speaker has made by asking a question at the end of the speech. The speaker will paraphrase the question and then concisely answer the question if he or she knows the correct answer.

Evaluative feedback is defined as making an evaluation about the speech, evaluating the quality of evidence, and critiquing the speaker's delivery, then conscientiously phrasing positive feedback and constructive growth opportunities.

Supportive feedback is when you attempt to bolster or enlarge the speaker by fully attending to the speech as it is being given, providing authentic praise orally after the speech and/or in a written evaluation.

Feedback Guidelines

How to Give Feedback

Refer to what a speaker does, make observations instead of inferences, and use I-statements

The following three guidelines adapted from management consultant and author Lynsday Swinton (2005), who wrote *"7 Tips for Giving Positive Feedback"*, will assist you in improving how you give feedback:

1. Refer to what a speaker does in his speech, not who the speaker is. Your feedback should relate to the behavior, not the person.
   To do this, use adverbs that relate to the actions rather than adjectives, which relate to speaker qualities. *Adverbs* are a word or group of words that serves to modify a feedback sentence. For example, instead of commenting "Mateo is confident," try saying "Mateo's spoke confidently. His direct eye contact and warm smile communicated that he was confident up on stage." If you focus on speaker behaviors instead of speaker personality traits, you will encourage change.

2. Make observations instead of inferences. *Observations* are based on concrete information that can be seen and/or heard. *Inferences* are conclusions or interpretations that follow our observations. Since inferences can be incorrect or based on our own perceptions, keep these distinct when providing feedback. When giving feedback, state what you observe, minus the judgment. For example, instead of saying "Latisha did not seem nervous up there," say "I noticed that Latisha looked right at me when she was giving her speech; she seemed to look at everyone in the audience." Be descriptive instead of prescriptive.

3. Use *I-statements* in order to describe the behavior. An I-statement is a statement that begins with the word "I." I-statements maintain a respectful attitude toward the receiver and are frequently used to take ownership for observations while avoiding destructive put-downs. Be exact in the words you use when making I-statements. Here is a three-part I-statement template:
   (a) Start your feedback sentence by saying "I."
   (b) Describe what you observed using specific examples.
   (c) Describe the effect it had on you.

Combine these pieces to form a sentence as follows: " __(a)__ noticed you __(b)__ in your speech. This made me feel __(c)__ ." For example: "I noticed you cited all of your references in your speech. This made me feel comfortable with your speech and confident in you as a speaker. I understood exactly where you found your evidence, and I knew from your sources that your evidence was credible."

YOUR VIEW

Consider a recent speech you have heard. If you were to have the opportunity to give feedback to the speaker, how would you phrase that feedback as a three-part I-statement?

_____

_____

_____

Receiving Feedback

While giving feedback can be hard, receiving feedback can be even harder (Swinton, 2005). Here are three tips for receiving feedback gracefully.

> **How to Receive Feedback**
>
> Welcome feedback from others, be willing to entertain new ideas, and do not ruminate on negative feedback

1. Welcome feedback from others. Be absorbent and porous like a sponge. Listen respectfully to the feedback you receive. According to Swinton (2005), author of several articles about giving and receiving feedback gracefully, said "Your powers of self-perception only go so far. People around you notice things, both good and bad, which you don't and you might learn from their feedback." Transparent, enlarging feedback after speeches can encourage your positive behaviors (Fujishin, 2006). Hearing out constructive feedback, without getting defensive, might assist you in honing your speech-giving skills.

2. Be open and willing to entertain new ideas about yourself and your speech-giving. Whether the feedback you receive is probing, evaluative, or supportive in nature, all feedback can be an adventure of self-discovery if you allow yourself to be open to it. Being receptive to peer and instructor feedback, without personalizing it, is an integral step in improving your public speaking skills.

3. Swinton (2005) also recommends to not ruminate on the feedback you received and concentrate only on the negative. As the receiver, you can determine what you take from the feedback and how you will modify or change your behavior. While you may need some time to sort out what you heard, do not become overly focused on it. Contemplate the feedback, accept the parts that are valid, learn what there is to learn, and then let it go.

YOUR VIEW

Consider your feedback behaviors. How can you improve how you give and receive feedback?

_____

_____

_____

_____

Noise

Being an effective communicator is more than being a skillful sender and receiver. Competent speech-giving also involves the minimizing or eliminating of communication barriers, or "noise," in your communications. *Noise* is defined as a barrier to communication. Noise blocks the process and hinders effectiveness. Anything that prevents understanding of the message is a barrier to communication, or noise.

Noise
is a barrier to communication.

According to Joseph Devito in his text *Human Communication: The Basic Course* (2008) and other researchers in the field of communications have posited that here are several different types of noise that can hinder effective communication: semantic, external, internal, perceptual, physical, and message noise. Six types of noise are reviewed next.

Semantic noise occurs when a word is used differently than you prefer and may cause you to focus on the word and not the entire message.

Six Types of Noise

Semantic, External, Internal, Perceptual, Physical, and Message

External noise is when bright lights, equipment, an attractive person, vivid clothing, or any other external or physical stimulus provides a potential distraction.

Internal noise is focusing on yourself, how you feel, your stresses, or choosing your responses to a message, rather than on the other person speaking. Internal noise is essentially cognitive interference.

Perceptual noise is when you feel the person is talking too fast, not fluently, is low in status, is unattractive, or does not articulate clearly. As a result, you dismiss the person.

Physical noise or physiological noise is when your body is calling for you to attend to it instead of the message or speaker, often due to hunger, stress, illness, sleep deprivation, or excessive anxiety.

Message noise is a distraction that happens when you focus on and limit yourself to understanding specific facts rather than the underlying idea or message.

Noise can be thought of as a filter; that is, the message leaves the sender, goes through a noise filter, and is then heard by the receiver. The filter muffles the message. The way to overcome filters is to become aware that you have them.

YOUR VIEW

What communication barrier have you recently experienced? How did this barrier hamper the transmission of the message you were receiving?

_____

_____

_____

Understanding Communication

Having an understanding of the communication process and the various components of communication will give you a solid start on the path to becoming a competent public speaker. The *Communication Inventory*, adapted from scholar Sharon Downey in her text *Interpersonal Communication Workshop (1994) and Communication Research Associates book Communicate!* (Joesting, 1995), will give you the opportunity to further explore your views about communication, to share your perceptions with others, and to gain knowledge of differing observations and impressions. There are no right or wrong answers in the inventory. The purpose is simply to give you the opportunity to clarify your views and to learn about the viewpoints of others, so that your understanding of communication is more complete.

Communication Inventory

Directions: Several statements are listed below. Circle "A" if you agree or mostly agree with the statement or think it is essentially correct. Circle "D" if you disagree or mostly disagree with the statement or think it is essentially incorrect. Complete these statements individually first. Then, you form small groups and attempt to arrive at a consensus. The groups should be prepared to justify and discuss their answers.

Individual	Group	
A D	A D	1. Communication occurs when one person sends a message to another person.
A D	A D	2. The more people have in common, the better they can communicate.
A D	A D	3. Communication is a natural process that requires little to no effort.
A D	A D	4. People can communicate with plants, animals, and other natural phenomena.
A D	A D	5. People can communicate with the dead, spirits, God, or supernatural phenomena.
A D	A D	6. Most communication transactions are quite simple when you understand the details.
A D	A D	7. Most of the world's problems are caused by poor communication.
A D	A D	8. How a person communicates has very little impact on what they communicate.

YOUR VIEW

How has this activity enhanced your awareness of communication? What did you learn about your views on communication that you did not know before?

_____

_____

_____

CHAPTER SUMMARY

This chapter identified and described three models of communication to assist you in getting "the lay of the land." The transactional model, used by most scholars today, moves away from previously endorsed linear models and recommends that communication instead be viewed as a two-way exchange between participants. This chapter then explained the seven elements of the communication process: sender, receiver, message, channel, context, feedback, and noise. Along the way, various components of the communication process were introduced, such as frame of reference, listening, the concept of place, and linguistics. Last, to complete your study of the term *communication,* was a focus on your own and other's perceptions of communication via the Communication Inventory.

CLIMBING THE MOUNTAIN: 3
Overcoming Speech Anxiety

Climb the mountains and get their good tidings. Nature's peace will flow into you as sunshine flows into trees. The winds will blow their own freshness into you, and the storms their energy, while cares will drop off like autumn leaves.

—John Muir

Does giving a speech feel like you are climbing a craggy mountain, or does it feel more like stepping over a tiny molehill on your front lawn formed by a burrowing gopher? If it feels like climbing a mountain, you are not alone. According to many polls and studies, the most common phobia that Americans have is not heights, snakes, spiders, or even death. It is glossophobia, the fear of public speaking. The word *glossophobia* comes from the Greek word "glossa," meaning tongue, and "phobos," meaning fear or dread. If you have very little glossophobia and even look forward to giving a speech, you are in the privileged minority.

Communication apprehension is another term for glossophobia. Leading researcher in communication apprehension James McCroskey defines communication apprehension as an "individual level of fear or anxiety associated with either real or anticipated communication with another person or persons." Communication apprehension is also known as stage fright, reticence, speech anxiety, or shyness.

Seventy-five percent of all Americans report having had intense communication apprehension at some point in their lives. For these people, and likely for you, public speaking does not feel remotely like cares dropping off like autumn leaves or flowing sunshine as in the 1901 John Muir quote above. For them, giving a speech is an anxiety-producing event. You may

Communication apprehension is another term for glossophobia or the fear of public speaking.

have heard stories from friends who dropped their public speaking class due to their fears, of people who panicked over giving a wedding toast, or of co-workers who failed to get their proposal adopted at work due to their intense worry about their presentation to their management staff. The fear of speech-giving might have hampered their success.

Some people also report that they feel alone, as if no one else experiences stage fright as profoundly as they do. Although their perceptions are normal, there are likely inaccurate. Even if other people do not display speech anxiety outwardly and pretend otherwise, communication apprehension is likely still operating below the surface.

Pretending that you do not have speech anxiety is not going to help you on your journey to be a more successful public speaker. Unfortunately, ignoring communication apprehension will not make it go away. The solution instead is to learn how to overcome much of your anxiety and create more confidence and calm.

The five steps to managing anxiety that will be comprehensively outlined in this chapter are the following:

> **Five Steps to Managing Anxiety**
>
> Assessing, Noticing, Accepting, Letting Go, Adopting Strategies

1. Assessing your own speech anxiety
2. Noticing if, when, and how anxiety affects you
3. Accepting anxiety if you have it
4. Letting anxiety go
5. Adopting strategies for staying centered

Step One: Assess Your Anxiety

The PRPSA (Personal Report of Public Speaking Anxiety) developed by James McCroskey (1970), is a considered to still be a highly reliable survey that focuses strictly on accessing public speaking anxiety. Following are thirty-four statements that we sometimes make about ourselves. The PRPSA is targeted toward college students, but is flexible enough to be utilized by anyone who wishes to examine her own level of anxiety. Just substitute the words "instructor" or "course outline" to fit your own experience. There are no right or wrong answers, but the results might give you some valuable insight into your own speech anxiety.

Personal Report of Public Speaking Anxiety (PRPSA) Self-Quiz

Directions: Indicate whether you believe each statement applies to you by marking whether you:

Strongly Disagree = 5   Disagree = 4   Neutral or Undecided = 3   Agree = 2   Strongly Agree = 1

_____ 1. While preparing for giving a speech, I feel tense and nervous.

_____ 2. I feel tense when I see the words *speech* and *public speech* on a course outline.

_____ 3. My thoughts become confused and jumbled when I am giving a speech.

_____ 4. Right after giving a speech, I feel that I have had a pleasant experience.

_____ 5. I get anxious when I think about a speech coming up.

_____ 6. I have no fear of giving a speech.

_____ 7. Although I am nervous just before starting a speech, I soon settle down after starting and feel calm and comfortable.

_____ 8. I look forward to giving a speech.

_____ 9. When the instructor announces a speaking assignment, I can feel myself getting tense.

_____10. My hands tremble when I am giving a speech.

_____11. I feel relaxed while giving a speech.

_____12. I enjoy preparing for a speech.

_____13. I am in constant fear of forgetting what I prepared to say.

_____14. I get anxious if someone asks me something about my topic that I do not know.

_____15. I face the prospect of giving a speech with confidence.

_____16. I feel that I am in complete possession of myself while giving a speech.

_____17. My mind is clear when giving a speech.

_____18. I do not dread giving a speech.

_____19. I perspire just before starting a speech.

_____20. My heart beats very fast just as I start a speech.

_____21. I experience considerable anxiety while sitting in the room just before my speech starts.

_____22. Certain parts of my body feel very tense and rigid while giving a speech.

_____23. Realizing that only a little time remains in a speech makes me very tense and anxious.

_____24. While giving a speech, I know I can control my feelings of tension and stress.

_____25. I breathe faster just before starting a speech.

_____26. I feel comfortable and relaxed in the hour or so just before giving a speech.

_____27. I do more poorly on speeches because I am anxious.

_____28. I feel anxious when the instructor announces the date of a speaking assignment.

_____29. When I make a mistake while giving a speech, I find it hard to concentrate on the parts that follow.

_____30. During an important speech, I experience a feeling of helplessness building up inside me.

_____31. I have trouble falling asleep the night before a speech.

_____32. My heart beats very fast while I present a speech.

_____33. I feel anxious while waiting to give my speech.

_____34. While giving a speech, I get so nervous I forget facts I really know.

Scoring Your PRPSA Self-Quiz

To determine your score on the PRPSA score, complete the following steps:

Step 1: Add all of the scores from questions 1, 2, 3, 5, 9, 10, 13, 14, 19, 20, 21, 22, 23, 25, 27, 28, 29, 30, 31, 32, 33, and 34.

Step 2: Using 132 as a base number, **subtract** the sum from step one from 132 to get a subtotal.

Step 3: Add all of the scores from questions 4, 6, 7, 8, 11, 12, 15, 16, 17, 18, 24, and 26.

Step 4: Now, add the sum in Step 3 to the subtotal in Step 2 for a final score. This is your PRPSA score.

Your score should be between 34 and 170. If your score is below 34 or above 170, you made a mistake in computing the score. The mean score is 115.

34-84 = Low Anxiety–this scores indicates a very low level of speech anxiety related to public speaking

85-92 = Moderately Low Anxiety–this scores indicates a moderately low level of public speaking anxiety

93-110 = Moderate Anxiety–Suggests moderate anxiety in most public speaking situations but not so severe that the individual cannot cope and be a successful public speaker

111-119 = Moderately High Anxiety–Suggests a moderately high anxiety about public speaking. People with such scores may tend to avoid opportunities to give public speeches.

120-170 = Very High Anxiety–this score indicates a very high level of speech anxiety related to public speaking. People with these scores will go to considerable lengths to avoid all types of public speaking situations

YOUR VIEW

What is your score? Do you think this assessment is an accurate measure of your level of speech anxiety? Why or why not?

_____

_____

_____

The higher your score, the higher your anxiety, according to this tool, and the more heavily you will need to rely on the techniques to reduce anxiety as discussed in this chapter. If your score is low, or if you already have extensive public speaking, broadcast journalism, or stage experience, or if you find giving a speech in front of others to be enjoyable, you may only need to skim the remainder of this chapter.

Step Two: Noticing the Effects

You should now have a clearer picture of your speech anxiety level according to the PRPSA. If your anxiety is middle to high, you may learn to reduce some of it by understanding how you uniquely experience it. *Speech anxiety* is a fear of speech-giving that manifests with physical, emotional, and psychological symptoms. Some symptoms are mild and easily manageable. Other symptoms are severe and challenging to contend with. If you find that your symptoms are profoundly impacting your life for more than a week, get assistance.

Speech anxiety is a fear of speech-giving that manifests with physical, emotional, and psychological effects.

Physical Effects

The *physical effects* of speech anxiety are what the body does in reaction to stress. Some people have very few physical reactions. Others tremble or shake and sweat or notice that their heart rate begins to quicken. Additional common physical symptoms include upset stomach, nervous coughing, and dizziness. These symptoms may have already started to happen to you, even if you have not yet given your first speech in the class.

Physical effects are what the body does in reaction to stress symptoms.

Psychological Effects

Psychological effects of speech anxiety are what the mind does in reaction to stress and often occur below the level of consciousness. Some people find that their mind begins to race, their thoughts become jumbled, or they have great difficulty putting their thoughts into any coherent order. Others

Psychological effects are what the mind does in reaction to stress.

lose short-term memory, repeat words and phrases, stutter, or demonstrate other speech disfluencies, such as excess "ums" and "uhs."

Emotional Effects

Emotional effects are the emotional reactions or feelings in response to stress.

The *emotional effects* of stage fright are the emotional reactions or feelings in response to stress. These symptoms are usually triggered by deep-rooted feelings of inadequacy or a conscious or subconscious fear of rejection. You question your abilities. Are you good enough? Will people notice your flaws? Will you not sound as smart as you are? These concerns are very real for some and occasionally cause low self-esteem, or feelings of helplessness, shame, or anxiety. The result of these emotions, if left unchecked and allowed to fester, can be negative self-talk. *Negative self-talk* is all the harmful things you tell yourself when you feel like a failure or are disappointed by your reactions. Two examples of negative self talk are saying to yourself that you have nothing important to say, or that members of your audience will find your speech foolish.

YOUR VIEW

What physical, psychological, or emotional symptoms do you notice, if any, before and during a speech?

_____

_____

_____

Step Three: Acceptance

Now that you have looked at what responses you have, if any, to the stressors of giving a speech, we will investigate what it means to accept your anxiety and move into a place of calmness.

The first step in acceptance is to realize that what some of you are experiencing is just an exaggerated reaction to the biologically programmed "fight-or-flight" response of your prehistoric ancestors, the very same response felt by our ancestors when confronting a danger. The body cannot differentiate between real and perceived stressors. Therefore, if you think you are in danger, even if you are not, your body triggers the same response of increased adrenaline and cortisol hormones. When there is a sudden boost of either of these hormones, regardless of the reason, you may experience the anxiety effects described in this chapter.

Although the fight-or-flight response to stress is innate, chances are that the stressor that triggers the anxiety itself is a learned fear, a result of upbringing or enculturation; that is, nurture instead of nature. Many people are taught, even if unintentionally, that giving a speech is a scary experience, or they have had a negative experience when giving a speech. These experiences create cognitive distortions, which are patterns of faulty thinking. This negative self-talk can impact thoughts, behaviors, and the experience of stress. Our thinking style is a habit that we can, with patience and practice, change.

Step Four: Letting Go

If speech anxiety is a learned state for some, based on childhood or early adult experiences and not something that is inherited and therefore cannot be changed, then for some people, public speaking anxiety can be relearned through cognitive restructuring.

Cognitive restructuring is changing the way you look at something which in this case, is speech-giving. Cognitive restructuring techniques were pioneered by Albert Ellis (1957) and Aaron Beck (1970), among others. *Cognitive restructuring* is the process of identifying and challenging irrational self-talk so that you can think more productive thoughts (Ellis, 1967). The word *cognition* is just another word for thought. There is an abundance of evidence that proves that how you think about giving a speech in public can greatly contribute to whether you find the event of speech-giving stressful.

Cognitive restructuring is the process of identifying and challenging irrational self-talk so that you can think more productive thoughts.

The basic premise of cognitive restructuring is that our emotions about public speaking and our anxiety behaviors that surround public speaking can be greatly affected by how we think about speech-giving. The process of recognizing, challenging, and changing cognitive distortions about giving presentations and negative thought patterns about public speaking can be accomplished by becoming aware of your inner dialogue about speech-giving. Perhaps it is time to change the way you think about public speaking. If you can consciously change your public speaking self-talk and alter your mental images about public speaking from negative to positive, you can accomplish several positive changes.

There are three steps to cognitive restructuring. These three steps were adapted from Hope, Burns, Hyes & Herbert's (2010) article called "Automatic thoughts and cognitive resructuring in cognitive behavioral group therapy for social anxiety disorder", Burn's (1989) book *The Feeling Good Handbook,* and Scott's (2007) article "Cognitive Restructuring for Stress Relief: A Little Cognitive Restructuring Can Bring Significant Change."

1. Becoming aware of negative self-talk and fears
2. Challenging cognitive distortion and faulty thinking
3. Replacing with realistic alternatives

Three Steps to Cognitive Restructuring

Becoming Aware, Challenging Distortion, Replacing with Realistic Alternatives

Becoming Aware

If you have any communication apprehension, the first major stride to reducing your communication apprehension through cognitive restructuring is to become aware of your internal self-talk and what triggers it. We all have automatic negative thoughts, but these increase when we are stressed. One method is to record your thoughts in a journal whenever you start to become stressed about your speech. Another technique is to write down every possible fear that you have in relation to public speaking on one sheet of paper. Some examples would be that you will faint or that people will laugh at you.

Identifying and Challenging Cognitive Distortions

Second, examine your journal and/or your list of fears that you generated. Look at each of the thoughts and fears and determine the probability and rationality of each concern you listed. Can you find any cognitive distortions? You can do this by asking yourself three questions:

Questions to Challenge Distortions:

1. How likely is _____to actually happen during my next speech?
2. What is the evidence to suggest the consequences of my giving a speech will be as disastrous as _____?
3. What are the other possible outcomes of my giving a speech that may not be so disastrous?

Identifying fear-based irrational thinking and cognitive distortions allows you to challenge that thinking for accuracy.

Replacing Errors with Realistic Alternatives

Last, replace cognitive errors with realistic and positive alternatives, because refuting irrational thoughts based on false beliefs will give these fears less power. Often the replacements for automatic negative thoughts become evident in the course of honestly answering the questions above. Sometimes this alone can reinforce for you that your cognitive distortions are not based on logical reasoning and you can replace these with more positive alternatives.

If you still are having trouble restructuring how you think about giving speeches, use this two-part response to construct more realistic, rational thoughts. The first part of the response should start with an honest acknowledgement of the irrational fear or cognitive distortion, followed second by the word "but," and finally a realistic, positive outcome of the situation.

Example: I will forget my entire speech when I get up there (COGNITIVE DISTORTION), but I know I can just look down at my notes if I forget and then I will remember (REALISTIC POSITIVE OUTCOME).

Example: People will laugh at me (COGNITIVE DISTORTION), but the chances of that genuinely happening are pretty low because I know my audience wants me to do well (REALISTIC POSITIVE OUTCOME).

YOUR VIEW

Do this two-part response for one fear or anxiety you listed or each possible negative outcome and then restructure it with a positive outcome statement. With this type of practice, you can change your self-talk and develop positive habitual ways to think about giving speeches.

_____

_____

_____

This article called "Letting Go of Anxiety" by Tina B. Tessina (2005) discusses other methods on how to accept and release anxiety.

These days, it seems that there's one disaster after another. Not only do we have to deal with an angry Mother Nature, but all sorts of fanatics and psychopaths are on the news every night. Add this to normal life issues, illness, financial stress and family troubles, and the triggers for anxiety abound. We are all in a time of high stress, and news events as well as personal life problems often bring up fear. If these fears are not dealt with, they can lead to "acting out" or behaviors such as drinking too much or creating problems in your relationships.

What we used to call worry, and have updated to anxiety, is a continuous stream of negativity at that keeps interrupting your mode of thought and that you find it hard to get away from. It's usually not focused on any one thing, but jumps from negative thought to negative thought. Worry drains and wastes your energy and makes you less likely to make good decisions. If you take that same rgy energy you're using running around in mental circles, and do something productive with it, it'll serve you better.

Often in my own life, I use a Zen concept of beginner's mind in the context of starting over. That is, to approach a new or difficult experience without expectations, willing to learn new things, willing to not be an expert, but to feel uncomfortable and incompetent, and to enjoy the experience of being a learner. This leaves one open to better experiences than would be otherwise possible.

Letting go, in the sense of trying not to control things makes every situation easier to handle. Another word for it is acceptance. In the long run, we gain more control by letting go. Rather an than fight what's going on, and try to deny bad things that happen use your beginner's mind it, to face it, do what you can, and learn from it,

Letting go in the sense of acceptance is an internal, private process. You don't need to let anyone else know you're doing it. Take charge of your negative thoughts (that's one thing totally in our your control) and turn them around—argue with them, fight them off, wrestle with them. Put energy into it. What you need to let go of is the things outside that you can't control. Other people, life's events, loss, disappointment. Stop trying to change what won't change, accept what is, let it be and live life as it is. Yes, I know it's easier said than done, but once you get a handle on it, is itself is easier. Fretting about what you can't control is an endless, useless waste of energy you can use elsewhere.

Tina B. Tessina, PhD (www.tinatessina.com), psychotherapist and author of *It Ends with You: Grow Up and Out of Dysfunction.* "Letting Go of Anxiety" written in 2005 is used with permission.

According to author Hugh Prather (2000) who wrote "The Little Book of Letting Go" and writer, speaker and trainer John Halderman who wrote "Top Five Wyas to Stay Calm and Reduce Stress", our last step in the acceptance process is to worry less, accept what is, and live life fully. You can do this by realizing that speech anxiety is often a result of negative self-talk or cognitive distortions that you can learn to minimize with practice. Understand that anxiety can be self-focused, which in its extreme form can even become narcissistic. If you are highly anxious, accept that, for whatever reason, you are expending a lot of your energy on your own negative self-talk and pessimistic mental images about giving speeches. What would happen if you shifted your focus—if you thought about what your audience needs, instead of how stressed you feel? If you thought that perhaps your speech might just go really well? You might notice a decrease in your speech anxiety, a quieter mind, and a calmer and happier disposition.

Step Five: Strategies for Staying Centered

You have assessed your own speech anxiety, noticed how anxiety affects you, accepted that it is there, and looked at strategies for letting it go. Even with all of these anxiety-reducing tips in your speech-giving toolbox, communication apprehension may still impact you at some point. Allow the following ideas to help you stay calm and grounded as you walk the *Speaker's Path* and climb what may sometimes seem like a sheer cliff on the side of a mountain. You will make progress in time if you persevere. As President Barack Obama so aptly put, "If you're walking down the right path and you're willing to keep walking, eventually you'll make progress." The next section will overview ten tools for creating calm in your life. Choose those tools that will work best for you.

Ten Strategies for Creating Calm

Exercise

The quote by Paul Dudley White illustrates the importance of physical activity in creating a happier, calmer state of being. He says, "A vigorous five-mile walk will do more good for an unhappy but otherwise healthy adult than all the medicine and psychology in the world." So if you are physically able, do some type of exercise within 48 hours of giving your speech, whatever is appropriate for your fitness level. Both aerobic exercise (e.g., running, cycling, swimming) and anaerobic exercise such as yoga or weight lifting have proven benefits. According to the Mayo Clinic's article "Exercise: 7 Benefits of Regular Physical Activity" in 2011, a workout at the gym or a brisk 30-minute walk can help you manage stress. Experts say that physical activity stimulates various brain chemicals such as endorphins that may leave you feeling happier and more relaxed. Your body releases endorphins in response to sustained physical exertion, also known as the runner's high. Endorphins are thought to contribute to feelings of euphoria and well-being. Additionally, exercise will work off excess adrenaline in your system, and as a result will help you feel more peaceful. You may also feel better about yourself when you exercise regularly, which can boost your confidence and self-esteem.

> **Ten Strategies:**
> Exercise, Stay Present, Be Kind to Yourself, Focus on Others, Practice Optimism, Breathe Deeply, Get Outdoors, Create a Calm Environment, Make Connections, Take Care of Your Body

Stay Present

When was the last time that you sat down to eat a meal and actually concentrated on the act of eating and the nuance of flavor and texture in your mouth as you mindfully chewed your food? Chances are that it has been a while. Usually we are doing other things besides just eating that take our minds miles away from what we are actually doing. When we allow our minds to wander, we are not staying in the moment. Taking control of our thinking and our internal dialog is what allows us to be present. It takes some practice but once you become aware of your wandering mind, you can start to train yourself to focus on what is right in front of you in the present moment, as a substitute for fretting about the past or future.

For example, if you become anxious about your next speech, be present with it. Observe your anxiety as if you were watching yourself from a few feet away. As you do so, label your anxiety from zero to ten and watch it go up and down, noticing that it doesn't stay at a high level of ten for very long. Understand that what you are experiencing is an exaggeration of your normal reactions to stress and that it is temporary. After all, there are some things that just cannot be harnessed no matter how hard we try and hold the reins. Trust that everything will fall into place just as it is meant to. So accept anxiety when it comes, wait a moment, and then allow it to pass. Stay in the here and now. As Henry David Thoreau once said, "You must live in the present, launch yourself on every wave, find your eternity in each moment."

Be Kind to Yourself

The Parker-Pope article (2011) in *The New York Times* , "Go Easy on Yourself, a New Wave of Research Urges," found that a surprising number of people who are kind and compassionate to others have little empathy for themselves. Their research suggests that "giving ourselves a break and accepting our imperfections may be the first step toward better health. People who score high on tests of self-compassion have less depression and anxiety, and tend to be happier and more optimistic (Parker-Pope, 2011)." Instead of berating yourself for what you perceive to be your failures and being self-critical, practice a little self-compassion. As Buddha said, "You can search throughout the entire universe for someone who is more deserving of your love and affection than you are yourself, and that person is not to be found anywhere. You yourself, as much as anybody in the entire universe deserve your love and affection."

The following ideas focus on how to be gentler on yourself. Accept yourself as you are instead of trying to be someone you are not. Forgive yourself for your imperfections. Change your negative thoughts into positive ones. Make a list of ten things that you like about yourself and repeat them to yourself until you feel confident. Celebrate your accomplishments and any small successes you achieve. Send yourself some flowers, a card, or buy yourself a small inexpensive gift. Read entirely for fun—a titillating novel, some romantic poetry, a children's book by authors such as Dr. Seuss or Shel Silverstein. Restart a hobby such as gardening, cooking, or basketball. Watch your favorite comedy and laugh fully.

Focus on Others

In addition to taking care of yourself, part of your success in public speaking may involve how well you take care of other people in your life. According to principles in what is known as *Systems Theory,* everything and everyone is interconnected. Because of this, a change in one person can produce a change in other people. For example, perhaps you can influence not just your outcome as a learner of public speaking, but the outcome of other people who are wishing to improve their communications or be less anxious about speech-giving. One way you can do this is by being present, being supportive, and by being positive.

Another method for being other-focused instead of self-focused is to concentrate on your audience before, during, and after your speech, instead of on yourself. Consider how your words can be a gift to the people in your audience. When you think of your audience, do not think of some homogeneous mass of people waiting to hear your message. Instead, think of the unique points of view of each of the individual members in your audience. Focus on what you have in common with your audience, on making connections. Whenever you begin to focus too much on yourself, shift your focus to back to others.

Practice Optimism

Positive thinking is a mental attitude that admits into the mind only thoughts, words, and images that are conducive to growth, expansion, and happiness. It is an outlook that expects good and favorable results. "Positive thinking will let you do everything better than negative thinking will," said motivational speaker Zig Zigler in his article "Positive Thinking". Even if your current circumstances are not as you wish them to be, expect only favorable results and situations. In time, your optimistic attitude will affect your life and circumstances and change them accordingly. When you expect success and say "I can," "I am able," or "it is possible," you fill yourself with confidence, hope, and joy.

Maintain your sense of optimism even in your speech-giving. Visualize yourself calmly getting up and standing in front of your audience. Picture the audience intently and respectfully listening to you. Hear the audience's applause at the end of your speech. Visualize yourself giving your entire speech in front of the room you will be speaking in. As psychiatrist and psychoanalyst Smiley Blaton said, "You can handle anything if you think you can. Just keep your cool and your sense of humor."

Breathe Deeply

Oxygen is the most crucial of all elements in the body. While it is technically not a nutrient, it is an oxidizing agent that forms new compounds that release energy into the body. Breathing in more oxygen is the most effective purification process for the blood stream. In addition, slow and deep breathing produces a stimulating effect of the parasympathetic nervous system, which sends relaxation signals to the brain.

Pay attention to your breathing. Observe if your breathing become too shallow. Find a quiet space where you can be alone without interruptions, sit in a comfortable chair, close your eyes, and practice breathing deeply. Deep breathing begins with a full exhale. Your ability to inhale is restricted when your lungs are not completely empty. After the exhale, breathe in slowly and deeply—in through your nose and down into your belly. Take several long, slow, deep breaths while imagining the tension washing slowly out of your body. Notice how you are able to calm yourself. Allow the powerful effects of deep breathing to improve your outlook, health, and vitality. As Zen Master and author of *Peace is Every Step: The Path of Mindfulness in Everyday Life* Thich Nhat Hanh said, "Breath is the bridge which connects life to consciousness, which unites your body to your thoughts."

Get Outdoors

There are many benefits going outdoors and being in nature's splendor. Research has shown that a connection to nature decreases stress levels, stimulates emotional healing, and increases immune function. Other studies suggest that an immersion in nature brings people closer to themselves and to others. A recent 2010 study in *Journal of Environmental Psychology* called "Vitalizing Effects of Being Outdoors and in Nature" found that being outside in nature makes people feel more alive, energetic, and resilient. Another article called "Spending Time in Nature Makes People Feel More Alive, Study Shows" by researchers at the University of Rochester in 2010 shows that experiences with nature can affect not just our mood, but our priorities. They found that when exposed to scenes of nature, peoples' values shifted from personal gain to a broader focus on community and connection with others (Ryan, 2010).

When you take time out of your hectic life to be present in nature, you get a feeling of being part of a community, of belonging to something bigger. Find time in your schedule to get away from buildings, artificial light and air, pollution, and noise. In its place, find serenity in nature. It just might transform you. As Dr. Richard Ryan, lead author and a professor of psychology at the University of Rochester, says, "Nature is fuel for the soul. Often when we feel depleted we reach for a cup of coffee, but research suggests a better way to get energized is to connect with nature (Ryan, 2010)."

Make Connections

Helen Keller once said that "Walking with a friend in the dark is better than walking alone in the light." Having a strong, supportive social network has been associated with lower levels of stress, increased longevity, and greater levels of happiness. Numerous research studies have shown that supportive friendships can provide emotional help during stressful times. It's important to have at least one person you can talk to about your feelings and the things that are going on in your life, someone you can really be yourself with. "Researchers have found that having even one close friend that you confide in can extend your life by as much as 10 years," says sociologist and relationship coach Jan Yager, PhD, author of *Friendshifts* (Yager, 1999). So, take the time to nurture a close friendship. Support your friend and allow her or him to support you. Confide in your friend about your feelings about your upcoming speech. Consider connecting with your friend a day or two before your speech date to do something enjoyable together. As labor leader and civil rights activist Cesear Chavez said about facing obstacles, "you are never strong enough that you don't need help."

If you don't have a close friend that will do, perhaps you can snuggle with your cat or enlist your dog to keep you company on a leisurely walk to the park. There is an abundant amount of research on pets and their impact on stress. In one study conducted at UCLA, they found that dog owners actually needed much less medical care for stress than non-dog owners. A pet can also ward off depression, lower blood pressure, and boost immunity.

Last, if you choose to define yourself as spiritual or devout, you may find your greatest solace in making a connection with something beyond human or animal. Embracing spirituality as a method for creating inner calm can take many forms, such as: observance, prayer, ritual, guided visualization, meditation, nature, music, community, or art. According to the 2010 Mayo Clinic article "Spirituality and Stress Relief: Make the Connection", "Some stress relief tools are very tangible: exercising more, eating healthy foods and talking with friends. A less tangible—but no less useful way—to find stress relief is through spirituality."

Create a Calm Environment

As German monk Martin Luther, once said, "Beautiful music is the art of the prophets that can calm the agitations of the soul; it is one of the most magnificent and delightful presents God has given us." If calm classical or smooth jazz music soothes you, listen to it. If listening to nature brings you joy, go outside and tend to your garden. Or, find music that is made for relaxation, therapeutic songs that mimic the sound of soft rain or the sound of waves. If you appreciate silence and quiet relaxes you more than sound, turn off your electronic devices and embrace the quiet. If you are a musician and making music calms you, play some soothing instrumental. Regardless of your sound preference, provide yourself with a relaxing space to quiet your mind.

Do not forget that scent can be as important as sound. Aromatherapy, which is the use of essential oils therapeutically, is very helpful as a relaxation aid. Whether it consists of a few drops of soothing essential oils in a bathtub, a scented candle, or incense, certain aromas can reduce stress and bring on a greater state of calm. According to the Sleep Aid Tips website in an article called "Relaxation with Herbal Aroma Therapy", some of the most relaxing and restorative oils that are useful to combat nervous tension and reduce stress include bergamot, chamomile, sage, jasmine, lavender, neroli, ylang ylang, and others.

Moreover, consider adjusting or dimming lighting, especially if you have fluorescent lights. One known side effect of being exposed to fluorescent lighting is overall stress. Think of all of this as creating a relaxing ritual for yourself before speech time, just like an athlete would before a big game. Rituals can be tremendously soothing during major transitions or stressful times.

Take Care of Your Body

Motivational speaker and business philosopher Jim Rohn once said, "Take care of your body. It's the only place you have to live." Taking care of your body starts with healthy eating and drinking, both of which are not about strict nutrition philosophies or depriving yourself of the foods and beverages you truly enjoy. Rather, healthy eating and drinking is about feeling great, having more energy, stabilizing your mood, and keeping yourself as strong as possible. Eat regular, healthy meals with equal servings of protein, whole grains, and vegetables. Try to eat a rainbow of fruits and vegetables every day. Colorful, deeply colored fruits and vegetables contain higher concentrations of vitamins, minerals, and antioxidants. Drink enough water. Monitor or reduce your intake of alcohol and caffeine.

Taking care of your body is also about getting enough sleep. Sleep is a necessary and vital biological function that is essential to a person's physical and emotional well-being. Roman poet Ovid Publius Ovdius Naso, also known as Ovid, once said about the power of sleep, "There is more refreshment and stimulation in a nap, even of the briefest, than in all the alcohol ever distilled." Yet, a recent survey found that many people sleep less than the recommended eight hours a night, which might result in sleep debt. According to Stanford researcher Dr. William Dement's website The Sleep Well, sleep debt is created when personal sleep requirements are not met

(Dement, 2010). He says this is especially true of students, medical residents, busy executives, shift workers, and new parents. While more research is needed to explore the links between chronic sleep loss and health, it's safe to assume that getting adequate sleep is too important to shortchange. For example, the Harvard Women's Health Watch article "The Importance of Sleep: Six Reasons not to Script on Sleep" in 2006 found that sleep loss may result in irritability, impatience, inability to concentrate, and moodiness. Studies have also shown that without enough sleep, a person's ability to perform even simple tasks declines dramatically. Further, too little sleep can also leave you too tired to do the things you like to do. Go to bed at your regular bedtime. Try to get eight hours of sleep.

YOUR VIEW

If you have some communication apprehension, develop a personal action plan before your speech anxiety becomes problematic. Reflect on these ten strategies for staying calm and grounded. Which three suggestions resonated with you the most?

1. _____

   _____

2. _____

   _____

3. _____

   _____

CHAPTER SUMMARY

This chapter overviewed five steps for managing speech anxiety, starting with assessing your own communication apprehension and concluding with several strategies to help you stay calm and grounded. The advice in this chapter should help you manage mild to moderate anxiety more effectively. However, if your fear of public speaking is extreme, or if it is compounded by social phobia or social anxiety disorder or other mental or physical health concerns, you may wish to seek professional help with a licensed therapist, psychologist, psychiatrist, or physician.

FOLLOW THE MAP:
Phase One of the Twelve Steps for Informative Speaking

4

Some people walk with both eyes focused on their goal: the highest mountain peak in the range. . . . they stay motivated by anticipating the end of the journey. Since I tend to be easily distracted, I travel somewhat differently—one step at a time, with many pauses in between.

—Hannah Nyala, *Point Last Seen:
A Woman's Tracker Story*

In this quote, Nyala (1997) describes how she stays motivated on a long and arduous trek, not by anticipating when the journey will come to an end, but by taking one step at a time. This chapter of The *Speaker's Path* will highlight a series of steps for PHASE ONE of Informative Speaking, which is preparing your speech. Think of these steps as a detailed speech development map to follow. Follow the map in the recommended sequence.

Preparation is the state of having been made ready beforehand, readiness, a preliminary measure that serves to make ready for something. According to Toastmasters International, a world leader in public speaking development, four million people around the world have become more effective speakers due to their involvement in Toastmasters. In all of the coaching, training, and teaching moments that Toastmasters provides, the same message comes across according to Toastmaster's Training Club Leaders series (2011), and that is that: People must spend time in preparation to deliver high-quality speeches. Most communication professors, corporate trainers, and speech coaches encourage people to prepare thoroughly and repeatedly practice their presentations.

Preparation is so vital to success in public speaking situations that experienced speakers will sometimes deliver lower-quality speeches because they feel less of a need to prepare. People with less experience and more anxiety often prepare more thoroughly, and thus deliver more accomplished speeches.

A number of variables influence exactly how much preparation a person needs. While there are a few people who report spending considerable time on preparation without becoming proficient at public speaking, for most people, effective instruction, preparation, and practice will give them the results they wish to obtain. Further, preparation and practice is one of the principle means for reducing speech anxiety.

YOUR VIEW
_____

Why do you think most experts agree that preparation is the key to success when it comes to speech-giving? If you have given public speeches before, have you fully prepared yourself? If so, what have you done to get yourself prepared?

_____

_____

_____

Two Phases of Informative Speaking

Developing and Organizing and Perfecting

Planning and pacing is integral to public speaking success. However, some do not plan because they are anxious. Others do not plan because they are extroverts or are skilled at communicating with people they know and mistakenly believe that because they can be the life of the party around their friends or co-workers, the same communication skills will transfer to public speaking. In order for your speech to turn out like you want it to, you will need to clarify your purpose or mission, then make a step-by-step plan on how to implement it. This will be accomplished in two phases, PHASE ONE and PHASE TWO.

Phase One: Developing Your Speech

Step One:	Review the Assignment
Step Two:	Consider the Audience
Step Three:	Clarify the Purpose of the Speech
Step Four:	Organize the Main Points
Step Five:	Support with Evidence
Step Six:	Construct an Introduction
Step Seven:	Add Transitions
Step Eight:	Create a Conclusion

Phase Two: Organizing and Perfecting Your Speech

Step Nine:	Complete Speech Preparation Guide
Step Ten:	Develop a Full-Sentence Outline
Step Eleven:	Cite Your Evidence
Step Twelve:	Design Visual Aids

PHASE ONE: Developing Your Speech

PHASE ONE of your walk on *The Speaker's Path* will highlight eight steps of informative speaking,, which encompass how to plan, prepare, and develop your informative speech. These steps are necessary because great speeches don't happen by chance. Great speakers aren't born great speakers. Great speakers prepare. As award-winning public speaker and speech evaluator Andrew Dlugan writes in his 2008 article "Speech Preparation #1: How to Prepare a Presentation," "proper preparation prevents presentation predicaments! (Dlugan, 2008)." This memorable quote on the importance of preparation is one that you should repeat to yourself often as you move into PHASE ONE of your journey.

Step One: Review the Assignment

Just as you would review a future employer's job description and research the company before interviewing for a big job, you should review the assignment criteria so that you understand exactly what type of speech you are being asked to give. Reviewing the assignment or criteria for your speech is your first step on *The Speaker's Path*. After you have studied the requirements for your speech, brainstorm a list of possible topics that meet the criteria you established. Brainstorming is a creativity technique designed to rapidly generate unrestrained and spontaneous ideas and solutions.

YOUR VIEW

Brainstorm three possible speech topics and explain how they each meet the criteria for the speech you have been asked to deliver.

1. _____

2. _____

3. _____

Step Two: Consider the Audience

Your topic selection and subject matter focus should not only be about what is required and what you prefer to talk about. It must also be about your audience—who they are, what they need, and how your topic will benefit them. The best topics are those that are targeted toward the intended audience, and the most effective speakers are audience-centered in their approach.

Audience-centered speakers take into consideration the answers to the following three questions when finalizing a speech topic:

1. What does the audience need?
2. What does the audience value?
3. What is the demographic makeup of the audience?

Audience analysis is choosing and focusing your topic based on the needs, desires, and values of your audience.

The process of targeting your topic to your intended audience is called *audience analysis*. Audience analysis consists of assessing the audience; making inferences about the needs, values, and demographics of your audience members; and then making sure the information provided to them is appropriate. It is your responsibility to reflect on what you know about your intended audience and to tailor your speech topic toward them. Your obligation as an audience-centered speaker does not stop there, however.

Before going further with audience analysis and your emerging topic, it is necessary to underscore how ethics play into being an audience-focused speaker. Ethics are a major consideration when formulating a topic and designing a speech. *Ethics* are defined as having a moral compass and a code of conduct. According to Jonathan Steele who wrote the article "Ethics in Public Speaking" on speechmastery.com, a website that specializes in improving communication skills, "Public speaking and those who attain mastery of public speaking have both mores and ethics they must follow. Failure to follow these could cost their credibility and future ability to speak (Steele, 2010)."

The National Speaker's Association Code of Professional Ethics (2007) states that ethics in public speaking includes not limiting others by means of economic, race, ethnicity, color, gender, age, sexual orientation, disability, religion, or nationality. You must be a steward of ethics who is responsible for valuing each of the diverse members of your intended audience. To accomplish this, choose a topic that creates bridges with your audience base, not walls. For example, even though you may not experience it this way, some members of your audience may find topics that possess adult humor or profanity to be offensive.

After some reflection, mull over the topics you generated, taking into account your intended audience and speaker ethics in your decision making. Then consider how to make your topic truly meaningful to your audience, a topic that leaves your audience wanting more from you as a speaker, not less—a topic that will enhance the lives of those in your audience. When you have taken time to think this all through, choose the topic that best meets the requirements, is most interesting to you, takes ethics into consideration, and has the maximum meaning and benefit to your intended audience.

YOUR VIEW

Reflect on the needs, values, and demographics of your intended audience. Which of your three possible topics will your audience most appreciate and why?

_____

_____

_____

_____

Step Three: Clarify the Purpose

This second step will assist you in illuminating the purpose of your speech. Why did you choose the topic you did? What do you want your audience to get out of your speech? Step Three asks you to answer these integral questions, so that you can walk *The Speaker's Path* with purpose.

> **Three General Purposes of Speech-Giving**
>
> To Inform, Persuade, or Entertain

To begin, review what you know about your audience from Step Two. Second, consider the criteria for the assignment. Third, before you develop your speech further, clarify and then write down your general purpose and your specific purpose. Getting clarity on the general and specific purposes of your speech will help you keep your mission in check and assist you in narrowing down and focusing your content.

The *general purpose* of your speech is the primary effect you want your speech to have on your audience. There are three general purposes or primary reasons why we give a speech:

> *General purpose* is the overall desired effect you want to have on your audience.

1. To inform or teach
2. To persuade or evoke a change
3. To entertain

The *specific purpose* statement is the most important sentences in your speech, because it illuminates your mission and goals and provides your speech with explicit focus. It is a thesis statement for speech-giving, the underlying theme of your speech. Everything you say in your speech should directly relate to your specific purpose. Use your specific purpose to guide you on your path to becoming a more effective public speaker.

> *Specific purpose* illuminates the mission of your speech and provides it with focus.

What are the general and specific purposes of your next speech?

_____

_____

_____

Step Four: Organizing the Main Points

You are now clear on your topic, audience, and mission. Step Four involves choosing your main points and the informative framework that you will use to organize these points into a logical sequence. Clear organization is vital to public speaking. The most prevalent weakness among speakers at all levels is the failure to organize material for the audience. Arranging the main points will help your audience remember your material.

Below are examples of sample speech topics and corresponding main points for the four most typical informative speech organizational frameworks: chronological, topical, pro/con, and spatial. The organizational pattern you choose will provide structure to the body of your speech. Once you have a pattern for arranging your speech content, it is time to further clarify the framework of your speech. This is accomplished by creating main points and sub-points. *Main points* support, develop, and explain the specific purpose of your speech. In outlines, main points are symbolized by roman numerals, for example: I, II, III.

Main points support, develop, and explain your specific purpose.

Informative Speech Patterns for Main Points

Chronological, Topical, Pro-Con, and Spatial Informative Frameworks

Chronological

Major events in our lives are organized by time (e.g. births, marriages, employment history, college degrees). This pattern is a natural way for arranging events in the sequence in which they occurred. As such, this sequence is sometimes called the time or sequential pattern. The chronological pattern shows time relationships, for example past, present, future. The *chronological pattern* is a method of speech organization in which the main points follow a time pattern. This framework is also used to demonstrate sequential steps to a process, or events in history.

Chronological pattern examples:

Turning Point	Grandma's Pie Recipe	U.S. Wars
I. Before	I. Make pie crust	I. World War I
II. During	II. Place filling in to crust	II. World War II
III. After	III. Bake pie	III. War on Terror

Topical

The topical pattern is a popular organizational framework for speech giving. The *topical pattern* is defined as a method of speech organization in which the main points divide the topic into logical and consistent sub-topics. This pattern demonstrates each of the parts to make up a whole. Think of this pattern as a pie cut in equal pieces. Topical pattern examples:

Favorite Colors	World Religions	Marriage Vows
I. Purple	I. Islam	I. Love
II. Orange	II. Buddhism	II. Honor
III. Green	III. Christianity	III. Cherish

Pro/Con

The pro/con framework consists of two main points that express two opposing viewpoints on a topic. The *pro/con pattern* is a method of speech organization that presents both sides of an issue. It is sometimes called the advantages/disadvantages pattern. When using this pattern, both sides should be given fairly even emphasis. Pro-Con pattern examples:

Abortion	Political Orientation	Proposition A
I. Pro-Choice	I. Republican	I. Vote For
II. Pro-Life	II. Democrat	II. Vote Against

Spatial

The points in the spatial pattern are arranged by geographical or physical sequence, or as they occur in physical space. This pattern can be effective in describing relationships between ideas. In all speeches arranged spatially, each main point must relate to each another. The *spatial pattern* is a method of speech organization in which the main points follow a directional pattern. Spatial pattern examples:

Continents	New Home	My Garden
I. Africa	I. Kitchen	I. Vegetables
II. Europe	II. Bedroom	II. Flower bed
III. Australia	III. Living Room	III. Herbs

YOUR VIEW

What organizational pattern will work for the type of speech you are giving? Why?

_____

_____

Next to the roman numerals, write your three main points:

I._____

II._____

III._____

Sub-points
are examples used to develop the main points.

Sub-points are the examples used to develop the main points. Sub-points support, expand, and explain main points. Each of your main points above should possess two to four supporting sub-points as evidence. Your next step is to consider what type of evidence you wish to incorporate under each of your main points.

Step Five: Support with Evidence

Evidence
is the supporting material in your speech, including facts, examples, and expert testimony.

Evidence is a term commonly used to describe supporting material in your speeches. Each of your main points must be supported or proven as true by at least two pieces of evidence. The three types of evidence that you will use to support your main points are facts, examples, and expert testimony.

Types of Evidence

Three Types of Evidence
Facts, Examples, Expert Testimony

Facts

Facts
are not in dispute and are verifiable by objective measures.

Facts give your other evidence an objective foundation and make your speech more than a collection of opinions, non-representative examples, anecdotes, stories, and prejudices. Facts are verifiable by objective measures and can include statistical data, dates, and historical events—although statistical data should be used sparingly so as not to overwhelm your audience. Because facts are not in dispute, they will provide powerful support for each point. However, you must avoid using nonfactual information as fact because doing so will destroy your credibility as a speaker.

How to Use Facts as Evidence

Most speeches will require that each main point possess, at minimum, one undisputable fact. How can you make sure the evidence you are using is a fact, and not just an opinion? To do so, make sure your evidence possesses a second level of editorial review. *Editorial review* is a tool to access the quality of the evidence you use in your speech. A second level of editorial review means that your evidence has been verified by a scholarly or highly reputable published source, and that it is factual. Editorial review is a form of quality control.

Examples

Examples are specific cases or illustrations that clarify, reinforce, or personalize your topic. Examples can help you illuminate complex concepts, assist you in proving a point, and help your audience visualize your meaning more clearly. Examples must relate to your topic and be audience-centered, vivid, easily understood, and memorable. Examples are not as weighty as facts.

Examples
are specific cases that clarify and reinforce your topic, including analogy, personal experience, and narratives.

There are three different types of examples: analogical examples, personal experience, and narratives.

An analogy is a connection that is established between two otherwise dissimilar ideas or things. *Analogical examples* illustrate a point or illuminate a connection by comparing the point to a known or more easily understood point. Analogical examples work well when you need to illustrate an idea or shed light on a connection.

A second type of example is personal experience. *Personal experience* can provide compelling support and real-life perspective when used appropriately and in moderation. Use personal experience when you need to present your ideas in human terms that relate to your experience or the experience of your audience.

The last type of examples that you may use to develop your main points are called narratives. *Narratives* are, in essence, extended examples. Narratives are short stories used to illustrate a point or an important truth. Storytelling can be a memorable and entertaining method of conveying information. Stories give meaning and context to what would otherwise be a collection of easily forgettable details.

Expert Testimony

Expert testimony involves a statement of opinion or inference from an expert. It is usually expressed in the form of quotations or summaries. Expert testimony can be a valid form of evidence when it involves the opinions of recognized experts or specialists in a field relevant to the topic of your speech. Be wary of assuming that respectable credentials alone or one expert's opinion will establish testimony as fact.

Expert testimony
is a statement of opinion or inference from an expert in the field.

YOUR VIEW

What facts, examples, and expert testimony will you use to develop your next speech? Why?

_____

_____

_____

_____

Information Literacy

Information literacy is a set of abilities requiring a speaker to recognize when evidence is needed, then have the ability to locate, evaluate, and use the evidence effectively. Information literacy is increasingly important due to the sheer abundance of user-generated information that is now available online. Increasingly, information is accessible online through unfiltered sources that do not possess editorial review. Unlike library books or databanks, web pages may be published by anyone. There are no quality controls on websites. Thus, it is essential to evaluate the quality of the web pages and other sources before using them as supporting material in your speech. To be information literate, you must access all of your research in four key areas: authority, accuracy, objectivity, and currency.

Criteria for Evaluating Information

The questions below, developed by librarian Rachel Sandoval of the West Valley College Library in 2009, will assist you in evaluating print and digital media (Sandoval, 2009).

Authority

Authority has to do with the source that the information is drawn from, and whether that information has an authoritative voice. Many of the books and databanks in an academic library have authority. Other forms of authority are the credentials that a person holds that indicate expertness in a particular field, the institution a person is affiliated with may be another, or if the author has "life experience" that adds credibility to their viewpoint.

Here are four questions to ask to determine if your source has authority:

◆ Can you identify the person(s) or organization responsible for creating and developing the page?
◆ Is it clear who wrote the material and are the author's qualifications clearly stated?
◆ What does the domain (.edu .com .org .gov) or URL tell you?
◆ Is there a way of verifying the legitimacy? Is there a phone number, address, or copyright?

Accuracy

Accuracy is defined as exact and precise conformity to an established fact. Sometimes people mistakenly assume that statistics, because they are numbers, are generally accurate. If you find statistics or evidence, and the website you find it on does not attribute the source of the evidence, do not assume accuracy. Even if the website cites the information or the statistic, the evidence presented should always be double-checked by measuring it against information on the same topic from another reputable source.

Here are four questions to ask to determine if your source has accuracy:

- ◆ Is the topic appropriate for the website?
- ◆ Can you verify the facts in another source?
- ◆ Is the information free of grammatical, spelling, and typographical errors?
- ◆ Is it clear who has responsibility for the information?

Objectivity

Information often has underlying assumptions or biases. *Objectivity* is the extent to which the information presented displays bias. While someone could argue that all information presents a bias of one sort or another, try to find evidence that is as objective as possible. Typically, this type of information is found in scholarly journals. If you are not using scholarly journals or library databanks, then you should thoroughly analyze the information to see if it is trying to get you to change your opinion, act, or buy a product.

Here are three questions to ask to determine if your source has objectivity:

- ◆ To what extent is the information trying to sway the opinion of the audience?
- ◆ Is there an evident slant or bias?
- ◆ Does the page try to sell product? Is there advertising on the page?

Currency

Currency is defined as being up-to-date or recent. It is always a good idea to get the most current research on a topic. Currency is especially important in scientific topics, current politics, and contemporary social issues. When looking at websites and other sources to support your speech, seek out the publication date or the latest revision date or the information contained within may be outdated and no longer credible. If the website or article does not have any dates, then reconsider using it. Also, since it takes month or years to public books or articles, you should keep in mind that the information found in the book or article will be older than the publication date.

Here are four questions to ask to determine if your source has currency:

- ◆ When was the page first placed on the web, updated, or revised?
- ◆ If the material is presented in graphs and/or charts, is the date that the data was gathered clearly stated?

- ◆ Are there any other indications that the material is kept current?
- ◆ Is old information archived, or does it just disappear?

Standards for Information Literacy

As the American Library Association Presidential Committee on Information Literacy (1989) says, "Ultimately, information literate people are those who have learned how to learn. They know how to learn because they know how knowledge is organized, how to find information, and how to use information in such a way that others can learn from them. They are people prepared for lifelong learning, because they can always find the information needed for any task or decision at hand." According to the ACRL, The Association of College and Research Libraries in the article "Information Literacy Standards for Higher Education" (2000) there are five standards of information literacy. Implement these five standards and you will become a competent researcher for your next speech. An effective public speaker:

1. Determines the nature and extent of the information needed.
2. Accesses needed information effectively and efficiently.
3. Evaluates information and its sources critically and incorporates selected information into her or his knowledge base and value system.
4. Uses information to effectively accomplish a specific purpose.
5. Understands many of the ethical, legal and socioeconomic issues surrounding information and information technology

Websites to Help Evaluate Webpage Quality

In a world of information overload, it is vital to not only find information but also determine its validity, reliability, and appropriateness. If you are still uncertain as to whether your evidence is of sufficient quality, go to one of the following websites to assist you in becoming more cyber smart.

American Library Association: www.ala.org/acrl/undwebev.html
UC Berkeley Library: www.lib.berkeley.edu/TeachingLib/Guides/Internet/Evaluate.html
UCLA College Library: www.library.ucla.edu/libraries/college/help/critical
University of Maryland Library: www.lib.umd.edu/guides/evaluate.html

YOUR VIEW

How do you know that your evidence has authority, accuracy, objectivity, and currency and meets the standards of information literacy?

_____

_____

_____

_____

_____

Evidence

Consider the facts, examples, and expert testimony that you have gathered for your speech. Use the list below to confirm if you have the quality and quantity of evidence you need to support your points. Circle the appropriate response. If you circled more than three "no" responses, you will need to reassess your evidence.

1. **Yes No** Is your evidence the most current possible?
2. **Yes No** Is your evidence relevant to your specific purpose or thesis?
3. **Yes No** Is your evidence representative of the whole body of research?
4. **Yes No** Is your evidence typical, reflecting all the data?
5. **Yes No** Is your evidence weighty enough to encompass the issue?
6. **Yes No** Is the source of your evidence reliable?
7. **Yes No** Is your evidence reasonably comprehensive?
8. **Yes No** Are the sources of your evidence objective and without bias?
9. **Yes No** Have the sources of the evidence included conflicting views?
10. **Yes No** Is your evidence for each main point equally developed?
11. **Yes No** Does most of your evidence have a second level of review?
12. **Yes No** Does your evidence reflect a wide variety of sources?
13. **Yes No** Did you use personal or hypothetical evidence sparingly?
14. **Yes No** Did you use your statistical evidence sparingly?
15. **Yes No** Did you avoid using anecdotal examples as evidence?
16. **Yes No** Did you simplify your evidence to make it comprehensible?

YOUR VIEW

Do you have the quality and quantity of evidence that you need to support your speech, or do you need to reassess? Why?

_____

_____

_____

Step Six: Create an Introduction

You cannot construct an introduction before you know what your main points are and have considered the quality and quantity of your evidence, or you will not know what you are introducing. Before getting into specifics on how to create an introduction for your speech, view the following flowchart for a speech.

```
INTRODUCTION
Attention getter
Orientation
Point preview
```

```
 I.  MAIN POINT
A. Evidence
     1. Example
     2. Example
B. Evidence
     1. Example
     2. Example
```

```
Transition to second point
```

```
II. MAIN POINT
A. Evidence
     1. Example
     2. Example
B. Evidence
     1. Example
     2. Example
```

```
Transition to third point
```

```
III. MAIN POINT
  A. Evidence
    1. Example
    2. Example
  B. Evidence
    1. Example
    2. Example
```

```
CONCLUSION
  1. Point review
  2. Closure
  3. Final Statement
```

A simple three-step way to remember how to organize a speech is this: *Tell us what you are going to tell us about, tell us about it, and tell us what you told us.*

In the introduction, you tell us what you are going to tell us about. Your introduction should be less than one minute in length for a five to ten minute speech. You should use three techniques in your introduction: attention-getter, orientation, and a point preview.

Attention-getter

Attention-getter gains the attention and interest of your audience right at the start of your speech.

The very first sentence you should say in your speech is called the *attention-getter*. It is different from your specific purpose statement in that it must gain the attention and interest of your audience within the first 20 seconds of your speech or people may choose to not listen to you. The attention-getter is also conceptualized by the hook metaphor, in that the attention-getter hooks your audience just as a fish gets hooked to a fishing line. Your attention-getter must relate to your topic, be appropriate to the audience, and be unique. Visual attention-getters are often effective and memorable because many people in your audience are likely visual learners.

There are several different types of attention-getters: startling fact, statistic, amusing story, visualization, hypothetical situation, rhetorical question, or audio or visual aids. Consider which attention-getter will work best for your speech.

Types of Attention-Getters

Startling Fact, Statistic, Amusing Story, Visualization, Hypothetical Situation, Rhetorical Question, Poem, Quote, Lyric, Video or Audio Clip

Startling Fact

A *startling fact* is objective and verifiable factual evidence that surprises your audience and, as a result, motivates them to pay attention. Startling facts should be externally verified by a second level of editorial review. This type of attention-getter works well if the fact comes from a reputable source and is cited.

Statistic
A *shocking statistic* can be effective on audiences who respond favorably to numerical data. Statistics are effective if the statistic clearly relates to your speech topic and purpose, is rounded, and is cited. Too many statistics can have the adverse effect of creating attention if the statistic does not come from a valid and reputable source.

Amusing Story
An *amusing story* can pull in your audience if the story is brief, descriptive, and appropriate to the tone of the speech. Only use amusing stories for speech topics that are light in nature. If your speech topic is serious in nature, the amusing story attention-getter can backfire.

Visualization
A *powerful visualization* will paint a picture of something in the minds of your audience members. Visualization can be a great way to gain the interest of your audience because it gives people a chance to use imagination when forming mental images. This type of attention-getter is effective if it is vivid, realistic, and relates to your purpose.

Hypothetical Situation
A *hypothetical situation* is an example that describes an imaginary or fictitious situation or event. This type of opening works well if you make certain that what you are describing is transferrable to the purpose of your speech. If the hypothetical situation you describe is not transferrable, this type of attention-getter falls flat.

Rhetorical Question
A *rhetorical question* is a question that is asked without the expectation of a reply. A rhetorical question can work well if the answer to the question is not obvious. The question is instead posed for the sake of encouraging its listener to consider a message or viewpoint. Rhetorical questions provoke curiosity that the speech then proceeds to satisfy, without the expectation of a reply. Sometimes novice speakers over-rely on the rhetorical question attention-getter and it loses its impact.

Quote, Poem, or Lyric
A thoughtful or provocative *quote, poem or lyric* can add emotional depth to your speech right from the beginning. Quotes work best when either you have written them, or a well-respected and famous author, musician, poet, philosopher, or leader has. A pithy quote has the power to enamor, enrage, inspire, or inform your audience.

Video/Audio Clip

A poignant *video/audio clip* works well as an attention-getter if it is short, cited, and neatly ties into your topic. Given that roughly half of a typical audience is composed of visual learners, this type of attention-getter can be quite powerful. However, it does not work when the speaker neglects to tie the clip into the purpose of the speech.

YOUR VIEW

What type of attention-getter will work best for your speech requirements and audience? Why? How can you make your attention-getter visual?

_____

_____

_____

Orientation

> **Three Components of Orientation**
>
> Relevance, Context, Credibility

Your speech introduction also consists of orientation and a point preview. The purpose of orientation, a term conceptualized by renown scholars Jo Sprague and Douglas Stuart in their groundbreaking text "The Speaker's Handbook" is to get the audience on the same page as you, right form the start. Orientation consists of relevance, context, and credibility.

Relevance

> *Relevance* shows your intended audience how your speech relates to them.

Relevance shows your intended audience how your speech relates to them, regardless of age, gender, culture, ethnicity, race, sexual orientation, income, religion, or other demographic variables. Relevance addresses the "what is in it for me" for each person in the audience. It makes your speech applicable. Often, speakers highlight shared values or common desires in a simple statement as a means of creating this connection. The importance of relevance should not be underestimated. If your audience does not believe your speech is relevant and valuable to them, they may choose not to listen.

Context

> *Context* is the circumstances that surround the situation where your public speaking address occurs.

Context is defined as the circumstances that surround the situation where your public speaking address occurs, or the specifics of your speech topic. It provides contextual information on the setting of your speech, such as pertinent information on the event or occasion. It also gives the audience necessary details, historiography, and/or background data about the subject matter of your speech. For example, if there are terms that need defining, a purpose that needs stating, or historical or background data on your subject that needs explaining so that your audience can more effectively follow your speech, briefly clarify that in your introduction.

Credibility

Credibility involves speaker trustworthiness, competence, goodwill, and integrity. Trustworthiness can be communicated by explaining your purpose, or why you chose the speech to begin with. Competence can be clearly developed by citing the sources of your evidence. If you think about it, integrity and honesty are hard to communicate verbally. Sometimes these factors are best relayed through your nonverbal communication or your reputation. Your reputation or status is the public estimation of your character, name, or deeds.

Credibility is the trustworthiness, competence, goodwill, and integrity of the speaker.

YOUR VIEW

Reflect on the three orientation strategies. What common theme will you use to demonstrate that your topic is relevant to all? What contextual information is required? How will you prove you are credible enough to speak on your topic?

_____

_____

_____

_____

Point Preview

A *preview* is at the very end of your introduction, after the attention-getter and orientation. The point preview serves as a clear transition into the speech body of your speech. The main point preview lists each of the main points in your speech in sequential order. The preview tells your audience what is coming up next, without giving your whole speech away. Numbered full sentence previews work well, but are not always necessary.

A *Preview* lists each of your main points in order at the end of your introduction.

Step Seven: Develop Transitions to Link Your Main Points

Transitions in speeches are much different than written transitions. In a written transition, you can sometimes use one word—for example, the word *next*. If your reader gets lost, all they need to do is re-read the paragraph prior and they will re-acclimate. However, in a speech the listeners cannot ask you to repeat what you just said if they become confused. Transitions in speeches are used in between each of your main points to signpost for the speaker two important cues: where you have been and where you are going. Transitions do not simply announce your main points, they are a bridge in between your main points. This is called a *two-part transition*.

Two-part transition tell your audience where you have been and where you are going.

Here are examples of one- and two-part transitions:

One-Part Transition
"Next, I will tell you about a different political opinion on the issue."

Two-Part Transition
"Now that we have talked about how the Democratic nominee views the issue, we will move into what the Republican nominee thinks about it."

Some audiences may prefer that you use numbers to further clarify your organization. Numbered transitions are the easiest to follow.

Here are some examples of number transitions:

Numbered One-Part Transition
"The second main point is on the cost of the hybrid car the Prius."

Numbered Two-Part Transition
"We've just spent some time on our first point, the gas-saving benefits of the hybrid car the Prius. Second, we will discuss how much this car costs consumers."

YOUR VIEW

Write a two-part transition between two of your main points for your next speech:

_____

_____

_____

You must clarify for your listener when you are moving from your introduction into the body of your speech, from main point to main point, and from the body to your conclusion. If your listeners do not know where you are at any given time in your speech, you probably have not told them often enough. You may be wondering if the audience really need all of these organizers. The answer is yes. And it will be quite easy for you to tell if you use transitions effectively. Either your audience will be able to follow you or they will not. If you want to sound logical, organized, and cohesive, use functional two-part transitions.

Step Eight: Construct a Conclusion

You told your audience what you are going to talk about in your introduction, and then talked about it in your speech body. Now, your speech conclusion gives you the opportunity to tell your audience what you told them. The conclusion should be shorter than your introduction, or roughly thirty to forty-five seconds for a five- to ten-minute speech. The three techniques that you will use are a review of main points, closure, and a final statement. The point review is the first words you will say in your conclusion. Closure is a technique that adds more meaning to your speech. It lets your audience know your speech is coming to a close. The final statement is the last sentence you say in your speech and provides a sense of finality.

> **Three Components to Conclusion**
>
> Review, Closure, and Final Statement

Review

A *review* is at the very beginning of your conclusion and serves as a clear signpost that your speech is coming to an end. Like the preview, the review lists each of the main points in order. Use different words than the preview to avoid excessive repetition. Numbered point reviews generally work well.

> A *Review* recaps each of your main points at the start of your conclusion.

Closure

Closure can be thoroughly or minimally developed, depending on your topic. Sometimes the closure and final statement are connected and can be hard to differentiate. Some techniques for closure are saying your specific purpose, reminding your audience of how the speech relates to them, or highlighting the moral of your speech or an underlying principle. It is critical in closure not to add new information into your speech, as doing so will confuse your audience. In addition, you should avoid using excessive pauses in your closure or your audience may misinterpret the silence and begin applauding too early.

> *Closure* lets your audience know that your speech is coming to an end.

Final Statement

A *final statement* is the very last sentence of your speech. It is different from closure in that it must impart a sense of finality. Some refer to the final statement as a farewell wish or clincher. Your final statement can relate back to your attention-getter if you choose. If your final statement is effective, your audience will applaud because they will know your speech is over. Some speakers like to thank their audience for listening as their final statement. Avoid using phrases like "that's it" or "I'm done." Remember to stay put after your final statement is over and accept the applause from your audience for a job well done.

> *Final statement* gives a sense of finality at the very end of your speech.

How will you develop your conclusion and achieve closure in your next speech?

_____

_____

_____

Before you move into Phase Two in the next chapter, complete this checklist to make sure you have completed Phase One.

Phase One Checklist

_____	Reviewed the assignment requirements
_____	Considered the audience in topic selection and content targeting
_____	Clarified the general and specific purpose of the speech
_____	Organized the main points into a logical sequence
_____	Supported each main point with ample quality evidence
_____	Created an Introduction
_____	Organized main points with two-part transitions
_____	Designed a Conclusion

CHAPTER SUMMARY

A speech, just like a challenging hike, can become overwhelming if you do not prepare and pace yourself or if you fall too far behind in your timing. The goal of this chapter is to provide you with a map to follow for speech development so that you can avoid feeling overcome with the task of developing your informative speech.

This chapter explained each of the eight steps in PHASE ONE, the first phase of Informative Speaking, which is preparation. It started with topic selection and audience analysis and moved into organizing and supporting your points, creating an introduction, and finally, designing a conclusion for your speech. The next chapter will overview the final four steps of informative speaking in PHASE TWO. To be an effective informative speaker, you should complete each of the two phases, one step at a time, at a steady pace.

NAVIGATING THE TERRAIN: Phase Two of the Twelve Steps for Informative Speaking

5

Walking is nearly as natural as breathing.
Most of us don't remember learning how—it's just something that happens.
And when it does—one foot in front of the other . . . thoughts are free to go skipping over the landscape like a thistledown in the wind.

—Cathy Johnson, *Nature Walks*

While walking may be as natural as breathing for some people as the Johnson quote implies, navigating the terrain in an attempt to achieve communication competence takes some well-intentioned effort. Competence is defined as the "state or quality of being adequately or well qualified in a specific range of skill." *Communication competence* is the degree to which a speaker's goals are achieved through effective and appropriate interaction with the audience.

Sprague and Stuart, authors of *The Speaker's Handbook* (1984) and experts on communication competence in the realm of public speaking, assert that the learning of public speaking as a skill often progresses through four stages of communication competence. These four stages are part of the Conscious Competence Ladder, which present a popular and intuitive approach to communication competence.

According to the Conscious Competence Ladder approach, consciousness is the first step toward gaining knowledge. This means you need to become aware of what you do not know about effective speech-giving. This discovery, although uncomfortable, is a necessary endeavor. You may find yourself to be highly competent in one aspect of communication such as developing visual aids, but have little skill in another, such as delivering your speech in a memorable and engaging manner.

Communication competence is the degree to which a speaker's goals are achieved through effective and appropriate interaction with the audience.

The Conscious Competence Ladder theory asserts that as you build expertise in preparing and delivering a presentation, you move from "unconscious incompetence" to "conscious incompetence." Then with practice, you move to "conscious competence" and finally reach the top of the ladder with "unconscious competence." The four stages of competence as first conceptualized by Sprague and Stuart (1984) are covered next.

Four Stages of Competence
Unconscious Incompetence, Conscious Incompetence, Conscious Competence, Unconscious Competence

Stage 1: Unconscious incompetence. In this stage, you are not aware that you are making errors in your public speaking, often due to lack of experience in giving speeches or to lack of self-awareness. You may be a naturally low self-monitor or are unaware that you need to learn this skill, so you may not have any motivation to learn how to enhance your skills.

Stage 2: Conscious incompetence. In this stage, you make the realization that you have a lot to learn about public speaking and effective communication. You become acutely aware that there is much room for improvement. In many cases, this awareness creates enhanced self-monitoring and sometimes even feelings of anxiety or being overwhelmed.

Stage 3: Conscious competence. In this stage, your hard work at improving your public speaking skills begins to pay off, but you still need to devote a lot of energy into each aspect of your performance. You are aware that the absence of such vigilance could mean a regression to more comfortable but less competent patterns. If you persevere despite the awkwardness that often accompanies learning new public speaking skills, your need for self-monitoring will lessen with time and practice.

Stage 4: Unconscious competence. In this stage, you have integrated the learned skills well enough that you do not need to devote conscious attention to maintaining competence because it comes naturally. Effective public speaking becomes relatively effortless, and maybe even fun.

YOUR VIEW

What stage of competence are you in when it comes to public speaking? What indications do you have that you are in that stage?

_____

_____

Constructivist Competencies

In addition to those already described, competent communication also requires a mastery of several other types of skills, known as communication competencies. The theory of Constructivism will guide this next exploration of different kinds of functional communication competence relating to speech-giving. Constructivism takes your skills to the next level into the realms of communication competence.

Constructivism, first theorized by Swiss psychologist Jean Piaget and American philosopher George Herbert Mead, seeks to explain individual differences in the ability to communicate. It does this by identifying what counts as proficient communication with respect to several core competencies. Some of these competencies were initially conceptualized by Professor of Psychological Sciences Brant Burleson from Purdue University in several scholarly papers and textbooks, most namely the article "Constructivism A General Theory of Communciation Skill" (2006) and the text he co-authored with John Greene (2003) called *Handbook of Communication and Social Interaction Skills*". This next section will underscore four core constructivist competencies for speech giving.

Cultural competence is a person's ability to know the social rules that govern the appropriate use of verbal and nonverbal language patterns and apply these rules to their communications with particular cultures. Cultural competence is the ability to gauge what communication pattern and style is proper and acceptable to a specific cultural group, then to communicate with the cultural group in ways the culture finds socially correct and acceptable. Cultural competence is an essential skill given the global village we live in.

Verbal competence is a communicator's skill in using language effectively. A person with high verbal competence appropriately applies specific linguistic rules and language norms to speaking and listening. It enables them to construct sentences that are comprehendible to diverse audiences. Verbal competence is also the talent of being able to accurately decode the words that others speak. Verbal competence is linguistic proficiency in areas such as syntax, morphology, structure, semantics, phonology, spelling, and grammar.

Nonverbal competence has to do with a communicator's being able to notice nonverbal subtleties in others' messages and "read between the lines" to extract the accurate meaning, whether intentional or unintentional. This competency also involves the ability to effectively encode nonverbal messages in a way that elicits a desired response from the audience. Nonverbal competence is especially important when communicating with indirect or high context audience members, because these communicators rely strongly on nonverbal messages.

Four Competencies

Cultural, Verbal, Nonverbal, and Perceptual.

Cultural competence is a person's ability to know the social rules that govern the appropriate use of verbal and nonverbal language patterns and apply these rules to their communications with particular cultures.

Verbal competence is a communicator's skill in using language effectively.

Nonverbal competence is the communicator's ability to effectively encode nonverbal messages

Perceptual competence
is the ability
to effectively
gather and utilize
information about
the social world.

Perceptual competence is the ability to effectively gather and utilize information about the social world, including experiences of ourselves, other people in our lives, and even social institutions. Perception is the process of observing, identifying, and interpreting things in the everyday world. Perceptual competence refers to how skillfully we make sense of our experiences. Perceptual competence is a core competency in effective communication because people often base their communication on their perceptions of self and others.

While people differ in their level of mastery in each of these areas of competence, effective public speakers should strive to expand upon their aptitude in all our areas. Functional communication competence includes the capability of mastering each of these types of competencies in your communication. The more skilled you are in each of these areas, the more competently you will communicate.

YOUR VIEW

Which of the four types of Constructivist competencies are you most and least skilled in?

_____

_____

_____

This chapter will assist you in cultivating constructivist competencies in informative speaking. It will also help you move up the conscious competence ladder to higher levels of communication competence.

PHASE TWO: Organizing and Perfecting Your Speech

Communication competence expert Mark Spitzberg (1988) defined communication competence as the ability to interact well with others by communicating with accuracy, clarity, coherence, and effectiveness. A speech is a type of interaction. PHASE TWO will help you organize and perfect your informative speech so that your interaction goes as planned. PHASE TWO is a follow-up of the steps already mapped out in PHASE

ONE of Chapter Four. PHASE TWO of your walk on *The Speaker's Path* will help you navigate the terrain by walking you through the final four steps of informative speaking, starting with Step Nine.

Phase Two: Organizing and Perfecting Your Speech

Step Nine:	Complete Speech Preparation Guide
Step Ten:	Develop a Full-Sentence Outline
Step Eleven:	Cite Your Evidence
Step Twelve:	Design Visual Aids

Step Nine: Complete a Speech Preparation Guide

Organizing your speech means arranging all of the material you have gathered so far in a manner that is orderly and easy to follow. Completing the appropriate Speech Preparation Guide and then developing this organizational device into an outline is a two-part process.

There are many benefits to organizing your speech into an outline. Here are a few:

- An outline provides a means to prepare your ideas in a logical and coherent manner.
- An outline permits you to review your speech as a whole before you give your speech. This quick scan will help you see what is needed to make the speech complete and what points could be left out.
- An outline provides an efficient way for you to assess the strengths and weaknesses of your speech as it is being constructed. When your points are laid out on paper, it is easier to make improvements.
- An outline enables you as a speaker to remember your points better, because writing something down often moves information from our short-term memory into our long-term memory.
- An outline will help you to be more relaxed and confident because you will know that you are organized and well-prepared for your speech.

The Speech Preparation Guide is your rough plan for your outline. Your outline is your specific plan for your speech. Before you begin arranging your content and evidence into an outline, complete one of the Speech Preparation Guide on the following pages.

Speech Preparation Guide — Informative

Speech Title: _____

Specific Purpose: _____

_____

Introduction:

Attention-getter: _____

_____

Context : _____

_____

Credibility: _____

_____

Relevance: _____

_____

Point Preview: _____

_____

Body:

Main Point One: _____

_____

Evidence: _____

_____

Evidence: _____

_____

Two-Part Transition: _____

_____

Main Point Two: _____

_____

Evidence: _____

_____

Evidence: _____

_____

Two-Part Transition: _____

_____

Main Point Three: _____

_____

Evidence: _____

_____

Evidence: _____

_____

Two-Part Transition: _____

_____

Conclusion:

Point Review: _____

_____

Closure: _____

_____

Final Statement: _____

_____

References:

_____

_____

_____

_____

Speech Preparation Guide — Informative

Speech Title: _____

Specific Purpose: _____

_____

Introduction:

Attention-getter: _____

_____

Context : _____

_____

Credibility: _____

_____

Relevance: _____

_____

Point Preview: _____

_____

Body:

Main Point One: _____

_____

Evidence: _____

_____

Evidence: _____

_____

Two-Part Transition: _____

_____

Main Point Two: _____

_____

Evidence: _____

_____

Evidence: _____

_____

Two-Part Transition: _____

_____

Main Point Three: _____

_____

Evidence: _____

_____

Evidence: _____

_____

Two-Part Transition: _____

_____

Conclusion:

Point Review: _____

_____

Closure: _____

_____

Final Statement: _____

_____

References:

_____

_____

_____

_____

Step Ten: Develop a Full-Sentence Outline

Your next step on *The Speaker's Path* is to convert your Speech Preparation Guide into a fully developed outline. Following is a sample outline on the topic of outlining to use as a guide.

Title: Putting Together an Effective Outline

<u>**Specific Purpose:**</u> To inform speakers how to develop and write an effective outline so that their speeches are well-organized and sufficiently supported.

<u>**Introduction**</u>:

Ralph Waldo Emerson once said, "By persisting in your path, though you forfeit the little, you gain the great."

What he means by this is that perseverance pays off. This is true for speech-giving as well. Effective speakers are not always the most extroverted or confident. Quite often, success boils down to being steadfast and prepared. Your outline is the key to preparation.

The introduction paragraph in your outline seeks to gain the audience's attention and interest as well as acquaint them with the subject matter and the tone of the speech. The introduction should be less than one minute in length. It will be in paragraph form. The introduction should consist of three related segments: attention-getter, orientation, and point preview. The attention-getter is the first thing you should say in your speech; it serves to pull the audience into your speech.

The second aspect of your introduction is orientation. Orientation helps to orient your audience to your subject and tone. Orientation might consist of credibility, relevance, and context. Credibility involves proving your trustworthiness, competence, goodwill, and integrity. Relevance shows your audience how your speech relates to them by providing your audience with a "what's in it for me." Context gives the audience necessary details about your topic or the speech occasion.

The last sentence in your introduction is the numbered point preview, which serves as a signpost and a transition to the body of your speech.

<u>**Body:**</u>

I. The structure of the outline must satisfy structural requirements.

    A. The main points and sub-points must follow specific criteria.
        1. Use roman numerals for your main points.
        2. Use uppercase letters for your evidence.
        3. Use Arabic numbers for your specific examples.

    B. The format of the body of your outline should adhere to a strict format.
        1. Double-space between your main points.
        2. Use clear margins and only one sentence per symbol.
        3. Use consistent outline symbols that follow the rules for outlining.

Transition one: Now that I have just told you about the structure of the outline, next I will tell you about subordination and development.

II. The outline must be properly subordinated and developed.

    A.   The points in the outline should be subordinated.
        1. Main points will develop and explain your thesis or purpose.
        2. Sub-points will develop, support, or explain the main point.

    B.   The body should be detailed with concrete, focused evidence.
        1. Use statistics, but use them sparingly.
        2. Use examples to include analogies and narration.
        3. Quotations can be used when presenting expert testimony.

Transition two: We have talked about how to develop your main points, now we will talk about how to arrange your points into a pattern that works.

III. Main points must conform to one, definite, overall pattern of arrangement.

    A.   Some patterns work well for informative speaking.
        1. The chronological pattern is used to show time relationships.
        2. The topical pattern is used to show parts of a whole.
        3. The pro/con format is used to demonstrate two sides.
        4. The spatial pattern is used to show spatial relationships between main points.

    B.   The patterns that work best for persuasive speaking will be discussed in the next chapter.

Conclusion:

This outline first covered structural requirements, second moved into subordination and speech development, and last discussed patterns for your main points. Now, the conclusion will provide closure and a sense of finality. It will be in paragraph form and is shorter than the introduction. The conclusion should not introduce new information. The conclusion will consist of three segments: point review, closure, and the final statement.

The first part of your conclusion is a numbered point review. The review serves as the transition from the body of your speech to the conclusion.

After the point review, closure will let your audience know that your speech is coming to an end. Closure can involve stating your specific purpose or underlying theme, or reiterating your pointing statement.

The final statement is the final words you say in your speech. It is commonly referred to as a closing statement, thank you, clincher, or farewell wish. The purpose of the final statement is to recapture interest and provide a sense of finality. The final statement often relates to the attention-getter, but does not have to. If you have a solid final statement and you state it with conviction, your audience will know when to applaud. If you do not have a strong final statement , there may be an awkward pause after your speech is over. In sum, following these simple guidelines for outline preparation will help you be organized and successful on speech day.

Step Eleven: Cite Your Evidence

It is important in speech giving to cite your sources, just as you would in any scholarly research paper, to avoid academic dishonesty.

Academic Dishonesty

Academic dishonesty is when a speaker attempts to show a possession of a level of knowledge or skill that he or she does not possess by cheating or plagiarizing.

Academic dishonesty occurs when a person does not cite evidence and intentionally or unintentionally attempts to show possession of a level of knowledge or skill that he or she does not possess. The two most common kinds of academic dishonesty are cheating and plagiarism. *Cheating* is the act of obtaining or attempting to obtain credit for academic or career work through the use of dishonest, deceptive, or fraudulent means. *Plagiarism* is representing the work of someone else as your own. It is your responsibility to know what constitutes academic dishonesty.

Cheating is:

1. Copying, in part or in whole, from someone else.
2. Submitting work presented previously somewhere else.
3. Altering or interfering with assessment or ranking.
4. Using or consulting any sources of materials not authorized.
5. Committing other acts that defraud or misrepresent.

Plagiarism is:

1. Incorporating the ideas, words, sentences, paragraphs, or part of another person's writings or speeches, without giving appropriate credit, and representing the product as your own.
2. Copying and pasting all or a portion of your speech, paper, or outline from another source without properly citing it and representing it as your own material.
3. Submitting a paper or speech purchased from a research or term paper service or from another person.

You might face steep consequences for academic dishonesty, depending on the seriousness of the infraction.

Source Credibility

Your speech is only as strong as your evidence. In other words, your speech is only as good as your sources. For example, *The National Enquirer* is a poor choice for accurate information and will make you seem less credible and believable. *The New York Times* is a better source. If your source has a conservative or liberal leaning, such as FOX NEWS or Mother Jones respectively, and you fail to note the politics of the source, you risk coming off as biased.

When to Cite

Whenever you paraphrase, summarize, or directly quote information that is not general knowledge, you must cite it in three places: the text of your outline if you are being asked to submit an outline, in your speech itself, and in a reference section if one is required.

How to Cite

Either use MLA (Modern Language Association) format or APA (American Psychological Association) format. APA style is the most universally accepted format for citing research.

The next section explains how to cite your sources using APA style in the text of your outline, your reference section, and your speech.

In-Text Cites

Whenever you paraphrase, summarize, or directly quote, sometimes it is required that you cite your sources in the text of your outline or paper. This is called *in-text cites.* If you do not, you could be plagiarizing.

In-text cites are source citations that occur within the context of your outline or paper.

Following are some guidelines.

◆ Cite your source in *every* main point or *every* sub-point, depending on the citation requirements.
◆ When three to five authors are cited, the phrase "et al." may be utilized after the first author's name, to connote the other authors. For example, Yao et al. (2012).
◆ There is no need to include an author's first name or a book's page number when using APA style. Only state the author's last name and the date (year only) of the publication or interview when using APA style in a paper or an outline.
◆ APA style does not use footnotes or endnotes. Only use quotation marks on direct quotes. For example, Sadr (2012) said, "It's important to cite your sources."

YOUR VIEW

Practice citing this quote below as if it were a piece of evidence in your outline.

"Nothing like a nighttime stroll to give you ideas," spoken by the character Mad-Eye Moody in J.K. Rowling's *Harry Potter and the Goblet of Fire,* written in 2000.

_____

_____

_____

In-Speech Cites

Begin by citing your sources in your introduction to establish credibility, although citing your sources just once at the beginning your speech is usually not sufficient. At the minimum, plan to cite once in each main point.

Following are some in-speech citing guidelines:

◆ It is not recommended that you cite each and every sentence or your citations may become tedious to your audience. Instead, cite a cluster of material at one time (if it is all from the same author).
◆ When citing statistics, it is important to mention *who* compiled the statistics, *when* they were done, *how* many people were surveyed, and *why* they relate to your speech.
◆ When citing an unknown author or interviewee for the first time, you must establish source credibility. Give relevant background information on the person or text that illustrates competence and/or expertise. When citing a source for the second time, you only need to include the author's last name.

Three-Step Process for Citing Sources in Your Speech

Fujishin Three-Step process is a three step process for citing sources during your speech.

Noted author and renown speaker Randy *Fujishin* (2006) developed a *three-step process* to cite evidence during your speeches. The three steps according to Fujishin are cite the source, state the evidence, and then restate the evidence.

Step One: **Cite the source** (the author and year of publication, and give it source credibility).

Step Two: **State the evidence** (clearly and succinctly, round statistics off).

Step Three: **Restate the evidence in your own words** (relate evidence to your speech).

YOUR VIEW

Review the steps above. Write down the source for the following quote and give the source credibility, write down the quote, and restate it in your own words. The quote is: "Walking is man's best medicine" by Hippocrates, between 460–377 B.C.E., a Greek physician who was considered one of the most outstanding figures in the history of medicine. To this day, he is still referred to as the "father of medicine" in recognition of his lasting contributions to the field of medicine.

_____

_____

_____

_____

References

Writing a Reference Section

A *reference* section is the same as a bibliography or works cited page. You should have used the information from the source in your paper, speech or outline in order to cite it in the reference section. References should be listed in alphabetical order. The reference page should be double-spaced in between each entry.

References are a list of your sources at the end of your speech or outline.

Here are examples of how to cite different types of sources in APA Style for your references:

Book
> Sprague, J., & Stuart, D. (2012). *The speaker's handbook.* San Diego: Harcourt Brace Jovanovich.

No author or editor
> *Second Harvest Food Bank Statistics.* (2012). Princeton, CA: Second Harvest Publications.

Journal article
> Cooper, M. Riese, M. (2012). Rhetorical criticism and Foucault's philosophy of discursive events. *Central States Speech Journal, 39,* 1–17.

Magazine article
> Gardner, H. (2011, December). Do babies sing a universal song? *Psychology Today,* pp. 70–76.

Newspaper article
> Duke, J. (2011, September 4). Basketball player loses position. *San Jose Mercury,* p. A7.

Pamphlet
> *Guide to Animal Welfare.* (2012). Chamber of Commerce. Washington, DC.

Interview
> Fikret, K. (2012, January 1). Instructor, San Jose State University. (408) 555-5555.

Web page

> Companies that don't test on animals. (2012, February 20). PETA's homepage, http://maratee.environlink.org/arr/peta/shop-guid/donttest.htm.

Step Twelve: Design Your Visual Aids

Some members of your audience are visual learners and will get more out of the images you use in your speech than they will the words you use. It is for this reason that you need to carefully consider what type of *visual aids* will work best in your speech. Your visual aids should always enhance the mission of your speech and must never distract from it or from you. After all, if your visual aid is distracting, then your visual is really not an aid. Consider which type of visual aid will most enrich the purpose of your speech.

In some studies, experimental psychologists and educators have found that retention of information three days after a speech or meeting is six times greater when information is presented by both visual and oral means than when the information is presented by the spoken word alone. Some studies by educational researchers suggest that up to 83 percent of human learning occurs visually. The studies suggest that three days after an event, people retain 10 percent of what they heard from an oral presentation, 35 percent from a visual presentation, and 65 percent from a visual and oral presentation. Thus, visual aids may help your audience to better retain the meaning of your speech. There are five types of visual aids to choose from.

Types of Visual Aids

Objects

Consider how you can make your presentation memorable with props or objects. An *object* will work well if it is practical, professional, and easy to see and maneuver.

1. Choose objects only after examining the space in which they will be presented. Stand at the back of the room to see if the object can be seen from there. If audience members in that area cannot see the prop or photo in detail, they will not be served by its presentation and, consequently, neither will you.

2. Confirm that your objects are large enough for every listener to appreciate. If an object is very small, take a picture of it and present it on a document camera or digital projector. A document camera can enhance the object if it is small and cannot be easily seen, such as a photo or coin.

3. Drawings as objects work well if you are artistic and if visuals cannot be better managed with technology.
4. Some speakers try to overcome size limitations by passing objects around the room during their speech. Rather than enlightening the listener, this practice often serves to distract the audience from your presentation.

Charts And Graphs

Charts/graphs are effective visual aids if relatively simple, focused, and comprehensible.

1. Use a line graph to demonstrate how something has changed over a period of time.
2. Opt for a bar graph to compare data. Keep your bar graphs in two dimensions as three-dimensional bar graphs are difficult to read accurately.
3. Consider a pie chart to show how percentages relate to each other within a whole.
4. Use an organizational chart to show chain of command, communication between departments, or how different departments or processes are related.
5. Try a flow chart to illustrate a series of steps in a procedure, decision, or a step-by-step process.
6. Put an appropriate amount of information and data on each chart or graph. Too much data can overwhelm the audience and be difficult to remember.

Computer-Generated Material

PowerPoint, Keynote, and other computer-generated visual aid programs have the power to aid your speech visually and enhance the experience of your audience. However, we have all seen speakers over-rely on technology at the cost of quality and as such create a PowerPointless instead of a PowerPoint. Computer-generated visuals work well if slides are brief, flawlessly prepared, and not overdone.

1. Prepare only five to ten slides for a five- to eight-minute speech. Make at least one slide for each component of speech, including your Introduction and Conclusion.
2. Keep slides simple. Minimize use of photos, clipart, or graphs to one or two per slide. Use animation sparingly, opting for "appear". Keep template design simple and consistent.
3. Cite sources throughout your slides, to include photos, graphs, and any other items than need to be credited to someone else. Do

not have a list of references at the end of your slide show, as your audience will likely not be able to connect your sources to your data.

4. Keep the sound for transitions to a minimum so as not to risk annoying your audience.

5. Use bullets and key words, except when citing an entire quote.

6. Contrast (light on dark or dark on light) your slide template and font so it is easy to read.

7. Darken the room slightly, or at minimum above the screen, so that your slides will be visible to all members of your audience.

8. Leave each slide up for about 20 to 30 seconds. If you need to discuss something else between two slides, insert a blank slide between the two slides so that your audience won't be distracted.

9. Stand next to the screen (not the projector or computer) so that your audience doesn't have to look back and forth between you and the screen. Do not face your slides or talk to your slides.

10. Always have a backup plan in case your technology fails.

Audio or Visual Clips

An audio or visual clip will add to your speech if it is short, explained well, and supports your purpose. Use DVDs, CDs, or audio or visual files from websites like YouTube to emphasize the main points of your speech.

1. Tell the audience why you are playing the clip. Explain what they are going to see or hear so that they know what to attend to.

2. Consider how your audience might perceive the audio or visual. Don't forget that moving images can distract your audience, and you may need to edit video and audio for time purposes.

3. A video or audio clip should be no more than 30 seconds long in a five- to eight-minute speech. Keep clips short, utilizing only the part that drives the message home. Members of the audience may stop paying attention or engage in side conversations if your clip is too long. Keeping clips short and interspersing them throughout the presentation gives them more impact.

4. Remember to ensure that everybody can hear and see everything. Use amplifying equipment if necessary. Keep the screen in full view for video clips.

5. Always have a back-up plan in case your technology fails.

Flip Chart

If you do not have access to technology, consider a flip chart as an easy, cost-effective way to illustrate key points for audiences when you have a crowd of fifty people or fewer to address.

1. Neatly print large, block letters and numbers on your flip charts so that the data will be visible from the back of the room.
2. Write in the top two-thirds of each flip chart sheet so that your words can easily be seen by all members of your audience.
3. Use dark colored markers such as blue or black as a contrast on the white paper. Avoid using lighter colors such as yellow, orange, beige, or pink as they may be too hard to read.
4. Make simple drawings on your charts if applicable to make the chart more interesting to the members in your audience.
5. Leave a blank sheet between each chart sheet, because flip-chart paper is often so lightweight that it can be semi-transparent.

Handouts

A speaker should thoughtfully consider whether a handout will enhance the purpose of the speech, as oftentimes handouts will have the opposite effect because your audience will be looking at your handout instead of listening to you.

1. If you have determined that a handout is appropriate for your speech and will enhance the purpose, either distribute the handout after your speech if you want the audience to act the way you proposed or to follow a course of action, or distribute the handouts before the speech if you want to guide your audience through the content.
2. Always bring extra handouts, just in case your audience is larger than anticipated.
3. Make sure that your handout does not distract from you or your message.

YOUR VIEW

What types of visual aids will best support your purpose? Why? How do you know if your visual aids will work on your audience? What will you do if, for whatever reason, your visual aids do not work or have impact you intended?

_____

_____

_____

_____

Visual Aid Checklist

Take this Visual Aid Checklist seriously. Check only the items below if they accurately describe your visual aids. You will have a good visual aid list when all the items are checked.

1. Is your visual aid appropriate?

_____ Does your visual aid help explain rather than complicate a concept?

_____ Is your visual aid consistent with the objectives of your speech?

_____ Could you give your speech just as well, or better, without the aid?

_____ Does your visual aid take advantage of classroom technology?

_____ Is your visual aid appropriate to the formality of the setting?

2. Is your visual aid easy to understand?

_____ Do you have too much information on one visual aid or slide?

_____ Is the sequence of your visual aids logical?

_____ Are your visuals or slides direct and to the point?

_____ Can a friend or co-worker understand all the information on your visual aid?

3. Is your visual aid easy to read?

_____ Will your audience have an unobstructed view of your visual?

_____ Is the font or template professional and large enough to read?

_____ Are all diagrams, pictures, or graphs to scale?

4. Is your visual aid interesting?

_____ Did you consider contrast, color, and balance in your design?

_____ If using multimedia slides, did you use simple animation?

_____ Did you use pictures, diagrams, charts, or graphs to add interest?

_____ Will your audience appreciate your visual?

5. Do you know how to use and set up your visual aid?

_____ Have you considered what you will do if your visual aids do not work?

_____ If using multimedia technology, is it already loaded on the computer?

_____ Have you practiced using your visuals or multimedia in your speech?

Phase Two Checklist

Before you finish this chapter, use this checklist for to make sure you have perfected your speech and completed PHASE TWO.

_____ Completed a Speech Preparation Guide

_____ Developed a full sentence outline

_____ Cited your evidence in your speech and in your outline

_____ Create innovative and professional visual aids

CHAPTER SUMMARY

This chapter was written with the intention of helping you build your communication competence in informative speaking. It walked you through the final four steps in a series of twelve steps on how to organize and perfect an informative speech. PHASE TWO of informative speaking first highlighted how to organize your content by completing a Speech Preparation Guide. It then reviewed finalizing the details of informative speech-giving, which are developing an outline, citing sources, and designing effective visual aids. The twelve steps of informative speaking as outlined in PHASE ONE and PHASE TWO underscore the crucial role of preparation and organization as a necessity for public speaking success.

CHART YOUR COURSE: Phase one of the Thirteen Steps to Persuasive Speaking

6

> *The world can doubtless never be well known by theory: practice is absolutely necessary; but surely it is of great use to a young man, before he sets out for that country, full of mazes, windings, and turnings, to have at least a general map of it, made by some experienced traveler.*

> —Lord Chesterfield, British Statesman, Diplomat, and Wit (1694–1773)

A map made by an experienced traveler is valuable to make your way along an unfamiliar path. Chapter Six starts to map out a comprehensive two phase strategy that will help you chart your course for your persuasive speech, PHASE ONE and PHASE Two of Persuasive Speaking. Chapter Six builds on your knowledge base of PHASE ONE and PHASE TWO of Informative Speaking. Therefore, Chapter Six assumes that you have mastered the Twelve Steps to Informative Speaking.

While all of the Informative Speaking skills you aquired in the previous chapters will transfer to persuasive speaking, the two styles of speech-giving are dissimilar. They can be contrasted in a variety of ways and appear on the opposite ends of a continuum. There are three primary points of contrast:

1. Informative speaking reveals options. Persuasive speaking urges us to choose from among options.
2. Informative speaking aspires for understanding. Persuasive speaking asks for commitment.
3. Informative speakers are gifted teachers. Persuasive speakers are motivational leaders.

Persuasive speaking, unlike informative speaking, involves directing, guiding, or appealing to the reason, emotion, or character of an individual or an audience. The goal of informative speaking is to teach. The goals of persuasive speaking are more complex: either to help the listeners to accept the idea, attitude, or action being presented by the speaker or to gain some sort of compliance in belief or action.

Persuasive Speaking

Persuasive speaking is similar, but distinctive from, argumentation, debate, and compliance gaining.

Argumentation is the act or process of forming reasons, justifying beliefs, and drawing conclusions and applying them to a case in discussion in an effort to influence others. Argumentation involves three key areas: (1) understanding and identifying arguments, either explicit or implied, (2) identifying the premises from which conclusions are derived, and (3) establishing the burden of proof. Persuasive speaking goes beyond identifying logical arguments, as it also encompasses emotional and character appeals.

Debate is a broader form of argumentation. *Debate* is the formal discussion of a motion before a deliberative body according to the rules of parliamentary procedure. Formal debate is a rule-driven contest between two or more opposing sides. In formal debate, there are generally at least two teams arguing opposite sides, the affirmative and the negative. Persuasive speeches do not typically have two or more sides advocating for differing resolutions or plans.

Compliance gaining is a term used to identify the act of intentionally trying to alter behavior. The term refers to how people try to get other people to do things, or comply. Compliance is separate, but not unrelated to persuasion. Compliance gaining targets actual behavioral changes, whereas in persuasive speeches, the changes in persuasion can be attitudinal. Thus, persuasive speaking also motivates changes in beliefs or even reinforces beliefs.

The pathway to charting your course for persuasive speaking is divided into two phases, PHASE ONE and PHASE TWO. This chapter of *The Speaker's Path* will underscore a series of steps for PHASE ONE of persuasive speech-giving, Steps One through Seven. Implement each of these seven steps as if you were following directions mapped out by a compass. Then, go on to Chapter Seven and complete the final six steps of PHASE TWO. By doing so, you will be able to navigate your journey into persuasion.

Phase One: Developing Your Speech
           Step One: Choose a Topic
           Step Two: Analyze the Audience
           Step Three: Clarify the Proposition
           Step Four: Determine Persuasive Plan
           Step Five: Ethos
           Step Six: Logos
           Step Seven: Pathos

Phase Two: Organizing and Perfecting Your Speech
           Step Eight: Organize Main Points
           Step Nine: Create an Introduction, Transitions, Conclusion
           Step Ten: Complete a Speech Preparation Guide
           Step Eleven: Build Outline using Persuasive Language
           Step Twelve: Cite Your Sources
           Step Thirteen: Create Visual Aids

> **Two Phases of Persuasive Speaking**
>
> Development and Organizing and Perfecting

PHASE ONE: Developing Your Speech

PHASE ONE of charting your course will emphasize the seven steps of the first phase of persuasive speaking, which is how to design and develop your persuasive speech. To get started on the pathway of persuasion, walk through each of the following seven steps in order, starting with choosing a topic.

Step One: Choose a Topic

Persuasion is a thoughtful act of attempting to change, influence, or reinforce thinking, beliefs, attitudes, intentions, motivations, behaviors, or actions. Persuasive speeches usually involve more planning and deliberation than informative speeches, because motivating people to change or act can be a challenging and arduous task. Due to this factor, five- to ten-minute persuasion speeches rarely achieve radical, lasting shifts in perception such as a change in a person's core beliefs or religious preference. Instead, short persuasive speeches can be influential in getting to people to behave in a particular way or to think about the world in a new light. Persuasion speeches can also create or strengthen attitudes or beliefs that your audience already possesses. Persuasion speeches argue one of three types of assertions: fact, value, or policy.

Assertion of Fact

Assertion of fact speeches argue whether something is true or is not true, whether something happened or did not, or whether something exists or

> **Persuasion** is a thoughtful act of attempting to change, influence, or reinforce thinking, beliefs, attitudes, intentions, motivations, behaviors, or actions.

> **Assertion of fact** speeches argue whether something is true or is not true, whether something happened or did not, or whether something exists or does not exist.

does not exist. Examples include historical controversy, predictions, or questions of existence. Here is where you as the speaker offer proof to support a statement of fact, and the audience determines whether you have convincingly proven the statement true.

Assertion of Value

Assertion of value or belief speeches argue whether something is good or bad, just or unjust, fair or unfair, or worthy or not worthy. Here is where you argue something is right or wrong, moral or immoral, or better or worse than another thing. You likely cannot factually prove that a belief or value is true or false, but you can supply convincing information to justify a belief or value, change that belief or value, or reinforce that belief or value.

Assertion of Policy

Assertion of policy speeches argue for a specific course of action that others should take, or how things should or should not proceed. Here is where you argue that some action should or should not be taken. The primary purpose is to get your audience to actually do something. In an assertion of policy speech, you try to convince the audience to act on some policy or to agree that some policy should be changed.

Clarifying the type of assertion you are arguing is the starting point for your persuasive speech topic. Once you are clear on what type of persuasive address you will be giving (fact, value, or policy), consider what topics will meet the criteria for your speech. Then, reflect on the golden rule in the art of persuasive speech writing, which is to look for a persuasion topic that genuinely interests you.

Assertion of value or belief speeches argue whether something is good or bad, right or wrong, just or unjust, fair or unfair, or worthy or not worthy.

Assertion of policy speeches argue for a specific course of action that others should take, or how things should or should not proceed.

YOUR VIEW

What type of assertion will you be arguing? Which topic best meets the requirements and type of assertion and is also the most interesting to you?

_____

_____

_____

Step Two: Analyze the Audience

Persuasive speaking is the type of speaking that most people engage in the most in both their professional and personal relationships. Persuasion can involve everything from arguing about politics or religion to talking about what movie to go see or what restaurant to go to. Persuasion is a regular event in the workplace as well, whether you are persuading someone to hire you or asking for buy-in on a new proposal. Since persuasion always involves at least one other person, persuasive speaking is at its essence connected to the receiver. The persuasive speaker must, in a sense, meet the listener halfway. Thus, persuasion is not entirely controlled by the speaker. Persuasion occurs when an audience or person assents to what a speaker says. Consequently, persuasive speaking requires extra attention to audience analysis.

Now that you have a topic, it is time to learn as much as you can about your audience, focusing on audience demographics and attitudes toward your topic, so that you can effectively target your speech toward your audience's needs, values, and population. You can do this be completing one of the questionnaires on the following pages, by having informal conversations, or by simply observing your audience and the room.

> **Three Types of Audience Profiles**
>
> Demographic, Attitudinal, Situational

Demographic Profile

One basic approach to audience analysis is to examine the audience's demographic makeup by conducting a *demographic profile*. *Demographics* are the statistical characteristics of a population. Demographic data include gender, race, ethnicity, age, disabilities, home ownership, employment status, and even beliefs and religious preferences. Knowing the demographics can assist you in choosing your proposition and approach. For example, the age of your audience may help you determine what humor and narratives to employ.

Demographic profile analyzes the audience's demographic makeup.

While a demographic profile can assist you in understanding your audience better, avoid making sweeping statements about any demographic characteristic. Demographics can only provide you with baseline information. It is important not to generalize your audience based on the demographic data you receive. If you choose to conduct a demographic analysis, use it for what it is, a guide and an indicator. Stay away from overly simplified assumptions and ensure that your speech is culturally sensitive and reflects the diversity of your audience base.

For example, gender is a socially constructed phenomenon and therefore means different things to different people. Some people's gender identity falls somewhere on continuum of masculine or feminine, not simply as male or female. Although you could likely make legitimate assumptions about gender, it would be inappropriate to assume that all men are sports fans and all women like to talk about relationships.

Another case in point relates to your audience's abilities and disabilities. As communication expert Bettina Brockman in her book *Some Same but Different: Unlearning of the Concept of Disability* (2012) wrote about the problem of immediately categorizing and labeling people with disabilities. She asserts that in lieu of defining a person via a label, "we instead need to get to know others first by understanding their needs (Brockman, 2012)."

Attitudinal Profile

While demographic data may help you in making basic inferences and predictions about your audience, learning about your audience's attitudes about your topic and proposition may provide more meaningful clues on how to proceed. This is called an *attitudinal profile*.

The goal of an attitudinal profile is for you to come to fully grasp the attitudes of your target audience. A *target audience* is the segment of your audience that you most want to influence and that you should target your persuasive appeals toward. To conduct an attitudinal profile, examine your audience base before giving your speech by means of posing qualitative questions about underlying attitudes and perceptions.

For example, is your audience already educated on your topic? How does your audience feel about your proposal? What is your audience's attitude toward you? The open-ended questions on the audience survey provided supply you with necessary clarity on how your audience perceives you, your topic, and your proposition. If the survey questions do not provide you with enough data and you require more information on your audience, consider conducting candid interviews with some audience members.

Situational Profile

Another important aspect of audience analysis to consider is the situation that you will be speaking in. A *situational profile* analyzes the surroundings of your speech or the context. Your best source for situational profile information may well be the person(s) who asked you to present in the first place, or another speaker at the same or similar event. An informal conversation with your contact person should provide you with what you need. Ask this person about the following two key areas: the audience and the room. In terms of the audience, learn how many people will be in attendance and if they are a captive audience or an audience by choice. Who are your customers and what occasion brings them together? As for the room, learn all you can about the setup of the room to include lighting, staging, speaking order, and sound system.

Attitudinal profile
An attitudinal profile analyzes your audience's attitudes toward and about your topic and/or proposition.

Target audience
A target audience is the segment of your audience that you most want to influence and that you should target your persuasive appeals toward.

Situational profile
A situational profile analyzes the surroundings of your speech or the context, including your audience and the room.

Audience Analysis Survey

Speaker:_____Speech Date:_____ Topic:_____

Speech Time: _____ Time limit: _____ Audience Size:_____

1. What is the basic demographic makeup of this particular audience?

_____

_____

_____

2. What situational characteristics of the room and the audience do I need to consider?

_____

_____

_____

3. What does this audience already know about my topic and/or proposition?

_____

_____

_____

4. How interested is this audience in my topic and/or proposition?

_____

_____

_____

5. What the audience's opinion of my topic and/or proposition? Why do they hold that opinion?

_____

_____

_____

6. How strongly does my audience agree or disagree with my topic and/or proposition? Why?

_____

_____

_____

7. What are my audience's biggest objections to my topic or to adopting my proposition?

_____

_____

_____

8. What would it take for me to persuade this audience to adopt my proposition?

_____

_____

_____

9. What else I should know about this audience before I give this speech?

_____

_____

_____

Audience Analysis Survey

Speaker:_____Speech Date:_____ Topic:_____

Speech Time: _____ Time limit: _____ Audience Size:_____

1. What is the basic demographic makeup of this particular audience?

_____

_____

_____

2. What situational characteristics of the room and the audience do I need to consider?

_____

_____

_____

3. What does this audience already know about my topic and/or proposition?

_____

_____

_____

4. How interested is this audience in my topic and/or proposition?

_____

_____

_____

5. What the audience's opinion of my topic and/or proposition? Why do they hold that opinion?

_____

_____

_____

6. How strongly does my audience agree or disagree with my topic and/or proposition? Why?

_____

_____

_____

7. What are my audience's biggest objections to my topic or to adopting my proposition?

_____

_____

_____

8. What would it take for me to persuade this audience to adopt my proposition?

_____

_____

_____

9. What else I should know about this audience before I give this speech?

_____

_____

_____

Analysis Summary

Reflect on the results of your audience analysis survey and any other types of audience analysis assessments you utilized. Before you go any farther on *The Speaker's Path*, take a few moments to answer the following questions about your audience, the situation, and about how your audience perceives your topic and proposal.

YOUR VIEW

What did your analysis teach you about your audience?

_____

_____

_____

Step Three: Clarify the Proposition

At this point of *The Speaker's Path,* you should be processing the data you received from your audience analysis. Once you have sufficient data to work with, review what you know about your audience from the audience analysis demographic, attitude, and situation assessments. Then, consider the type of assertion you will be arguing, and the criteria for the assignment. If you have not received the information you need to formulate your speech plan, do further audience analysis.

The next phase of your journey is clarifying your proposition. The specific purpose in a persuasive speech is called the proposition. Before you go any further in putting together your persuasive speech, formulate your proposition or action plan. The fact, value, or policy proposition statement is the most important sentence in a persuasive speech. Illuminating this hopeful outcome now will help you keep your mission in check as you gather evidence for your speech. The *proposition* is the desired effect you want to achieve, the action you want your audience to take, your proposal or assertion, the change you hope to create, or the outcome of your speech. Everything you say or do in your speech should support your proposition statement.

Once you define your desired outcomes and identifying a proposition that can achieve this outcome, according to Sandra Mireles who wrote the article "How to Measure Outcomes and Evaluations", the next step is to identify ways to measure the outcome or prove that it occurred or will occur. At the end of your presentation or soon thereafter, you should be able to gauge whether your audience will, or plans to, adopt your proposal.

Proposition
The proposition is the desired effect you want to achieve, the action you want your audience to take, your proposal or assertion, the change you hope to create, or the outcome of your speech.

This is known as an outcome measure. An *outcome measure* is the evaluation of the results of a plan, process, action, or program and the comparison with the intended or projected results to determine if success is the outcome. An outcome measure can be used to measure the success of your speech. Consider how you will measure whether or not your proposition is adopted.

YOUR VIEW

What is your proposition statement? What is the outcome measure?

_____

_____

_____

Step Four: Determine Persuasive Plan

*Audience
adaptation*
is the process of
ethically using the
information you
have gathered
when analyzing
your audience to
help your audience
clearly understand
your message
and to achieve
your persuasive
objective.

Audience adaptation is the process of ethically using the information you have gathered when analyzing your audience to help your audience clearly understand your message and to achieve your persuasive objective or gain support for proposition. Your *persuasive plan* is the detailed formulation of your persuasive strategy based on audience adaptation. Your comprehensive persuasive plan will dictate what type of supporting material you start accumulating. Using the right type of supporting material for persuasive speeches is a bit more complicated because you will need to thoroughly consider not only if your evidence is solid, but also if your evidence is the right kind to use to influence your audience.

Audience Types

Persuasive plan
Your persuasive
plan is the detailed
formulation of
your motivational
strategy.

Developing a persuasive plan that is ethical and adapted to your audience is integral to effective persuasion. According to public speaking experts Susan and Steven Beebe (2005) in their text *Public Speaking Handbook*, "If you only analyze your audience but do not use the information to customize your message, the information you've gathered will be of little value. Using your skill to learn about your listeners and then to adapt to them can help you maintain your listener's attention and make them more receptive to your ideas (Beebe & Beebe, 2005)."

To begin, review the audience analysis results and determine what type of audience you are trying to persuade. Consider what they know and how they feel about you, your topic, the occasion, the proposal, and themselves. What is your audience's reaction to your proposition? Does your audience appear to be in favor, or is your audience seemingly opposed? Are you considered to be credible to your audience, meaning does your audience view you as trustworthy, professional, and competent?

There are seven audience types or profiles. A *highly favorable audience* views you as exceedingly credible or fully supports you proposition and may even already be acting on it. A *favorable audience* considers you to be credible and to some extent approves of both you and your proposition. A *neutral audience* is on the fence; they have mixed feelings about your credibility or your topic. Often a neutral audience chooses not to weigh in on one side or another. An *uninformed audience* does not have enough knowledge about your credibility or your topic to make a determination. An *apathetic audience* type is an indifferent or detached audience, an audience who does not have strong emotions about you or your topic. An *opposed audience* is in opposition to your proposal and/or is in mild disagreement with you. A *hostile audience* openly opposes you and/or strongly resists your proposal.

> **Seven Audience Types**
>
> Highly Favorable, Favorable, Neutral, Uninformed, Apathetic, Opposed, Hostile

Audience Type Continuum

Determine your audience type by using this continuum:

```
◄──────────────────────────────────────────────────►
Highly favorable    Favorable    Neutral      Opposed    Hostile
                                 Uninformed
                                 Apathetic
```

YOUR VIEW ──────────────────────────────────────

What is your audience type in relation to you and your proposition? How do you know if your assessment is accurate?

_____

_____

_____

Targeting Your Rhetoric

Once you know what your audience type is, you want to think about what rhetorical appeal is appropriate to that audience type. *Rhetorical appeals* are the persuasive strategies or proofs of ethos, pathos, and logos. Aristotle was the first to identify these three persuasive appeals in his book *Rhetoric*, written 350 B.C.E., and translated by W. Rhys Roberts (Roberts & Aristotle, 2012). Aristotle defined Ethos (Credible) appeal as convincing the

Rhetorical appeals are the persuasive strategies or proofs of ethos, pathos, and logos.

audience by the character of the speaker. He termed Pathos (Emotional) appeal as persuading by appealing to the audience's emotions. Last, he classified Logos (Logical) appeal as motivating by the use of reasoning.

Even though you will likely need to use all three appeals as evidence in your speech, one of these strategies will become your primary strategy. Your *primary strategy* is the persuasive appeal that you will use more than the others based on your audience analysis. The reason you pick a primary strategy is that different strategies will work on different types of audiences. The most skillful persuasive speakers consider their audience first, and then target their appeals toward their audience. The rhetorical devices you utilize should not be haphazardly applied across situations. Instead, purposely aim your persuasive efforts at your context and listener.

For example, if you use excessive emotional appeals on an opposed audience, you may find that your audience feels manipulated and is irritated by your strategy. It is often best to rely on logic more than emotion when your audience is opposed. At the other end of the spectrum, if your audience is favorable, why would you inundate the audience with more factual evidence than needed when they have already made up their minds? Often the best way to persuade a favorable audience into action is to use pathos as your primary appeal, instead of relying primarily on logos.

Now that you have your audience type, your next step on *The Speaker's Path* is to strategize your rhetorical approach using the Audience Type Matrix. The *Audience Type Matrix* will assist you in gathering the evidence that will best persuade your audience to respond to your proposition.

Primary strategy
Your primary strategy is the persuasive appeal that you will use more than the others based on your audience analysis.

Audience Type Matrix

Type		Primary Appeal	Reasoning
Favorable	⇨	Pathos	They want to be emotionally compelled to take action.
Neutral	⇨	Logos	They need more factual information to make up their mind.
Uninformed	⇨	Logos	They do not have what the data they need in order to make a decision.
Apathetic	⇨	Pathos	They need to become emotionally engaged to be persuaded.
Opposed	⇨	Logos	They need you to employ sound reasoning and give them the facts.
Hostile	⇨	Ethos	They will only listen to someone they find highly credible.

YOUR VIEW

Which persuasive strategy should be your primary appeal, and why?

_____

_____

_____

Persuasion is a thoughtful process that requires advanced planning. You now have your audience type and primary appeal clarified, and your persuasive plan in place. It is time to put your plan into action by learning how to incorporate ethos, pathos, and logos appeals into your speech.

Step Five: Using Ethos

In *Rhetoric*, Aristotle wrote, "Of the modes of persuasion furnished by the spoken word there are three kinds. The first kind depends on the personal character of the speaker; the second on putting the audience into a certain frame of mind; the third on the proof, or apparent proof, provided by the words of the speech itself. Persuasion is achieved by the speaker's personal character when the speech is so spoken as to make us think him credible."Aristotle believed that the most important of the three persuasive appeals is Ethos.

Ethos is Greek for "character." Ethos was originally defined by Aristotle in *On Rhetoric* as being trustworthy. He stated that we are more likely to believe people who have good character. He later broadened this definition of ethos to add that we are more likely to be persuaded by someone who is similar to us, whether by their intrinsic characteristics or the qualities they adapt. Aristotle does not include the concept of either a speaker's authority or reputation in his definition of ethos. These attributes reflect more modern translations of credibility. *Ethos* is now defined more broadly as the strategy of using your credibility or ethical appeals. It includes the character traits of honesty, integrity, trustworthiness, dynamism, and goodwill.

Audiences tend to listen more closely to people they find credible. Before you can convince an audience to accept anything you have say, they have to accept you as credible. The ethos of a speaker can be measured by three related characteristics: trustworthiness, similarity, and competence.

> **Three Persuasive Appeals**
>
> Ethos, Pathos, and Logos

> *Ethos*
> is the strategy of using your credibility or ethical appeals to persuade.

Characteristics of Ethos

Trustworthiness, Similarity, and Competence

Trustworthiness

An audience is more likely to be persuaded by someone whom they trust, and this is largely independent of the topic being presented. If the audience has faith in you, if they believe you care about them and your topic, then they expect that what you are telling them is truthful.

A person's trustworthiness is a major part of his or her character. Your trustworthiness is enhanced if the audience believes you have a strong moral character, as measured by concepts like honesty, goodwill, and integrity. Unfortunately, trustworthiness is hard to gain and easy to lose.

Consider how you can communicate trustworthiness to your audience. For example, one way to demonstrate it to your audience is to show that you sincerely care about them by showing up to your speech on time, making eye contact, and sharing personal stories. You can further establish rapport with your audience by delivering your speech in a dynamic and engaging and way.

Similarity

Your audience is more receptive to being persuaded by someone with whom they can identify or whom they perceive as being like them. Like trustworthiness, this aspect of ethos is contingent on the speaker primarily and is largely independent of the topic.

What characteristics do you share with your audience? If you share any qualities with your listeners, bring them up in your speech. If you can demonstrate that you are similar, your audience will likely be more receptive to you. This is called the *similarity principle*, which means that people trust people who are like them. Thus, when an audience is trying to decide whether to trust a speaker, they often do not have time to find out how trustworthy the speaker actually is, so they take a shortcut by assuming that someone who is similar is trustworthy.

If you do not share many similarities with your audience, you can still demonstrate that you are similar to your audience by adapting to your audience. A subtle shift in your language, mannerisms, attire, demeanor, or overall style can have a marked effect. Remember to maintain authenticity, however, or your efforts will backfire on you.

Competence

Your expertise and reputation will influence how your audience perceives your competence. Expertise is what you know about your topic. Reputation is what your audience knows about what you know about your topic.

Your reputation is determined by your experience, demonstrated skills, and achievements. Audience members will generally listen more closely to a speaker with a solid reputation or one who they perceive as being knowledgeable or experienced in a given subject area.

One way to boost your perceived competence is to use statements to position yourself higher in the minds of your audience members. You can do this by reviewing your qualifications, degrees, or experiences. Another method for establishing competence is citing your research so that your audience perceives you as being an expert on your subject. It is your obligation, if you wish to be seen as credible, to prove to your audience that you are competent to speak on your topic and that you have a high knowledge base.

To determine how credible you are as a speech-giver, ask yourself the following nine questions:

1. Does your audience respect you?
2. Does your audience believe that you respect them?
3. Does your audience like you?
4. Does your audience trust that you like them?
5. Does your audience believe you are honest?
6. Does your audience perceive you as possessing integrity?
7. Does your audience consider you to be reliable?
8. Does your audience know your reputation?
9. Does your audience consider you to be an expert?

If you answered in the affirmative to most of these questions, you are well on your way to becoming a credible and inspiring speaker. If you did not, consider how you might boost your ethos appeals.

YOUR VIEW

It what ways can you develop ethos in your speech? Give two specific examples:

_____

_____

_____

Step Six: Using Logos

Logos is synonymous with a valid logical argument. Logos is using logical appeals, sound reasoning, and factual data. Some speakers shy away from logos because they think it might be dry. This is a mistake. Do not underestimate how important logic is in your speaking. Logical analysis is critical to your success as a speaker because (1) if your speech is not logical, your audience will not be able to follow you, and (2) if your arguments are weak, your audience will discount you.

Logos is using logical appeals, sound reasoning, and factual data to persuade.

According to renown public speaking consultant Andrew Dlugan in his 2010 article called "What Is Logos and Why Is It Critical for Speakers?," you can develop strong logos by following three general principles regarding your premises. Premises are facts, claims, evidence, or a previously proven conclusion. First, he says that the premises in your speech must be easily understood by the audience before they can be persuaded. Second, your arguments must be able to stand on their own. Make sure your premises do not have holes in them and address any objections outright. Last, base your premises on concrete and specific facts and examples (Dlugan, 2010).

Logic is the reasoning process of the speaker. *Reasoning* is the process of drawing inferences or conclusions from evidence. Logical reasoning includes deductive reasoning, inductive reasoning, and reasoning by causation. Each of these three types of reasoning will be addressed.

Reasoning is the process of drawing inferences or conclusions from evidence.

Forms of Reasoning
Deductive, Inductive, and Reasoning by Causation

Deductive reasoning is a kind of reasoning that moves from the general to the specific and attempts to show that a conclusion necessarily follows from a series of premises.

Deductive Reasoning

Deductive reasoning consists of constructing or evaluating one or more *deductive arguments*. It is also called deductive logic. It contrasts with inductive reasoning, in that a specific conclusion is arrived at from a general principle. Thus, deductive reasoning moves from the general to the specific.

Deductive reasoning attempts to show that a conclusion necessarily follows from a series of premises. Generally, a speaker starts with one or more *premises,* then derives a *conclusion* from them. Premises can be facts, claims, evidence, or a previously proven conclusion. In a deductive argument, *if* your premises are true, *then* your specific conclusion must also be true.

While deductive arguments can be sound or unsound, valid or invalid, deductive reasoning usually is a credible form of reasoning. A deductive argument is considered to be sound if its premises are true. An invalid deductive argument is one in which the truth of the premises does not guarantee the truth of the conclusion. In invalid arguments, the conclusion does not necessarily follow, even though it is claimed to.

Deductive reasoning consists of three key areas: one or more major premises, one or more minor premises, and a conclusion. When all three components are stated, it is called a *syllogism*. In most deductive arguments, one of the premises is not stated and is merely inferred.

An oft repeated example of a deductive syllogism is:

Major Premise: All men are mortal.
Minor Premise: Socrates is a man.
Conclusion: Therefore, Socrates is mortal.

The first premise, the major premise, states that men have the attribute of being mortal. The minor premise states that Socrates is a man. The specific conclusion states that Socrates must be mortal because of his classification as a man. Deductive reasoning moves from general theory to a precise finding.

Use deductive arguments in your persuasive speaking as a means of proving to your audience that a problem exists that needs to be solved or that a solution or proposition is sound. Deductive reasoning assumes that the basic law or rule from which you are arguing is applicable in all cases. This can let you take a rule and apply it. For example, deduction is used by some scientists who take a general scientific law and apply it to a certain case, because they assume that the law is true.

Inductive Reasoning

Inductive reasoning is the opposite strategy. This form of reasoning contrasts with deductive in that a general conclusion is arrived at by specific examples. *Inductive reasoning*, also known as induction, is a kind of reasoning that constructs or evaluates observations of individual instances.

Inductive reasoning Inductive reasoning is a kind of reasoning that constructs or evaluates observations of individual instances.

The premises of an inductive argument indicate some degree of support, which is called an inductive probability. Inductive reasoning suggests truth and infers it, but does not ensure it. Inductive reasoning consists of inferring general principles or rules from specific facts. Inductive reasoning allows for the possibility that the conclusion will be false, even where all of the premises are true.

An example of inductive reasoning is the following:

1. 80 percent of Americans between the ages of 16–24 own a smart phone.
2. Jose is a 19-year-old American.
3. Therefore, the probability that Jose owns a smart phone is 80 percent.

Unlike deductive arguments, inductive arguments are not evaluated by soundness or validity. Instead, inductive arguments are considered to be either strong or weak. Even if an inductive argument is seemingly valid, it will never be the case that if the premises are true, the conclusion must also be true. The most that an inductive argument can hope for is a high probability that its conclusion is true. In other words, a good inductive argument is such that if the premises are true, then the conclusion is most likely true. Inductive reasoning deals with inference. Thus, we can infer that Jose most likely owns a smart phone.

One technique for using inductive reasoning is to derive a general rule in an accepted area and then apply the rule in the area where you want the audience to change. Or, give your audience a lot of detail, then explain what it all means. The key is to present a strong, inductive argument such that it is improbable that the premises stated are true and the conclusion is false. This type of reasoning can be used to persuade an audience to change attitudes, values or behavior based on the likelihood that your perceptions or observations are most likely correct.

Cause-and-Effect Reasoning

Cause-and-
effect reasoning
is a type of
reasoning that
assumes that one
thing is caused by
something else
and that every
cause has an
effect.

Cause-and-effect reasoning assumes that one thing is caused by something else and that every cause has an effect. This variety of inductive reasoning is also called causal reasoning. However, like other forms of inductive reasoning, it cannot be assumed that a causal relationship constitutes proof or absolute truth, as there may be other unknown factors and processes involved. Instead, cause-and-effect reasoning is concerned with establishing the presence of causal relationships among events. Causal reasoning may be used to direct scientific research and eliminate unlikely hypotheses for understanding certain phenomena.

When you are presenting a causal argument, show the cause-and-effect that is in operation. Help the audience comprehend why things have happened or will happen. Or, show the linkage between what happens first and what happens next. When using causal reasoning, go beyond correlation and coincidence by giving irrefutable evidence of causality. If you cannot show causal linkage, then you may be successful just by asserting it, because few people will challenge a cause-and-effect assertion. To be ethical however, you should only use causal reasoning when you have good reason to believe that events or causes are systematically related to other events or effects, or you may be committing a logical fallacy.

Avoiding Logical Fallacies

Logical fallacy
is a fallacy or
error in logical
argumentation.

The word *fallacy* comes from Latin, meaning "deceit," "trick," or "fraud." A *logical fallacy* is a fallacy or error in logical argumentation. Although sometimes these types of errors are hard to catch, learning to recognize logical fallacies can help you to be a more ethical speaker. According to Keneesaw State University English Hagen (2002), there are several types of logical fallacies, some of his are outlined below.

Avoid misleading your audience when you speak persuasively by being aware of some common fallacies:

Appeal to Flattery

Appeal to flattery is inflating the audience's ego with superficial flattery in order to persuade them into action. When speakers strive only to

**Eight Logical
Fallacies**

Appeal to Flattery, Bandwagon Appeal, Scare Tactics, Overgeneralization, Red Herring, False Analogy, Slippery Slope, and Non-Sequitur gain support by molding their words and deeds to inflate the audience's image of themselves or to boost audience members' self esteem, they are pandering.

Bandwagon Appeal

The belief that something should be done because it is popular is called Bandwagon Appeal. Bandwagon appeals urge people to follow the same path that the majority of people appear to already be following. In old-time political campaigns, politicians used to travel on horse-drawn bandwagons, urging citizens to "jump on the bandwagon" or join the crowd.

Scare Tactics

Scare tactics are coercing a favorable response from your audience by prey-ing upon the audience's fears or insecurities. Scare tactics are veiled threats. Instead of threatening a probable consequence, or causality, scare tactics highlight the possible negative outcomes to the extreme, while merely sug-gesting causality.

Overgeneralization

Overgeneralizations are statements speakers make that are so general that they oversimplify or exaggerate reality. Speakers that make sweeping gener-alizations and stereotype in an effort to preduct often do so at the expense of ignoring important evidence that may speak to the contrary.

Red Herring

An argument that distracts the audience's attention from the core issue by raising irrelevant issues is called a red herring. The phrase "red herring" comes from the practice of dragging a fish across a road to confuse tracking dogs by throwing them off the trail. Red herrings are utilized to hide weak arguments.

False Analogy

False analogy is an elaborate comparison of two things that are too dis-similar. Analogies are comparisons. They are most helpful when a speaker is trying to explain something that is unfamiliar to his audience by using more familiar terms to logically compare. Speakers must compare two sub-jects carefully to ensure that they have essential features in common and are not false in nature.

Slippery Slope

When a person stands on a slippery slope, one small misstep can force him to fall. The slipper slope fallacy occurs when an argument exaggerates the possible consequences of a long chain of events, often with the inten-tion of frightening the audience. Slippery slope fallacies exaggerate the consequences.

Non-Sequitur
This phrase means "it does not follow", meaning that one sequential event may not necessarily cause the other. Non sequitur is a conclusion that has no apparent connection to the premise. Non-sequiturs occur when speakers omit an integral step in an otherwise logical chain of sound reasoning.

YOUR VIEW

It what way can you develop logos in your speech while avoiding logical fallacies? Give an example:

_____

_____

_____

Step Seven: Using Pathos

Pathos
is when you use psychological appeals to arouse feelings in the audience.

Pathos is when you use psychological appeals to arouse feelings in the audience (e.g., anger, sadness, excitement, pity) in an effort to motivate your audience. Pathos is a powerful motivational tool that will be discussed in detail in the following section. But first, caution is required. Pathos should not be used in isolation, but should instead be used as part of a trio, in combination with both ethos and logos. While an appeal to pathos can cause your audience to identify with your point of view and feel what you feel, be wary of how you rely on and use pathos appeals in your speeches. The major criticism of pathos focuses on the overemphasis of pathos at the expense of logos and ethos.

Maslow's Hierarchy of Needs
is a theory that suggests that people can be motivated to fulfill needs in a specific order, from basic safety and health needs to personal actualization.

Psychologist Abraham Maslow first introduced his Hierarchy of Needs more than sixty years ago (Maslow, 1943) This influential theory is a type of pathos appeal that still remains valid today in the field of psychology and communications. *Maslow's Hierarchy of Needs* posits that all people are motivated to fulfill essential human needs. According to the article "Hierarchy of Needs" by author and educator Kendra Cherry, who wrote the Everything Psychology Book (2010), Maslow believed that these five needs: Physical, Safety, Belongingess, Esteem, and Self Actualizaiton, play a major role in motivating behavior. Therefore, a speaker who uses Maslow as a tool for incorporating pathos may be particularly persuasive, depending of the audience type. One way to use Maslow as a pathos appeal is to compel the audience to want to fill a particular need by use of visualization, imagery, or emotional stories or images.

Maslow's Hierarchy of Needs

Physical, Safety, Belongingness, Esteem, and Self-Actualization.

Physical needs include the most biological, instinctive, and intrinsic needs that are vital to survival. These are also known as physiological needs. This first level of needs is what all mammals need to live, from insects to primates, such as water, oxygen, food, and sleep. Building these needs into your speech can be particularly persuasive, because no one in your audience can go without them. Physical need motivators are clean air and water, adequate sleep, basic shelter, and healthy food.

Security needs are also known as safety needs and include our need to feel safe and secure. Security needs are important for survival, but are not as life-threatening as the physical needs. Examples of security needs include a desire for locked doors, steady employment, and health insurance. You can actualize your proposition using security motivators by compelling your audience to want to feel safe or by offering financial, health, or employment security to your audience.

Belongingness needs are the next level up on the hierarchy. These are also known as love, affection, or social needs. Maslow believed that all human beings need to feel connected to others. Maslow noted that once physical and security needs are met, people can concentrate on meeting relationship belonging needs. You can enhance your speech with belongingness motivators by sharing stories with your audience about friendship, love, community, or the importance belonging to a group or team.

After the first three needs have been satisfied, *esteem needs* become increasingly important. These needs reflect our personal worth. These include the need for recognition, accomplishment, and rewards. People in the esteem needs category are motivated by recognition, attention, accomplishment, and status found through the acquisition of material goods. One way to persuade your audience using esteem needs is to enhance your audience's desire for obtaining more status or prestige in their lives.

Self-actualization is the summit of Maslow's motivation theory. These needs can only be fulfilled when all of the other needs lower on the hierarchy have been met. Self-actualization is being at peace with all aspects of your life, including your relationships with others and with yourself. This highest level is about practicing selflessness and giving back to others. Self-actualization motivators are truth, harmony, wisdom, community service, and justice. You can persuade your audience to adopt your proposal by encouraging your audience members to reach their full potential as human beings.

Other Pathos appeals include:

Adventure—appealing to an exciting, risky, or remarkable experiences
Conformity—appealing to correspondence in form, manner, or character
Deference—appealing to respect and esteem due a superior or an elder
Fear– appealing to being afraid of or being alarmed by something or someone
Consequences—appealing to something produced by a cause or necessarily following certain conditions
Pity– appealing to something to be regretted or a sympathetic sorrow or one who is suffering

To incorporate emotion into your speech, first decide which pathos appeal would be most effective for the intended audience by anticipating or predicting the highest motivators. Then, shape a message that focuses on creating the receiver's needs or emotions by using vivid storytelling, guided visualization, or imagery. Compelling and memorable visual aids may also work to build pathos. Last, persuade the receiver that the desired action would satisfy those needs. When trying to persuade an audience to adopt your proposition, appeal to the audience's needs or emotions.

YOUR VIEW

It what ways can you develop pathos in your speech? Give two specific examples:

_____

_____

_____

Phase One Checklist

_____ Reviewed the speech requirements and determined a topic
_____ Analyzed the demographics, attitude and situation
_____ Clarified the proposition and how it will be measured
_____ Considered the audience when developing a persuasive strategy
_____ Developed content using ethos, pathos, and logos

CHAPTER SUMMARY

This chapter was developed as a means to walk you through the first phase in a sequence of thirteen steps on how to prepare a persuasive speech. It highlighted PHASE ONE: Speech Development. These first seven steps explained how to consider your audience and clarify your proposition and persuasive plan.

Chapter Six also showed you how to support your speech using ethos, pathos, and logos appeals. Ethos, pathos, and logos are known as the three pillars of persuasive speech-giving. These three persuasive appeals were the secret to being a persuasive speaker over 2000 years ago are still being used today.

The following chapter will review Steps Eight through Thirteen in PHASE TWO.

FURTHER ALONG THE TRAIL :
Phase Two of the Thirteen Steps for Persuasive Speaking

7

With the first step, the number of shapes the walk might take is infinite, but then the walk begins to define itself as it goes along, though freedom remains total with each step. The pattern of the walk is to come true, is to be recognized and discovered.

—A.R. Ammons, *A Poem Is a Walk*

Step by step, one foot in front of the other—that is how you progress on *The Speaker's Path*. You have just completed the first seven of thirteen steps in developing a persuasive speech in PHASE ONE. This next chapter, which starts with organization, will spotlight PHASE TWO of your walk through persuasion, taking you further along the trail.

Organization is a necessary component of competent persuasive speech-giving. If you are disorganized and ill prepared, your audience is likely to not pay attention and get very little from the information you provide. Conversely, a well-practiced and orderly speech will keep your audience interested and leave your audience members glad they took the time to hear your insights.

When your speech development process is organized and a clear timeline is established and adhered to, you will reduce anxiety, actualize higher levels of communication competence, and most importantly, free up time for fun with friends and family.

Some people possess natural organizational skills. They find cataloging, systematizing, and arranging a breeze. Many others, however, find the task of organizing to be burdensome and mystifying. Take the following Organization Quiz adapted from Katherine Balpataky's quiz "How Organized Are You?" (2004) to learn how organized you are.

Organization Quiz

Directions: Read the statements below and rate your reactions to each, from 1 (you rate yourself low, this statement is not at all true for you) to 5 (you rate yourself high, this statement is true for you).

1. _____I waste a lot of time looking for receipts and files that I need.
2. _____I am often late for meetings and appointments.
3. _____I would be terrified if I were notified of an impending audit.
4. _____I do not have enough space in my office or room.
5. _____I do not have a good system for managing the payment of my bills.
6. _____I do not have a systematic method for purging outdated emails and texts.
7. _____I frequently have to return to my home, office, or car for forgotten items.
8. _____I do not use my time planner (e.g., calendar, Outlook, iPhone) effectively.
9. _____I do not have a system for managing work in progress.
10. _____I am often late completing my projects at work, home, and/or school.
11. _____My office desk is covered with paper.
12. _____ I often discover that I have double-booked by daily schedule.

To score this quiz, add your totals.

If you scored less than 25 points on the quiz, you might be the kind of person who has a color-coded clothes closet at home, knows exactly where to find a stamp when you need one, has a system in place for managing and paying your bills, has an emergency road kit in your car, and would never let mayonnaise expire in the refrigerator. In other words, you are an organized person. You are planner and can see what needs to be done.

If you scored 25–40 points, you are on the right track in terms of organization, but there is room for improvement. A score of between 45–60 points indicates that your level of organization is low and could hamper your communication competence.

Regardless of how you define yourself in terms of organization, to be a successful public speaker you will need to devote quality time toward organization. There is no way around this reality. If you fail to plan, you are in essence planning to fail. An uncluttered existence does not happen overnight. It requires time and effort. However, the end result will make life a lot easier and ultimately feel like a weight has been lifted off the shoulders.

YOUR VIEW

What is your score? How can organization help you achieve success in public speaking?

_____

_____

_____

Phase Two: Organizing and Finalizing Your Persuasive Speech

Organization and planning is essential to effective persuasive speaking. The intent of this chapter is to assist you in systematically organizing and finalizing your persuasive speech. The previous chapter emphasized PHASE ONE of the Thirteen Steps of Persuasive Speaking, Steps One through Seven. This chapter will take you further along the trail to PHASE TWO, Steps Eight through Thirteen. To complete your journey of persuasion, walk through each of the following six steps in order.

Phase Two: Organizing and Finalizing Your Persuasive Speech

Step Eight:	Organize the Main Points
Step Nine:	Create an Introduction, Transitions, and Conclusion
Step Ten:	Complete a Speech Preparation Guide
Step Eleven:	Build an Outline Using Persuasive Language
Step Twelve:	Cite Your Sources
Step Thirteen:	Create Visual Aids

Step Eight: Organize the Main Points

You are now clear on your topic, your audience, your proposition, and your persuasive plan. You have also had the opportunity to investigate how to use Aristotle's three persuasive appeals. Step Eight asks you to define your main points and decide how to arrange your main points into a logical sequence.

Main points are the core of your speech. Select your main points carefully, phrase them precisely, and arrange them strategically. One of the most important items to consider when building a persuasive argument is the structure. Like a house, if a speech is well-structured and soundly built, it will withstand a few flaws in the detail. However, if you build a house made of straw or on uneven ground, a gentle breeze might blow it over.

A well-organized persuasive speech does not just happen by chance. You have to make it happen by making choices about what to include and where to include it. Those choices should be guided by the four subsequent principles of organization, as recommended by communication scholar and noted author of several textbooks Joseph DeVito (2005, 2008). Allow these principles to guide you, but know there may be times when you decide you need to go against them.

The *Principle of Balance* means that the three major parts of the speech (Introduction, Body, and Conclusion) should be in proportion to each other, or should be balanced. The introduction should take about 10–20 percent of your speaking time, the body roughly 70–80 percent, and the conclusion about 10 percent of your total speaking time. The percentage of time each main point takes will vary, but the general rule is that each main point should be approximately the same length.

The *Principle of Unity* means that everything you include in your speech should relate to the proposition. If the evidence presented in your speech does not relate to your proposal or your target audience, even if you are really fond of it, it should be removed from your speech.

The *Principle of Coherence* means that the relationships among the three main points of a speech should be logical and clear to the audience. For example, in a persuasive speech, you may want to establish the existence of a problem before addressing any possible solutions to that problem.

The *Principle of Emphasis* means that the most important ideas should be stressed by giving them more air time. Settle on which are the major and minor points in your speech, and emphasize them appropriately so as not to confuse your audience.

With these four DeVito principles in mind you can begin to organize the main ideas of your persuasive speech.

Below are examples of sample persuasion speech topics and corresponding main points for each of the four organizational frameworks: reasons, problem/solution, problem/cause/solution, and Monroe's Motivated Sequence.

Reasons Pattern

The *reasons pattern* explains either the three reasons to justify why you should support the proposition, or the three reasons to refute why the audience should not be against your proposal.

The *reasons justification pattern* can be effective on an audience that is already mildly favorable. The *reasons refutation organization pattern* is best for an audience that is opposed to your proposition.

Reasons Justification

First, anticipate the audience's motivations or rationale for wanting to adopt your position. List each of the three major justifications as grounds for your main points, acknowledging them one at a time. Then, persuade your audience to accept your proposition because they already validate your rationalization.

Example:

Proposition: You should exercise for at least 30 minutes four times a week.

   I. Regular exercise will reduce stress and affect your sense of well-being so you feel more content.

  II. Regular exercise will help you keep your weight in check so that you do not have to worry about your weight.

III. Regular exercise will positively impact your cardiovascular health, so you do not suffer from heart disease.

Reasons Refutation

First, accurately predict the audience's objections to your proposal and list them as your main points, acknowledging each opposing argument one at a time. Then systematically refute each opposing view by providing rational reasons why each objection is not an issue.

Example:

Proposition: You should exercise for at least 30 minutes four times a week.

   I. Some people do not believe that they have enough time to exercise, but they can find 30 minutes to spare.

  II. Some people are worried that exercise equipment will be too expensive, but most equipment isn't costly.

III. Some people are concerned that they are too "out of shape" to start an exercise program, but they should just start slowly.

Problem/Solution

This persuasive pattern works on various audience types, most notably uninformed or neutral. It proves that a problem exists and offers a feasible solution.

Problem

The first step in the *problem/solution pattern* is to argue that a widespread problem exists. Prove to your audience, beyond a doubt, that there is an obstacle that needs to be overcome, and that something is wrong with current conditions. Adapt the problem to your audience by explaining how the problem impacts them personally. Make them buy into the issue. Assist your audience in taking ownership of the problem.

Problem/ Solution persuasive pattern proves that a problem exists and offers a feasible solution.

Solution

The second step to the problem/solution format is the solution itself. Give your audience a precise and practical method of solving the problem you previously posed. Explain the resolution step by step in sufficient detail. Ascertain if a similar solution has been applied before, and if so, explain and cite a model solution to demonstrate to your audience how the proposed solution has already worked in the past. You may also wish to refute objections your audience may have to adopting your solution.

Example:
Proposition: If you have the right to vote, you should exercise it in the next election.
    I. Many of you do not have a voice in local, national, and international affairs.
   II. Voting will give you a voice in major decisions that impact your life and the lives of others.

Problem/Cause/Solution

Problem/Cause/ Solution pattern extends the Problem/Solution pattern by adding a main point on what causes the problem to have occurred.

The *problem/cause/solution pattern* extends the problem/solution pattern by adding a main point on what causes the problem to occur. This pattern is most persuasive for speeches that require logos as the primary appeal.

Problem
The first main point proves there is a problem that warrants the audience's attention. In this point you describe a need. Explain who is involved, how widespread the problem is, and how long has the problem has existed. Give details to prove that a problem exists and show the audience how the problem impacts them so that audience believes that they are connected to the issue.

Cause
The second main point provides a diagnosis, analysis, and evaluation of the problem. It lists the reasons why the problem exists and extrapolates on the causes that contribute to the problem.

Solution
The third main point highlights a solution and calls the audience to action. Here you will show the plan and the practicality. You will need to be very specific. If possible, find a model of the solution and explain it fully. You will need to manage any objections and provide proof that your solution will work.

Example:
Proposition: Driving hybrid cars will save you money.
    I. The price of gasoline is currently over $4 a gallon in the United States.
   II. Gasoline prices are on the rise due to global consumption, politics, and overall demand in recent years.

III. Hybrid vehicles have an environmentally friendly combination of gas and electric hybrid technology which gives you higher gas mileage and therefore saves you money on gas.

Monroe's Motivated Sequence

This pattern stretches the problem/solution pattern out by adding a third main point, but in a different way than the problem/cause/solution pattern does. *Monroe's Motivated Sequence* adds a main point called Visualization. This main point illuminates the positive consequences of adopting the solution and the negative consequences of not adopting it. It also is more prescriptive in terms of the introduction and conclusion, also known as the Attention and Action. This organizational framework build in pathos appeals and tends to work well on all audience types.

Monroe Motivated Sequence pattern takes the problem/solution and adds a point called visualization that elucidates the positive and negative consequences of adopting the solution.

Attention

The first step to Monroe's Sequence is to gain the attention of your audience. Open with an attention-getter that corresponds with your audience analysis and survey results. Provide background information and establish your credibility and competence, give your audience a reason to listen via pointing.

Need

Show that a problem exists in the lives of your audience members. For example: food insecurity, cancer, toxic waste, public transportation, or lack of role models. The problem needs to be proven with credible evidence. Prove to us that there is an issue that needs our attention.

Satisfaction

Now that you've established that there is a problem or need, the next step is to explain how your solution to the problem. Use and cite valid evidence to explain how you can meet the need. In this step you should also address and meet any objections your audience has.

Visualization

Create a visual image for your audience by explaining what you or others saw, felt, experienced, and/or witnessed. Illustrate to your audience members the positive consequences of supporting your proposition and the negative consequences if they choose not to. You used logos and ethos in the previous steps, now you can appeal to emotions and desires (pathos).

Action

This is your call to action where you state your proposition, which is the action you wish the audience to take. The easier the solution, the more likely your audience will do it. Your purpose in this final step or conclusion is to get your audience to take action.

Example:

Proposition: You should contribute five cans of food to Second Harvest food bank.

   I. More than 5,000 people in your community suffer from food insecurity and poverty.

  II. Second Harvest food bank feeds 3,000 people in your community each month.

 III. You can make a difference in others' lives by contributing to Second Harvest food bank.

YOUR VIEW

What pattern will you use? Why?

_____

_____

Write your two or three main points next to the roman numerals below.

I. _____

_____

II. _____

_____

III. _____

_____

Meeting Objections

Meeting objections is addressing and refuting your audience's objections to your proposition.

As you have likely noticed, most persuasive organizational patterns will require that you address and refute your audience's objections to your proposition at some point during your persuasive argument. This is called *meeting objections*. Objections are not necessarily obstacles. More often they are opportunities to advance your proposal. If you take the time to learn the grounds, reasons, or causes of the opposing arguments and then refute the objections one at a time, your speech will benefit enormously. If you neglect to manage opposing arguments, the objections will still be in your audience's mind when your speech comes to an end. Managing opposing views by meeting objections is a fundamental aspect of any persuasive effort.

There are two steps to meeting objections:

1. State the opposing point of views fairly and concisely. This means that you should clearly state the objection, without over analyzing it or giving it too much air time.
2. Refute the objections by posing valid counter-arguments. Explain why the objections do not need to be a concern. Use logos and reputable sources to argue your view whenever possible. Here are two examples of how to meet objections:

GOVERNMENT SUBSIDIZED HEALTHCARE: Some people believe that all Americans deserve equal access to government-subsidized healthcare regardless of whether or not they pay taxes (Opposing View). However, government provided healthcare will be substandard at best, even though the cost is estimated at three trillion dollars. Further, it erodes personal responsibility and limits individual freedom (Refutation).

GLOBAL WARMING: Some people dismiss global warming as a media stunt based on political hype (Opposing View). Yet, scientific evidence has proven just the opposite—that one third of the summer sea ice in the Arctic is gone, that the oceans are 30% more acidic. The atmosphere over the oceans is priming us for devastating floods (Refutation).

Review your audience profile information to determine why your audience may not adopt your proposal and consider how you will refute the concern.

YOUR VIEW

What is one major objection for your proposal, and how will you refute it?

_____

_____

_____

_____

Step Nine: Create an Introduction, Organizers, and Conclusion

This section is a review of how to develop an Introduction and Conclusion, as well as how to use two-part transitions. This iteration will assist you in achieving your proposition.

Introduction

Just like your informative speech, the introduction consists of an attention-getter, orientation, and a point preview.

An *attention-getter*, the very first sentence of your speech, sets the tone for your entire persuasive presentation. The purpose of the attention-getter is to pull your audience in. The attention-getter should be reflective of your primary persuasive appeal of either ethos, pathos, or logos. For example, a logos attention-getter might be reliable and valid statistical evidence, a pathos attention-getter an emotional narrative, and an ethos attention-getter a personal example that communicates trustworthiness or competence. Your attention-getter is different from your proposition, which you should not be stated until later in your speech. If you give away your proposition at the start of your speech, your speech may be less persuasive.

Orientation consists of relevance, context, and/or credibility. The goal of orientation is to orient your audience to your persuasive topic and to establish the tone of your speech.

Relevance shows your audience how your speech relates to them. It is usually one statement that addresses the "what's in it for me" concern that your audience has. If you do not take the time to establish a logical or causal connection between your persuasive topic to your target audience, your speech will fall flat. In this part of the organizational sequence, you are tasked with convincing each member of your audience that your speech matters to them.

Context gives the target audience necessary details so that your listeners fully understand and appreciate the inter-related conditions of your topic and the setting of your persuasive speech. Context might include background information on your subject or your assertion, or an explanation of key terms or concepts. Context provides your audience with a framework so that they can follow your arguments.

Credibility, or ethos, involves trustworthiness, competence, goodwill, and integrity. To demonstrate trustworthiness, consider demonstrating to your audience why the topic is important to you. For competence, you should cite your research and establish that you are prepared to speak on your subject. Good will is communicating to your audience that you genuinely care about them and your topic. Your likelihood of motivating your audience to adopt your proposition will be magnified if you establish that you are credible. In your introduction.

A *point preview* is at the very end of your introduction and serves as a clear transition to the speech body. It lists each of the main points in sequential order. Numbered previews work well in persuasive speeches, just as they do in informative speeches.

YOUR VIEW

What ideas do you have for developing your introduction to meet the needs of your target audience?

_____

_____

_____

Two-Part Transitions

Just as in an informative speech, in a persuasive speech you must also clarify for your listener when you are moving from main point to main point. If you want to sound logical, organized, and cohesive, add clear _two-part transitions_. A _two-part transition_ tells your audience where you were and where you are going.

Conclusion

You have told your audience what you are going to talk about and talked about it. In your conclusion, you will tell your audience what you told them via a review, closure, and a final statement or clincher.

The _review_ is at the very beginning of your conclusion and serves as a clear signpost that you have completed your arguments and your speech is coming to a close. Like the preview, the review lists each of the main points in order. Use different words than the preview to avoid excessive repetition.

A _closure_ follows your point review, just like in your informative speeches. In persuasion, sometimes it is best to save your proposition until you are at the closure point in your conclusion—to sell your audience on your proposition first via ethos, pathos, and logos, and then tell them exactly what you want from them later. In some situations, assertions or persuasive organizational frameworks warrant that the proposition is asserted earlier in the speech. Whichever is the case, you must have a proposition strategy.

The _final statement_ is the very last words of your speech, and should impart a sense of finality. The final statement is different from the closure. Do not discount the importance of a memorable final statement. While the _primacy effect_ is a cognitive bias that results in a listener recalling primary information such as the attention-getter better than information presented later on in the conclusion, the _recency effect_ is also an element of persuasion. This means that while your attention-getter may provide an unshakeable first impression, your audience members often recall the last words that you say in your speech almost as much. As author David Sousa in a primacy-recency effect article based on his text *How the Brain Learns* (2005) observes, "During a learning episode we remember best that which comes first, second best that which comes last, and least that which comes just past the middle."

YOUR VIEW

What ideas do you have for designing a persuasive conclusion?

_____

_____

_____

Step Ten: Complete a Speech Preparation Guide

The Speech Preparation Guide is the rough plan for your persuasive outline. Complete a Speech Preparation Guide for your next speech. Remember to add your references to the end of the Speech Preparation Guide.

Persuasive Speech Preparation Guide

Speech Title: _____

Proposition: _____

_____

Introduction:

Attention-getter: _____

_____

Context: _____

_____

Credibility: _____

_____

Relevance: _____

_____

Point Preview: _____

_____

Body:

Main Point One: _____

_____

Evidence: _____

_____

Evidence: _____

_____

Two-Part Transition: _____

_____

Main Point Two: _____

_____

Evidence: _____

_____

Evidence: _____

_____

Two-Part Transition: _____

_____

Main Point Three: _____

_____

Evidence: _____

_____

Evidence: _____

_____

Two-Part Transition: _____

_____

Conclusion:

Review: _____

_____

Closure: _____

_____

Final Statement: _____

_____

References:

_____

_____

_____

_____

Persuasive Speech Preparation Guide

Speech Title: _____

Proposition: _____

_____

Introduction

Attention-getter: _____

_____

Context: _____

_____

Credibility: _____

_____

Relevance: _____

_____

Point Preview: _____

_____

Body:

Main Point One: _____

_____

Evidence: _____

_____

Evidence: _____

_____

Two-Part Transition: _____

_____

Main Point Two: _____

_____

Evidence: _____

_____

Evidence: _____

_____

Two-Part Transition: _____

_____

Main Point Three: _____

_____

Evidence: _____

_____

Evidence: _____

_____

Two-Part Transition: _____

_____

Conclusion

Review: _____

_____

Closure: _____

_____

Final Statement: _____

_____

References:

_____

_____

_____

_____

Step Eleven: Build an Outline Using Persuasive Language

Before you start the process of constructing your comprehensive persuasive outline or speech manuscript from your Speech Preparation Guide, you should also consider word choice and what makes the words of a speech memorable. Effective public speakers know that a little focus on language choice goes a long way. To this end, successful speech makers employ rhetoric, which is also known as the art of persuasive language. Convincing persuasive speeches rely on rhetorical language because the speaker must use this type of discourse to motivate the audience to action.

The following are some rhetorical techniques you may wish to build the content of your persuasive speech:

Action Verbs

Just as you would want to use action verbs throughout your resume and cover letter to market yourself to a perspective employer to convey your skill sets, so should you use action verbs in your speech. Action verbs express action or activity. *Action verbs* are something that a person, an animal, a force of nature, or thing can *do*. Use action verbs to make your speech seem more exciting, urgent, and memorable.

Adjectives

Adjectives are one of the simplest components of persuasive language and for this reason, perhaps, they are overused with little thought for their meaning or purpose. *Adjectives* are the part of speech that modifies a noun or other substantive by limiting, qualifying, or specifying. When used carefully throughout a speech, adjectives are appropriate for creating emphasis. Adjectives are important for attaching emotive value to the noun. Your choice of adjectives may convey your attitude.

Adverbs

There are two forms of adverbs that will be addressed here, the assumptive adverb opening and use of adverbs as intensifiers.

The *assumptive adverb* uses an adverb to make something appear true. This can be accomplished in two ways. You can start with a statement that you want be accepted without question, then follow up with a statement that is desirable and easily accepted. Or, you can start with a statement that is easy to accept and follow up with the statement you want people to accept. Assumptive adverb include "obviously," "naturally," "evidently," or "clearly."

> **Twelve Language Techniques**
>
> Action Verbs, Adjectives, Adverbs, Concrete Language, Imagery, Repetition, Rhetorical Questions, Perceptual Language, Personal Pronouns, Pithy Language, Possibility, or Simplicity

An *intensifier adverb* amplifies the effect of a verb by using an adverb that intensifies the meaning and particularly the emotional content. Use the intensifier to subtly suggest to the other person what emotions she should feel. Use intensifiers adverbs to accentuate or reduce the emotional content of a verb.

Concrete Language

Concrete language is the opposite of abstract language. The word abstract derives from the Latin *abstractus*, which means "removed from." The term is conventionally employed to describe ideas and words that are removed from material reality. By contrast, *concrete language* identifies things perceived through the senses, such as touch, smell, sight, hearing, and taste, not just by our intellect. Your audience members can readily relate to concrete words because they refer to tangible ideas and concepts.

Imagery

Imagery language is using words to create dramatic visual images in the mind of the audience. Imagery can make a speech more captivating and memorable, or it can elicit emotive responses. Imagery techniques include metaphors, similes, and personification. These techniques can be used for a range of purposes: simplifying complex ideas, making comparisons, or highlighting a personal viewpoint. An image, once created, can stick in your audience's memory and then so too does the proposition that went with it.

Repetition

Repetition is the act of repeating key phrases or words for dramatic effect or to add emphasis. Catchy repetitive language can encourage your audience to attend to your message more closely. This device was illustrated by Martin Luther King Jr. when he repeated "I have a dream" in his famous address. When used well, repetition will draw your audience in, reinforce key ideas, and make your speech unforgettable.

Rhetorical Questions

While rhetorical questions do not always make captivating attention-getters, they can be effective persuasive devices because they invite the audience to pause and reflect. *Rhetorical questions* are most commonly used for effect only, without the expectation of a response. The natural reaction of your audience to a question mark, though, might be to consider what the answer to your question may be.

Perceptual Language

Perceptual language is when a speaker uses words to indicate how he is observing or interpreting a situation, event, person, place, or idea. Perception means to become more aware of through the senses. Perceptual language encompasses visual sensory words such as "appears" or "looks like" or feeling descriptor words such as "feels like." Speak about what you perceive rather than asserting what is. Talk about what you are seeing, hearing, or otherwise directly sensing, without further interpretation or analysis. Or, communicate about how things make you feel or about how something affects you, whether happy, sad, or angry, or other distinct emotions.

Personal Pronouns

Personal pronouns are influential little words that can add significant power to your persuasive speech. This persuasive strategy needs to be used with finesse and caution. If you use too few personal pronouns, you will seem distant. If you use too many, you may come off as manipulative. The three types of personal pronouns that will be discussed are the use of singular and plural "you" and "we".

The *singular "you"* refers to just one person. One of the best ways to get someone's attention when he is half-listening is to startle him by saying a "you." This personal pronoun will often jolt him back to listening fully. When you say "you," you are firing an arrow directly at another person and your words may be attended to more fully.

The *plural "you"* refers to a group of other people, as in your audience. As with many of the rhetorical devices mentioned, use care when employing the technique. For example, if your audience does not like or agree with you, or are a difficult force to overcome, the use of the plural "you" can result in a backlash. Further, if your audience is dissimilar or in disagreement, they may resent being addressed as one entity.

Effective use of the pronoun "we" can have a positive effect. The *pronoun "we,"* as opposed to using "I" or "you" can bring a speaker and an audience together, bonding the two of you as a single unit.

Pithy Language

Pithy language refers to words that are precisely meaningful, forceful, and brief. These short sentences or phrases can really make a point. Sometimes a pithy, summarizing sentence or phrase works better than a longer more descriptive one. In general, pithy language works well at the start of a main point, and again at the end, to signal completion of an idea or thought. Do not overuse pithy language, however, or you may appear to your audience to be either terse, emotionally cold, or without substance.

Possibility

To use the language of possibility, the speaker must move away from the language of certainty. *Possibility language* communicates to your audience that anything is possible. Instead of saying "will," "must," or "cannot," use possibility words such as "could," "may," or "might." You can also use verbs that imply possibility, such as "believe," "discover," "imagine," "ponder," "speculate," "suppose," or "wonder." When a speaker talks about possibilities rather than absolutes, she generates wonder and cultivates the imaginations of the audience.

Simplicity

Simple language is defined as being modest or free from vanity. Sometimes speakers think they need to impress the audience with complex vocabulary, assuming that it will make them appear intelligent. However, language that is too complex may overwhelm or not make sense to your audience. Your audience may end up putting their energy into trying to define your words, instead of on your underlying message. Simple language keeps your listeners engaged in your speech.

Build an Outline

Your next step on *The Speaker's Path* is to convert your Speech Preparation Guide into a full-sentence outline that incorporates the rhetorical principles of language just described. The structure of the outline should satisfy the same structural requirements as the informative outline. The main points and sub-points must follow specific criteria. Use roman numerals for your main points, uppercase letters for your evidence, and Arabic numbers for your specific examples.

Your outline should be detailed with concrete, focused evidence. It must be properly subordinated and developed. Main points will develop and explain your thesis or purpose. Sub-points will develop, support, or explain the main point. Main points must conform to one, definite, overall pattern of arrangement.

YOUR VIEW

How will you use persuasive language to develop the content of your outline?

_____

_____

_____

Step Twelve: Cite Your Sources

The outline or manuscript should possess academic-quality APA or MLA Style in-text cites and references, if you will be submitting it for someone to approve such as a manager or professor. This section summarizes the comprehensive directions on how to cite your evidence from Chapter Five. If you require more citation specifics, refer back to Chapter Five.

When to Cite

Whenever you paraphrase, summarize, or directly quote information that is not general knowledge, you should get into the habit of citing it in three places: the text of your outline if you are being asked to submit an outline, in your speech itself, and in a reference section if one is required.

How to Cite

Either use MLA (Modern Language Association) format or APA (American Psychological Association) format. APA style is the most universally accepted format for citing research. The next section explains how to cite your sources using APA style in the text of your outline, your reference section, and your speech.

In-Text Cites

Whenever you paraphrase, summarize, or directly quote, you must cite your source in the text of your outline or paper, which is known as an *in-text cite*. If you do not, you could be unintentionally plagiarizing. "This is one example of an APA Style in-text cite" (Jimenez, 2012). Or, according to Nguyen (2012), "this is a second example of an APA style in-text cite." Either of these two in-text citing methods should be suitable for citing your sources in your outline.

Following are APA in-text cite guidelines.

◆ Cite your source in *every* main point or *every* sub-point, depending on the citation requirements.
◆ When more than one author is cited, the phrase "et al." may be utilized after the first author's name, to connote the other authors. For example, Patel et. al. (2012).
◆ There is no need to include an author's first name or a book's page number when using APA style. Only state the author's last name, and the date (year only) of the publication or interview when using APA style in a paper or an outline.
◆ APA style does not use footnotes or endnotes. Only use quotation marks on direct quotes.

In-Speech Cites

Begin by citing your sources in your introduction to establish credibility, although citing your sources just once at the beginning your speech is usually not sufficient. At the minimum, plan to cite once in each main point. It is not recommended that you cite each and every sentence or your citations may become tedious to your audience. Instead, cite a cluster of material at one time (if it is all from the same author). Do not forget to add source credibility the first time you cite orally. It is your task to prove that your research comes from a credible source by listing the qualifications of the source when you first cite it.

As was discussed earlier in the text, there are three steps to citing evidence during your speeches (Fujishin, 2008). The three steps are: cite the source, state the evidence, and then restate the evidence.

Example: "Randy Fujishin, who wrote the text *The Natural Speaker* and who is famous for his finesse at delivering public speeches, developed the Three Steps as a method for citing your sources in your speech. Fujihsin said to first cite your source. He said that second, you should state your evidence, and then last, restate your evidence in your own words. If you use this simple oral citing methodology in your speech, your audience will know exactly where you evidence came from, and how your evidence related to your topic."

References

References are virtually the same as a bibliography or works cited page. You have to have referred to the information from the source in your manuscript, speech, or outline in order to cite it in the reference section.

Your reference list should appear at the end of your outline or manuscript. The reference list provides the information necessary for an audience member, reader, instructor, or manager to locate and retrieve any source you cite. Each source you cite in the text of your outline or manuscript must appear in your reference list. Likewise, each entry in the reference list must be cited in the text of your outline.

References should be listed in alphabetical order by author's last name. Authors' names are inverted with the last name first. Start with the earliest publication date when you have multiple articles written by the exact same author or set of authors. For examples of how to cite different types of sources such as Twitter, a pamphlet without an author, or a YouTube video in APA or MLA style for your references, refer to apastyle.org or mla.org.

Step Thirteen: Design Your Visual Aids

You are already aware that some members audience members may be more motivated by the visual aids you use in your speech than they will by the words you say. Given this reality, take some time to reflect on what type of visual aid will best persuade your target audience to adopt your proposition. You may decide to use an object, chart, graph, multimedia visual, slides, audio or visual clip, or drawings—or a combination of the above. Once you have determined what type of visuals to use in your speech, you will want to implement the advanced technique of using color to your advantage.

Many studies support the benefits of using colors wisely. Although effects of color choice on the psyche are often subliminal, they can have a powerful impact on audiences. *Color symbolism* is the use of color to represent traditional, cultural, political, or religious ideas, concepts, or feelings or to evoke reactions. The general rule for colors are that cool colors, such as blue, green, or silver, are calming to the audience, and that warm colors, such as red, yellow, and orange, are exciting colors that may stimulate your audience. Black, blue, red, purple, and green are considered to be the most visually appealing visual aid colors.

Black can represent ideas such as power, sophistication, elegance, formality, professionalism, mystery, gravity, fear, sadness, and anger. Black makes a simple, no-nonsense, powerful visual statement. The color black implies that the presenter is serious, knowledgeable, and professional.

Blue is the hue of water and the sea, with all the symbolic references that the element of water suggests. Blue usually indicates flow and purity, just as water does. Blue can also symbolize peace, calm, stability, security, and loyalty. Blue gives the impression of trustworthiness and being accessible.

Red can symbolize many things, from blood to love. Red symbolizes strong emotions such as action, excitement, energy, strength, danger, passion, and aggression. Red is a power color. It infers the presenter is in charge. It can also be used as a motivational tool to stimulate listeners to action.

Purple combines the stability of blue and the energy of red. It symbolizes power, nobility, luxury, and ambition. Purple is associated with wisdom, creativity, mystery, and femininity. According to some surveys, almost 75 percent of children prefer purple to all other colors. Purple may have a calming effect on your audience.

Green is the color of nature. It can represent healing, eternity, peace, the environment, good luck, and youth. Green suggests stability and endurance. Green is the color of choice when dealing with earth-friendly topics. It is also the color of comfort, life, and money.

Further, light backgrounds such as white paired with dark red, blue, green, or purple have the most impact, and give better visual acuity. This is true for computer-generated slides, handouts, flip charts, charts, or graphs. Contrast is especially important when persuasive speech-giving in a large auditorium.

Color symbolism is the use of color to represent traditional, cultural, political, or religious ideas, concepts, or feelings or to evoke reactions.

YOUR VIEW

What type(s) of visual aids will work best on your audience type and be most persuasive to your audience? Why? How will you use color to enhance your visual aids?

_____

_____

_____

Before you complete this chapter, review this checklist to make sure you have completed Phase Three.

Phase Two Checklist

_____	Organized the Main Points into a pattern
_____	Developed an Introduction, Transitions, and Conclusion
_____	Completed a Speech Preparation Guide
_____	Used Persuasive Language to Build Outline
_____	Cited Sources in Text, in a Reference Section, and in Speech
_____	Created Compelling Visual Aids

CHAPTER SUMMARY

Persuasion is a process aimed at changing an audience's attitude or behavior toward some event, idea, object, or other person(s). This chapter followed up on PHASE ONE in Chapter Six to take you further along the path of persuasion. The objective of this chapter was to walk you through PHASE TWO, the last seven steps on persuasive speech-giving.

This chapter's purpose was to teach you how to organize and perfect the content and structure of your persuasive speech. It first reviewed how to organize your speech by completing a Speech Preparation Guide and supplementing your outline with persuasive language. Then it reviewed the final steps of citing sources and creating convincing and colorful visual aids.

Being persuasive is not magic, and it is not luck. It is skill. When you follow each of the thirteen steps in PHASE ONE and PHASE TWO, you will no doubt be better skilled at influencing your audience.

WALKING WITH PURPOSE:
Elements of Delivery

8

Walk and be happy, walk and be healthy.
The best way to lengthen out our days is to walk steadily and with purpose.

—Charles Dickens, British novelist, 1812–1870

This next phase of your journey must be walked with purpose; that is, determined, resolute, and full of meaning. You have learned how to develop and organize the content of your speech, and have prepared what you are going to say. At this point on *The Speaker's Path* focus your walk on your delivery. What you say in your speech is the content, how you structure your presentation is the organization, and how you say your address is the delivery. *Delivery* is all of the nonverbal components to your speech-giving, such as eye contact, gestures, and movement. This chapter overviews the basic components of purposeful speech delivery, starting with the four delivery modes.

> *Delivery* is all of the nonverbal components to your speech-giving.

Modes of Delivery

For a seasoned speaker, the process of delivering a purposeful speech is second nature. For others, the delivery methods are unfamiliar and thus it is challenging to determine which speaking mode is best to use for the given situation. Over the last few decades, four basic styles of delivering public speeches have developed: manuscript, memorized, impromptu, and extemporaneous. Each has its advantages and disadvantages. This next section will provide a synopsis of all four methods of delivery.

> **Methods of Delivery**
>
> Manuscript, Memorized, Impromptu, and Extemporaneous

Manuscript Method

Reading an entire presentation word for word is known as the *manuscript method*. According to public speaking consultant Angela DeFinis who wrote "4 Methods to Deliver a Great Speech" (2009), some speeches must be delivered in manuscript style such as "critical updates to the media from the government, reports at a professional meeting or convention, or a political address from an elected official". She asserts that in these highly formal contexts precision of language is an extremely important component of the overall performance because every word may be analyzed.

In the manuscript mode, speakers write down everything they plan to say, one word at a time. Then, they bring their full manuscript to the podium and read it to the audience verbatim. Or, the speaker uses a teleprompter. A *teleprompter* is an electronic device that, unseen by the audience, scrolls a prepared speech line by line as a prompting aid to the speaker. It may look easy when experienced anchor people give a polished, manuscript speech on television, but it requires a great deal of skill and practice.

So too, the writing of a manuscript speech requires talented word-smiths who know the nuances of writing speeches that will be read. For most of the rest of us, this type of speech is difficult to construct. To begin with, some people assume that they write the same way that they talk. Written and oral communication are two very different styles of transmitting information. For example, written communication is more formal and uses full sentences. However, most of us speak less formally in fragments or phrases instead of full sentences.

The challenge is to make the written word sound spontaneous and genuine. Otherwise, this type of speech can come across as dry and dispassionate. Novice teleprompter or speech readers sometimes squint and stare at the words, which causes them to look stiff and unnatural.

Reading a verbatim speech from an essay or from a teleprompter effectively is all about not actually appearing to be reading. This sounds like a simple task, but is really just the opposite. If your face is contorted and your eyes are down at your notes or glued to the teleprompter, it will be obvious that you are reading. If you are going to read your speech from a manuscript or a teleprompter or some other electronic device, you must thoroughly rehearse your material so that you do not come across as uncomfortable. DeFinis of Definis Communications further advises that "the delivery must be closely choreographed with the message to lift the speech from the page and into the hearts and minds of the audience."

Although challenging to accomplish successfully, the manuscript method has three advantages. The first advantage is that there is no danger of forgetting a part of your speech, unless you somehow lose your manuscript or your technology fails. Second, a manuscript speech allows you plenty of time to choose the most effective language beforehand. Third, the use of manuscript assures precise timing. Unfortunately, many manuscript delivery deliveries sound as if they are being read, which prevents the speech from sounding natural. Most people don't read aloud as well as they think they do.

Memorization Method

A second method, called the *memorization method*, also begins with a written manuscript but differs in that the manuscript is memorized word-for-word and not used during the delivery. Memorized delivery has some of the same advantages as manuscript delivery. The two advantages of this method are that you may choose the most effective language beforehand, and your speech may be timed precisely.

However, in the memorized method of delivery, the disadvantages outweigh the advantages if your speech is more than a few minutes in length. The first disadvantage is that the presentation may sound prepackaged, just like the manuscript mode. A second disadvantage is that word-for-word memorization puts a tremendous burden on your memory for any speech longer than four minutes. If you forget a word or a sentence, you may omit important portions of your speech without knowing it. Or, even worse, you may find that you do not know where you are, what you have said, or what comes next. This method is rarely used these days as a result, except perhaps for brief speeches such as a toast at a wedding or a short congratulatory remark at a retirement dinner. A third disadvantage is that while a rare number of speakers can use this method effectively, too often this style results in a stilted and inflexible presentation. This is because the speaker is more concerned with remembering the material than with the reactions of the audience.

Unless you are an experienced actor or orator, memorizing a speech longer than four minutes in length is not a recommended method due to these disadvantages. It can result in an expressionless presentation that leaves your audience in doubt as to your sincerity and even your knowledge of the subject. If you do choose to recite some or all of your speech from memory, however, make sure you know it so well that you do not risk blanking out in front of your audience or fumbling with your words.

Impromptu Method

The third method, called the *impromptu method*, is the opposite of the first two. Impromptu style is unrehearsed or rehearsed just a little and is in many ways spontaneous and improvised. This method demands that the speakers organize their ideas and choose their words at the time of delivery.

Memorization method, is a written manuscript memorized word-for-word.

Impromptu method is unrehearsed or rehearsed just a little and is spontaneous and improvised.

Impromptu speaking is used on occasions when people must speak "off the cuff," with little or no chance for preparation beforehand. One example of when you might use an impromptu speaking mode is at a job interview, when you answer the question "Why should I hire you?" In a job interview, you should research the company first and plan your approach ahead of time even though you have no idea what you will be asked by the hiring manager. Similarly, impromptu speeches are also often not completely without some form of preparation, no matter how slight.

Mark Twain wrote "It usually takes me more than three weeks to prepare a good impromptu speech." While you most likely have closer to thirty seconds than three weeks to prepare an impromptu speech, if you are in a situation where you might be called on to do an impromptu talk, it is a good idea to at the least think over what you might say in your speech before you reach the podium. Take your time to walk up to the front of the room, to gather your confidence and consider your approach. There is usually no need to rush right into your speech. Even a minute or two of preparation time will likely pay off.

Another suggestion for impromptu delivery style is to only choose to speak on topics you are extremely familiar with. For example, Ian Schleter of Siglap Toastmaster's Club asserts on its website that to be an effective impromptu speaker, you should "speak on specific illustrations, experiences and examples from your past that you are knowledgeable on, and that you have a desire to share with other people (Schleter, 2007)."

Last, if you are going to give an impromptu speech, break your talk down into small parts and clarify your purpose in your mind as a means of mentally preparing for the speech in the allotted time you have. Take a deep breath, and before you even start your talk, think through a logical beginning, middle, and ending progression of your speech. The typical organizational format for an impromptu speech contains: a brief yet compelling introduction, one or two main points that each possess one descriptive example as supporting evidence, a couple of simple transitions, and a concisely worded conclusion.

One advantage of impromptu speaking is that since it is by nature spontaneous, it rarely sounds overly rehearsed or canned like the memorized or manuscript methods can. Instead, it often allows a speaker's personality to shine through. This style can be engaging, emotional, genuine, and passionate. Your speech will sound natural, much like ordinary conversation.

There are several disadvantages to this method of delivery. Its major drawback is its tendency to sound unprepared, unless the speaker has a lot of experience in impromptu speaking. Another drawback, which derives from the impossibility of doing research, is the speaker's lack of opportunity to use statistics, facts, or compelling examples to illustrate ideas clearly unless he or she is an expert on the subject. Another liability is the speaker's tendency to ramble or use unnecessary phrases such as "you know" or "um" to gain thinking time. Finally, the impromptu method can also leave a speaker feeling awkward or embarrassed because his speech was not refined or logical.

Extemporaneous Method

The fourth method is a combination of the strengths of the other three styles. In the *extemporaneous method*, speakers prepare outlines of the ideas of their speeches beforehand, just like in manuscript of memorized styles. As such, timing and organization can be premeditated. However, the speaker does not memorize an exact pattern of words, nor does the speaker bring a manuscript to the podium or read from a teleprompter. Instead, she chooses the words with which to clothe her ideas as she is speaking, much like the impromptu mode. Yet, the extemporaneous mode isn't completely off the cuff like impromptu. On the contrary, the extemporaneous speech is thoughtfully and thoroughly prepared, planned, and practiced.

Extemporaneous method is a prepared beforehand, with the words chosen at delivery.

When speaking in the extemporaneous mode of delivery speakers use keyword notes, a brief outline, or a computer-based slide presentation program such as PowerPoint or Keynote to stay on track. Full-sentence comprehensive notes are manuscript style, and if they are right there in front of you, will probably be too tempting to read. As long as the speech structure is carefully planned and the major ideas and themes are memorized, keyword notes are all that most speakers need. Extemporaneous speeches are previously planned but delivered with the help of few notes.

This is the most recommended method of speech-giving by most experts in the field because it combines the best qualities of the aforementioned modes. As consultant DeFinis (2009) says about her communication skills training business and clientele, "This is the method we recommend for the majority of people we work with." It is often the required approach for speech-giving in university-level public speaking classes as well.

The major advantage of the extemporaneous method is that it sounds more like "telling" your speech than like "reading" it, almost as if you are having a conversation with your audience. Audiences feel connected to the speaker because of the direct eye contact used in this method. A second advantage is that audiences are often tolerant of a speaker who looks them in the eye and addresses them directly. This is true even if the speaker occasionally needs to look down at his notes to jog his memory, or if the flow of words is not fluent. The last advantage is that the extemporaneous method gives the speaker the best opportunity to make use of positive and negative feedback from the audience. It allows the speaker to survey the audience and gauge their reactions to the material, and then make necessary adjustments.

The only disadvantages to the extemporaneous method are that it requires that you create speech notes and that you must practice with those speech notes numerous times before speech-giving in order for your speech to come off as polished. Since the disadvantages are so few, and the advantages so numerous to this speaking style, it is the one mode that will be highlighted most prominently in this chapter.

YOUR VIEW

What mode of delivery will be most suitable for your next speech?

_____

_____

_____

Speech Notes

It is rare for novice speakers to be able to effectively give an organized, structured, and detailed speech that is over four minutes in length and within the time limits of the speech without the use of some type of speech notes. Those who try to give a speech impromptu without notes often come off as disorganized or unprepared. On the other hand, speakers who overly rely on notes and read their entire speeches or outlines in manuscript style lose the connection with the audience and are perceived as less confident and interesting. Preparing effective speech notes can be an asset to your speech-giving.

You have already constructed a fully developed outline. Instead of reading your outline verbatim, it is recommended that you convert it into simple, key word speech notes. Consider making key word notes on note-cards or on one sheet of paper or using computer-generated presentation programs as your notes. If you are using computer generated slides such as Power Point as your notes, bring a laptop or tablet and position it so that it is in easy view in front of you. If necessary, request a separate small table so that you always see your laptop, tablet, or electronic speech notes.

Whatever type of notes you decide on or are required to use, use key-words to remind you of what you wish to say, instead of full sentences. Anything more than keyword speech notes might negatively impact your credibility, because your audience needs to see your eyes to believe in you.

Below is a guide for using computer-generated and traditional paper key word speech notes to your advantage.

Computer-Generated Speech Notes

If using *computer-based speech notes* generated by a presentation program such as PowerPoint or Keynote, or other multimedia speech notes—for example, those on a tablet or an iPad—try the following seven tips for success:

1. Use notes that correspond to each slide or image.
2. Do not face the screen, your laptop, or your tablet. Face your audience.
3. Try to use your notes as little as possible during your speech.
4. Always use notes as unobtrusively as possible except when reading a direct quotation or complicated statistics. In these cases, face the screen so that your audience can see that you are taking special care to be accurate.
5. Avoid writing your notes in too much detail. Use keywords only. Except for long quotes or complicated statistics, limit the number of lines you put on your speech notes and indent them, so you will be able to find your place in an instant.
6. Type your notes in a font style and size that you can easily read from where you will be standing.

Computer-generated speech notes use a computer-based presentation program such as PowerPoint, Keynote, or other multimedia notes as a guide.

Traditional Paper Speech Notes

If using *traditional paper speech notes* such as note cards, try the following eight suggestions:

1. Use standard three-by-five or four-by-six-inch rigid paper note cards or one sheet of paper. Cards are recommended because they are easy to hide in one hand or on the podium. Cards also work well if you are worried that your hands might shake your note paper during your speech.
2. Always use speech notes as unobtrusively as possible except when reading a direct quotation or complicated statistics. In these cases, hold your notes up so that your audience can see that you are taking special care to be accurate.
3. Make sure your notes are legible.
4. Number or staple multiple note cards, so you will be able to put them in order quickly if you happen to drop them or find they are disarranged.
5. Write on only one side of your cards or paper. Even though your audience will expect you to use notes, turning the cards or paper over is distracting. Moreover, if you have something written on the back

Traditional paper speech notes use a keyword outline or note cards as a guide.

of your note card, the audience members in the front row will no doubt try to read it.

6. Avoid writing your notes in too much detail. Use keywords only. Except for cards that have a long quote or a complicated statistics, limit the number of lines you put on a card and indent them, so you will be able to find your place in an instant.

7. Hold note cards in one hand so that you can still gesture freely with the other hand.

Overall, your speech should be so well rehearsed that you find you rarely need to use your notes. They should only been used when you absolutely need them. Speech notes only serve as a guide to jog your memory when delivering your speech. The extemporaneous method requires spontaneity and good eye contact. Overly detailed notes or full-sentence notes will entice you to read your cards from top to bottom, which will destroy two-way communication.

Practice

A great speech on paper is not a great speech unless it is delivered effectively. Therefore, once you have designed your notes, you must commit time to practice. Practice means to perform something repeatedly in order to polish your speech. The number one thing that you can do to improve your delivery is to practice with your entire presentation using your speech notes at least five and ten times. Below are eight tips regarding speech practice.

Practice
is when you perform your speech repeatedly in advance

1. Allow ample time for practice. In other words, do not begin practicing the night before you give your speech. Begin practicing two to three days before your speech is scheduled. Practice enough to develop a conversational delivery, but not to the extent that you unintentionally memorize your speech.

2. Always rehearse with the same speech notes and visuals that you plan to use when delivering your speech. If you rewrite or redesign something, run it through a practice session to make sure that you have not made an error that will throw you off during your speech. Be comfortable and familiar with your speech notes and visuals.

3. Consider running through your speech as if you were delivering it to your intended audience. After you have practiced alone or in front of a mirror, try to find a person or two to serve as your audience. Have them sit or stand 20 feet away from you. Each time you practice in front of people, practice looking up and smiling.

4. Go through the entire speech during each practice because being consistent helps. If you hit a trouble spot or two during practice, do not stop and start your entire speech over. Chances are that, if you do, you might do this while delivering your speech. Instead, practice from start to finish each time.

5. Do not deliver your speech the same way each time you practice it. Changing wording each time will help you find creative ways of saying something that incorporates your own sense of speaking style and keep you from memorizing.

6. Rehearse your speech aloud with the same volume that you plan to use in delivering it. Although it is helpful to visualize giving your speech in your head, it is equally beneficial to practice in your speaking voice. If possible, rehearse your speech in your front or back yard so that you can work on your volume.

7. Time your speech in practice. If you have been given a time limit for your speech, conform to it in practice.

8. Practice the way you will approach the speaker's lectern because you are on stage the moment you leave your chair or walk into the room. If possible, practice at least once in the room where you will be delivering your speech or a similar room. Anything you can do in practice to approximate the real thing is worth the effort.

If you create effective speech notes and thoroughly practice with them, you may be able to obtain the most sought-after of all delivery skills, which is called dynamism. The concept of *dynamism* refers to the energy of a speaker, the ability of a speaker to engage and audience, the rapport a speaker has in front of a group, and the power a speaker has at the podium. Dynamic speakers are perceived as more influential, credible, persuasive, and believable. If you have a lifeless, dull, and flat delivery, you will lose your audience no matter how great your words. Use effective notes and practice so that you can deliver your speech in a dynamic way.

> *Dynamism* refers to the energy of a speaker, the ability of a speaker to engage and audience, the rapport a speaker has in front of a group, and the power a speaker has at the podium.

YOUR VIEW

What have you learned about speech notes and practice that you will apply to your speech-giving so that your next speech is delivered in a dynamic way?

_____

_____

_____

PREP Model for Delivery

<table>
<tr><td>

The PREP Model

Professional,
Receptive,
Energetic,
Polished

</td><td>

The **PREP Model** is a simple and essential guide to help you cultivate a dynamic nonverbal delivery. Nonverbal delivery includes your appearance, facial expressions, posture and stance, eye contact, gestures, voice, and movement. According to some researchers, the majority of the meaning expressed in a speech is nonverbal (without the use of words). That means how you say your speech is often more important than the words you use in your speech. As such, it is important to consider what you want your nonverbal actions to say about you when you are up in front of an audience. If you wish to convey dynamism and professionalism, follow the PREP Model.

</td></tr>
</table>

Professional is exhibiting the standing, practice, character, spirit, or methods of a professional.

Professional

Professional is defined as exhibiting the standing, practice, character, spirit, or methods of a professional, as distinguished from an amateur. Just as you should always dress for the job you want as opposed to the job you have, so to you should consider how your attire may impact how the audience perceives you as a speaker. Choose the same type of attire that you would wear to a job interview. Professionalism is more than just clothing choices, however. A professional also radiates self-control and composure. If you want to be perceived as professional, behave as you would in the business context. Smile when appropriate. Use professional language, avoiding slang and jargon. Make sure that your organization is clear.

Receptive is being open and positive.

Receptive

Receptive is being open and positive. It is the quality of being ready, willing, or qualified for receiving. If you wish to be perceived as receptive, focus on your audience instead of yourself, your notes, or your visual aid and respond appropriately to audience reactions. Use open and expressive nonverbal communication to convey that you perceive the audience favorably and you want them to perceive you in the same light. Keep your eyes on your audience, focusing on one audience member at a time.

Energetic is possessing or exhibiting enthusiasm or vigor in abundance.

Energetic

Being *energetic* means possessing or exhibiting enthusiasm or vigor in abundance. The liveliness level of a speaker can have a remarkable impact on how engaged the audience will be. If you want to be perceived as vibrant and animated, engage your audience with your eye contact, facial expressions, vocal delivery, and expressive gestures and movements. Allow your personality to shine. Your audience deserves to see the best of you, so bring up your

Polished
energy level and volume, even if you are feeling tired, stressed, or anxious.

To be *polished* means to be refined, skillful, smooth, and almost flawless. To achieve this, rehearse your speech to such an extent that you seldom, if ever, rely on your notes. Exude poise, sophistication, class, and composure. You should also use smooth transitions so that you speech flows naturally, and speak loudly enough so that every audience member can hear you, even those in the back of the room.

Polished is to be refined, smooth, and almost flawless.

Now that we have discussed how to improve your nonverbal delivery in general terms, we will highlight specific aspects of your delivery, one precise skillset at a time, starting with eye contact.

Delivery

Eye Contact

Giving an effective speech requires many things as you have now learned, from organization to creating speech notes, but the most important aspect is likely making eye contact with your audience. *Eye contact* is meeting your audience with your eyes. While steady eye contact is considered impolite or aggressive in some cultures, eye contact is an important aspect of social interaction in American culture. In fact, when a speaker averts her eyes, she is often perceived as untrustworthy, superficial, or unreceptive. This is another great reason why you should avoid writing your notes in too much detail.

Compents of Delivery
Eye Contact, Paralanguage, Gestures, Facial Expressions, Platform Movement, Appearance

Eye contact is meeting your audience with your eyes.

When making presentations, eye contact is crucial to your success. Your goal for should be to maintain eye contact with your audience at least 90 percent of the time. You will only be able to do this if you convert your outline to basic notes and if you practice with your notes several times. This means not looking up at your projected slides or down at your paper notes. Instead, look at all faces of your audience members, including the people who are frowning or seeming to not be paying close attention.

You can do this by creating simple speech notes and practicing with them. Another trick is to not look up or down to plan your words or to recall your content. Remember, your speech should be so well-rehearsed that you hardly need to use your notes, so that your eyes can be with your audience almost the entire time.

Try to make eye contact with every single person in your audience at least once. Because eye contact is to a speech as a handshake is to a greeting, lock eyes with the audience member for about as long as you would shake hands, or roughly three seconds. Once you have made eye contact with a member audience, move on to someone new. Look directly into the eyes of a person and communicate a thought, then when you would normally look away, just move to another set of eyes.

As communications expert and public speaking and sales consultant Robert Graham says in his article "The Windows to the Soul: Mastering the Art of Eye Contact" on his website grahamcomm.net, "Pick a person, stop and talk to him or her for an entire thought or sentence. Then, at a natural transition in your talk, find somebody else in the room." He says that instead of thinking of the group as one massive entity, pretend that you are having individual conversations with one audience member at a time. He adds, "All of us are comfortable in conversations. So think of speaking to a group as having a bunch of small conversations."

If looking at someone directly in the eyes is too intimidating for you, pick a spot directly between or slightly above the listener's eyes on his or her forehead. Do not look at a spot on the wall or way above the person's head, as he will be able to tell that you are not really looking at him. Or, try letting your eyes go slightly out of focus so that the person is hard to see clearly. This has the added benefit of softening your gaze, which may make you appear to be more sympathetic and approachable.

Not only does eye contact builds rapport with your audience, but eye contact gives you immediate feedback. Eye contact with audience members will help gain an understanding of your audience. You can see if they are listening, interested, worried, excited, bored, or delighted.

By employing some of these strategies for good eye contact, you will make your listeners feel more connected with you and increase the likelihood that they will respond favorably to your speech.

YOUR VIEW

What are two ways that you can improve your eye contact?

_____

_____

Paralanguage

All of us are aware that the meaning of what we say is contained partly in the words we use, but also that how we say things contains powerful meaning. The word, "Okay," for example, can mean completely different things, even in the exact same sentence, depending on how it is said. The "how" something is said is referred to as paralanguage. *Paralanguage* is defined as vocal features that accompany speech and contribute to communication such as vocal quality, projection, and pace. Specifically, paralanguage can be broken down as follows: pace, projection, pitch, and pauses. These are known as the Four Ps.

Paralanguage is vocal features that accompany speech.

Pace

The *pace* is the rate at which you speak, or the tempo at which you put your thoughts together out loud. *Rhythm* is the pattern of the sounds you produce. The rhythm and pace, be it slow, fast, or somewhere in between, communicates a great deal. If you speak at a pace that is too quick, your audience may perceive you as being anxious, agitated, overly excited, or extremely urgent. However, if you speak at too leisurely a pace, your audience may lose interest in what you are communicating, or they may think you are uncertain or even dull. Generally speaking, in U.S. culture, a moderate pace is considered to be more credible, as long as you speak at a rate slow enough that the audience can follow and fast enough that your audience does not become disengaged.

Since most speakers talk too fast due to nervousness, when you feel you are speaking too slowly, you may just be speaking at the right pace. Many of us want to get the presentation over as quickly as possible, and it shows as we speed through our delivery. So do not rush through your words, particularly when you start or end your speech as it may take a few seconds for your audience to hear and understand what you have said. It will take even longer for them to make the transition from one topic area to another. To make slowing down your pace possible, you must be realistic about your time constraints and the amount of material you have. Avoid the temptation to force more content into your speech so that you have to talk faster.

Most communications experts advise two key techniques in terms of pacing. First, as discussed, you should speak fast enough to keep people from becoming bored, yet slow enough for people to absorb fully what you're saying. The second piece of advice is that you vary pace and rhythm when you speak.

To add color to your speech, consider changing the pace and rhythm of your delivery between topics or main points. If you can change the pace or rhythm of your speech at the right time, it can add emphasis to certain ideas. When making a key point, for example, slow down your pace so that the audience understands it is important. Slowing down can emphasize key ideas or inject gravity. Or, when you want to convey an exciting event, urgency, high emotional states, or add humor, quicken the pace and adjust your rhythm.

To keep audiences attentive, you need to fluctuate your tempo at appropriate times because when you deliver a speech at the same rate of speed, you are depriving yourself of a means of power. Ronen Cohen of First Level Leadership Group, a group that develops leadership skills, says about the importance of tempo in his article "Persuasive speech is evident: for it is measured in how you regulate the . . . " that your thoughts should regulate your pace. He says that if you are aware of your thoughts

The Four Ps

Pace, Projection, Pitch, and Pauses

Pace
is the rate or tempo at which you speak.

Rhythm
is the pattern of the sounds you produce.

when speech-giving, you will automatically modulate your speed at the right time in your speech. First Level Leadership Group advises that you be prudent in how often you change your pace, however: Don't change your tempo too quickly because "tempo, like a healthy diet, is best when balanced."

Projection

No matter how well organized, researched, and polished a speech may be, if the listeners cannot hear what the speaker is saying, the speech will not be successful. Although it is possible to speak too loudly for a given room or audience, most novice speakers have the opposite problem. They cannot be heard in the back of the room. While this may be due to feeling nervous or anxious, it is most often attributed to the fact that novice public speakers do not realize that they are not effectively projecting their voice. For the inexperienced speech giver, just about any volume level may sound too loud. This is understandable, because the natural volume for conversations in one-on-one conversations or small groups is lower.

projection
is the strength of speaking whereby the voice is used with volume and with power.

Voice projection is the strength of speaking whereby the voice is used with volume and power. It is the degree of loudness and the intensity and clarity of sounds. Appropriate volume and projection communicate confidence and authority. What is appropriate public speaking projection? It is speaking loud enough for your audience and the context of your speech. How do you know if your volume and projection suit the situation? Project your voice and bring up your volume so that you think it can be easily heard and understood by all members of your audience. Then, as a safeguard, ask your audience how your volume is at the start of your speech. They will give you feedback if you are talking to loud or too softly. Try to mostly stay at that volume throughout your entire speech.

Minor variations in loudness can be appropriate, however. There may be sentences or sections of your speech where it is advisable to increase or decrease your volume as a means of emphasis. Thus, some variation in volume may be effective. When done appropriately, moderating your projection and volume may enhance the purpose of the speech. While you should vary your vocal delivery for interest and to accent key words or phrases, do not ever drop your volume so low that someone in your audience has to ask you to speak up.

One way to develop vocal projection and volume is to rehearse your speech a few times in your backyard, front yard, in a large room, or even at a local park. You may feel a little silly if someone observes you doing this, but this technique, regardless of how embarrassing it may feel, will likely help you improve your speech-giving vocals. When you are practicing, maintain a mental image of broadcasting or propelling your voice to the far corners of the yard or room. Visualize your voice as being like an arrow moving in a large arc from your stomach, through your throat, and to your intended target. When you are practicing, do not speak at the same volume that you do when talking with a couple of friends. This volume will be too low for speech-giving, especially in a larger room. Instead, bring your volume up a couple of notches and get used to how your voice sounds when magnified.

Another method to improving projection is by deep breathing into your diaphragm. Volume and projection are controlled by the diaphragm, not the throat. The diaphragm is a muscle located between the abdominal and thoracic cavities, just beneath your ribs. The diaphragm is responsible for pushing out air that is sufficient enough to project the sounds you make. Exercising the diaphragm is crucial to vocal projection and volume. One technique for enhancing how you use your diaphragm is to practice inhaling as much air into your lungs as possible. Breathe through your mouth and nose deeply into your belly until your lungs are filled. Slowly push the air back out of your lungs. Quickly releasing your breath does not exercise your diaphragm. Breathing out very slowly will force your diaphragm to take control and become stronger. Deeply inhale and slowly exhale in this manner several times. When you feel you're taking enough air into your lungs, begin rehearsing your speech.

To summarize, although you want to be loud and project your public speaking voice to the far corners of the room and even occasionally alter your volume, keep in mind that you should never yell like a drill sergeant. Too much volume at the wrong time, or throughout your entire speech, may be assaulting to your audience.

Pitch

The *pitch* of the voice is defined as the rate of vibration of the vocal folds. The sound of the voice changes as the rate of vibrations varies. As the number of vibrations per second increases, so does the pitch, meaning the voice will sound higher.

Pitch is the rate of vibration of the vocal folds.

Pitch is the main acoustic correlate of tone. To understand pitch, think of music. Music has high and low notes as do people's voices. Every person's voice has a natural pitch, with women's voices tending to be higher than men's. Everybody has a pitch range that they habitually use. This is called vocal range. *Vocal range* is the measure of the breadth of pitch, the span from highest notes to the lowest notes.

When the vocal range is very small, the effect is called monotone, or one tone. Monotone is the succession of sounds or words uttered in a single tone of voice. According to a recent study cited in the U.K.'s *The Telegraph* in 2012, monotone voices in men are sometimes associated with strength and power. Yet that same phenomena in a speech is considered boring or flat by some audiences. This may be because often those who speak in a monotone communicate very little nonverbal expressiveness.

On the opposite end of the continuum is a voice that has a range of pitch that is very large. When the voice drops and falls in quick succession like a melodic song, it can make a speaker appear not as intelligent as she actually probably is, or it can convey things like anxiety or tenseness. Further, bringing your pitch up at the end of your sentences designates the statement as a question and can make you seem hesitant or indecisive. Thus, it is recommended that you drop your pitch at the end of your sentences, unless you are trying to ask a question or wish to appear uncertain.

Here are three recommendations for improving your pitch:

1. Renown public speaking coach and Toastmaster's consultant Andrew Dlugan advocates that you play with your pitch to see how high and low you can go. He recommends to vary your pitch by speaking in a woman's voice if you are a man, or in a man's voice if you are a woman. He also suggests that you read a couple of sentences from a novel or a famous quote out loud, starting at a really low pitch. With each sentence, he instructs that you raise your pitch a note and see how high up you can get. Then he advises to try it again, starting at the highest pitch and working your way down (Dlugan, 2009).

2. Another suggestion is to practice changing your vocal pitch with different emotional experts recommend content. For example, a *sad* voice takes on a different pitch than a *happy* voice, which is distinct from an *irritated* voice. Choose a child's storybook that has vivid characters and begs to be read in a variety of tones and emotional affect. Use a different voice aloud for each character. Change your pitch and affect with each character, like an actor would when reading a script.

3. Last, according to The Voice Lady Nancy Daniels in a 2012 article called "A Simple Exercise for Overcoming a Monotone Voice" on voicedynamic.com, there is a simple but effective exercise to begin expressing emotion. She says that you should practice effective pitch variation by standing in front of a mirror and saying the words "I am capable" as if you were really excited, asking a question, and last, without any expression. She says that you should notice a difference. If you don't, she recommends that you do the exercise over and over again until you start to hear the pitch changes. She also suggests that you record your voice while you are doing this and then play it back and listen to the tone changes. She ends with, "without an expressive delivery, a well-crafted speech or presentation is not nearly as effective as one that sparkles with color (Daniels, 2012."

Pauses

In music, it is the pause of silence between the notes that makes the melody. *Pauses* in speech-giving are using silence instead of filler words, un-words, or filler phrases. In many American contexts, silence is not highly valued, and therefore pauses are avoided at all costs. This likely is because for many people, silence is awkward and uncomfortable. Instead, people use the *filler words* "like," "you know," and "basically" to take up the silent spaces. *Un-words* are another type of filler such as "uh," "er," and "um." People also use *filler phrases* such as "I think," "you know," and "what I'm trying to say is." Filler words and phrases and un-words are generally never written into a speech, and thus add next to nothing when a speaker utters them. Yet these insidious vocal slip-ups are so present in most oral presentations that there is even an entire book devoted to the topic called *Um: Slips, Stumbles and Verbal Blunders and What They Mean* by Michael Erard.

Speakers tend to use fillers in their speeches because they are often processing meaning at a deeper level than surface thoughts or well-rehearsed phrases, while at the same time feel the expectations of people around them to speak. As a result, people often add in fillers because they are not sure what else to do with the space or because they are unprepared. Consequently, the use of fillers in speech-giving is often highest when speakers fail to adequately prepare and practice their speeches. This is because the brain needs to generate words off the cuff, instead of pulling them from long-term memory.

In the article "How to Stop Saying Um, Uh, and Other Filler Words" (2011), award winning communications strategist Dlugan says that "while some audience members may adopt a zero tolerance policy when it comes to filler words and phrases and un-words, since fillers are so common, an occasional filler word will likely not trump your appeal as a speaker. Nonetheless, he and other experts advise that you should strive to minimize your use of filler words because they represent vocal static and can weaken your perceived credibility (Dlugan, 2011)

How do you know if you are using um words or filler words and phrases? If your self-esteem can deal with the knowing, there are two simple but effective ways to learn about your useage. You can either recruit a friend in the audience to count your use of fillers Or, you can review your own speech video or audio file and track your use yourself. Your goal in assessment is to establish how often you are inserting filler words, phrases, and un-words, and to determine if they distract from your message or power as a speaker.

If you find you are only using filler words rarely or intermittently, you are ahead of the pack. If you learn that you use filler words, phrases, and

Pauses
are using silence instead of filler words, un-words, or filler phrases.

un-words more than you ever imagined, then you will first want to slow down your pace to give your brain time to catch up to your words. It doesn't have to be a drastic change; even a modest reduction in pace will help.

Another technique is to replace the filler word or phrase with silent pauses. *Pauses* and *silence* are two of the most neglected delivery tools in public speaking. Thus, instead of fearing a few silent moments in your presentation, be open to embracing them. Appropriate use of pauses and silence can add meaning to your speech-giving. Soundless pauses can help you achieve impact, add emphasis, build suspense, and create anticipation concerning what you're about to say. The pause will allow your audience time to absorb your message. In other words, use silence as a partner, not something to avoid. Pause to underscore major points or when you're about to transition to another idea or at the end of a thought or paragraph.

Be conscious of all four major paralanguage variables just discussed: pace, projection, pitch and pauses. Then, devise a plan for working the four Ps into the delivery of your next speech.

YOUR VIEW

What are two ways that you can you improve your paralanguage?

_____

_____

Gestures

Gestures
are arm and hand
movements that
communicate
nonverbally to
express a meaning.

Gestures are simple arm and hand movements that communicate non-verbally to express a meaning. There are four different types of gestures: emblems, illustrators, regulators, and adapters (Martin & Nakayama, 2011).

Emblems are gestures that have specific verbal translations, such as when you wave your hand as someone is leaving to say farewell. Emblems, like all gestures, are not universal and vary from culture to culture. Thus, misunderstandings can easily occur, oftentimes without the speaker even knowing it. What might be a sign of approval for one culture may be a social insult in another. Keep this in mind that what one gesture means to you may mean something quite different for the members of your audience.

Illustrators are gestures that go along with speech-giving, illustrating what is being said. Illustrator gestures are useful as they add detail to the mental image that the person is trying convey in a speech. The timing of illustrators should be synchronized with the speech. The preparation for the gesture should start before the words are said. If there is a small lag between words and gesture and the gesture comes late, it is usually noted by the audience and as such can make a speaker appear manipulative. Make sure you start your illustrator(s) before you say the words.

Regulators are gestures that regulate the flow of a conversation and determine who should talk and when. For example, when you are talking and someone interrupts you before you are finished, you might put out your hand as if to say, "I am still talking, hold on a minute." These same regulators can be used in speech-giving. If you are asking your audience a question and a response is required, you may wish to use a regulator to indicate to your audience that you wish them to respond.

The final type of gesture is called an *adapter*, which is related to managing and conveying our emotions. Adaptor gestures can convey a feeling in a general way, such as rubbing your eyes when you are tired. Sometimes affect such gestures should be avoided because they give away anxiety or are overly dramatic. For example, gestures such as covering the mouth or playing with hair can communicate nervousness or insecurity. However, when adaptors are used effectively, they add spice and emotion to what is being said in the speech.

Here are five recommendations for using gestures in your speech:

1. Take notice of the emblems, illustrators, regulators, and adapters of people in normal conversation. Observe how they correlate gestures with their words. Observe the speaker to determine which gestures you think work effectively and mimic those in your own speaking. However, avoid making the same gestures over and over as monotony breeds distraction. Gestures should be natural, unanticipated, and in synchrony with the meaning of the words spoken.

2. Create opportunities for making gestures during a speech. Try out some possible illustrators and emblems in your practice sessions to see if the gestures match your personality and the context of the speech. For example, attempt a gesture by moving your hands and arms to draw pictures in the air to indicate the size of an object or the general shape of something. You might also try using your hand or index finger to direct the listeners' attention to some place, object, or person.

3. Incorporate regulators into your speech by using phrases such as "On the one hand . . . on the other hand," and by numbering your points "The second point I wish to discuss is . . . ". Or, incorporate regulators as transitions to show that you are moving from one part of your speech to another. For example, use your fingers to enumerate points or place both palms on the podium and then move both hands, with palms facing each other, from one side to the other in front of you.

4. Observe your own gestures during practice. Begin your speech with your hands together and your speech notes on a table, podium, or lectern. Then, as you speak, notice that your hands will often naturally separate and come together again. When you are observing your hands, make sure that your hands are at your waist level or higher, so they can be easily seen by the audience. Finally, monitor your gestures to see if your movements are too gregarious or too slight or restrained. Gestures that are too subtle or reserved might convey hesitancy or nervousness. Gestures that are too controlled might communicate discomfort or lack of trust. Gestures that are too expansive may convey aggressiveness or may appear overly dramatic.

5. Last, hold your arms out from your elbows and away from your body, so that your gestures are not lost against the backdrop of your body. Think of a food server at a restaurant and the three ways that a server carries out the plates of food to his hungry customers. Either he lines up the food on his arms, carries the food on a round high tray near his shoulders, or transports the plate above his head. Your gestures should be in "food-server style," not above your head or below your elbows. That is, gesture in the upper zone of your body, in between your waist and the top of your head, keeping your arms away from your body.

Gestures are one of the greatest assets of a speaker. Yet gestures must be appropriate to the context of your speech and cultures represented in your audience or they may communicate something you did not intend. Gestures should also be used naturally and judiciously, or else they may overwhelm the content of the speech and distract your audience from your purpose.

YOUR VIEW

What are two ways you can improve your gestures?

_____

_____

Facial Expressions

Paul Ekman, a psychologist who has been a pioneer in the study of emotions and their relation to facial expressions, found from his cross-cultural research that while there is no universal nonverbal cue, there are six universal facial expressions based on emotions. The following is Ekman's (1972) list of basic emotions from his research entitled "Universals and Cultural Differences in Facial Expressions and Emotion", which are: anger, disgust, fear, happiness, sadness, and surprise. He concluded that the best method for expressing emotions between human beings is through the face (Eckman, 1972). Other researchers agree that the muscle movements in your face are the best means to convey your emotional state to your audience.

Facial expressions are a form of nonverbal communication and are a primary means of transmitting social information and emotions. What this means for you as a public speaker is that you cannot neglect the importance of facial expressions in your communications. After all, your face is what most people in your audience are going to be concentrating on reading cues from. Think of *facial expressions* as a gesture executed with facial muscles instead of hand and arm movements. Sometimes novice speakers forget to bring their facial expressions to the front of the room, and instead leaves them at their chair. Seek instead to enhance your delivery with facial expressions as a means of communicating emotions. Enhance the same type of facial expressions that you normally use when having a conversation. The face can communicate without even using the mouth to speak. We can use facial expressions to help someone accept a statement that we are making, or to communicate sincerity, interest, and other emotions.

Facial expressions are gestures executed with facial muscles.

How can you make your facial expressions count in your speech? To begin, smile. Smile not just by means of a slight upturn at the corners of your mouth, but authentically and from your eyes. Imagine standing at a lectern and seeing those in your audience. Those in attendance are looking to you to mirror their expressiveness. If your face displays displeasure, your audience will be less likely to want to listen to you. So smile even though you may not be thrilled at the prospect of giving the speech, or even if your nerves are on edge. There is an old saying that "a smile is a curve that straightens out a lot of things." If your topic is not too serious, smile at the beginning and then on throughout your speech. A smile brings out friendliness and conveys kindness and sincerity.

Humor is another method of adding facial expressiveness. Fitting humor, meaning humor that is used in the right context and with an audience that is receptive, can be a wonderful tool in creating an entertaining and light-hearted facial expressiveness. Humor can break down barriers so that the audience is more receptive to you and your speech The best way to inject humor into a presentation is by telling a brief and humorous personal narrative, recommends international expert on humor in speeches Steven Boyd in his article "Using Humor in Your Speech". Boyd advises that if no one smiles or laughs at your storytelling, to just move on as though you meant for your words to be serious. He suggests that this approach will take the pressure off you and your audience. Boyd also advises "If you don't laugh or smile at the cartoon, joke, pun, one-liner, story . . . then you certainly cannot expect an audience to do so. A key to using humor is only using humor that makes you laugh or smile."

Your face is the nonverbal cue that your audience will most spotlight on, from your eyebrows down to your smile. Your face is also a primary means of effectively communicating emotions cross-culturally. Do your best to bring your facial expressions up with you to the stage when you are giving a speech, instead of leaving your personality at your chair. Your audience will thank you.

YOUR VIEW

How can you can improve your facial expressiveness?

_____

_____

Platform Movements

Platform movements are movements that a speaker makes that involve the entire body.

Platform movements are movements that a speaker makes that involve the entire body. Some speakers shy away from platform movement, viewing the lectern, podium, or front of the room as a small box that they feel they must never exit. They freeze instead of incorporating movement, figuratively boxing themselves in. Instead of staying in the same spot throughout the entire speech, try moving out of the box.

If you are new to platform movements and are not sure how to proceed, do not aspire to add physical movement to every moment of your presentation. It will likely be distracting and may appear disingenuous. Instead, think through your talk and pick out a few moments when you could add in some minor movement.

One technique is to use the *walk and plant* in your speech-giving. In the walk and plant, you deliberately walk two to four steps to your left or right, and then pause and plant (stop) for at least 20 seconds. The simplest way to start adding platform movement to your presentation is to coordinate your walk and plant with your speaking points. As you move from point to point and as you transition, you can also move from spot to spot on the stage. Do not keep moving back and forth or you may communicate, unintentionally, that you are nervous. Instead, walk and then plant.

But what about if you have a lectern or are speaking from a podium? Should you still walk and plant and have platform movement? Or, should you stay still and never move out from behind the blockade? The answer is to incorporate platform movement, even when at a podium or lectern. Try not to stay behind a barrier throughout your speech, or you may well be creating a barrier between you and your audience. A barrier creates distance, instead of connection. Thus, instead of treating the lectern or podium like a child that you would never leave unattended, feel free to intentionally and purposefully move about from time to time.

When you are behind the lectern, stand about a foot away from it so that you are not tempted to lean on it or grab the edges. The only two items that should ever be on the podium or lectern are your speech notes or speech outline, and perhaps some water. If you are using speech notes, consider placing them on the lectern before you speak. Always take a few moments at the lectern before you start your presentation to make sure your notes are organized.

Remember when you approach the podium, lectern, or front of the room, the audience's eyes will already be on your every move. Even if you are feeling anxious, move up to the front with assuredness and poise. Act as if you are confident, even if you aren't. The more confident you appear, the more confident you will feel. In terms of what to do after the speech is over, master speaker trainer and public speaking coach Arvee Robinson-who wrote the article "Lectern Etiquette", explains how to use a podium or lectern appropriately when your speech has concluded. He says "Wait patiently at the lectern, enjoying the applause, until the emcee takes charge of the lectern. Think of a relay race where the runner passes a baton to another runner before slowing her pace. Once the baton is passed, the passing runner is finished."

Another suggestion for adding platform movement is to synchronize some basic acting skills into your speech-giving. You don't need to turn your presentation into a one-person theater show, but when you are telling stories or revealing truths, try incorporating a little movement to paint a picture for the audience. Help your audience to visualize your example by performing it to a modest extent. Since you are not trying to audition for a Broadway musical, there is no need to go all out in terms of your acting. Melodramatic overacting when delivering a speech might not go over well with your audience. As an alternative to overacting or not acting at all, pull in just a bit of the stage performer in you for your presentation. For example, if you are talking about a time you were texting a friend, show us yourself doing a simulation of your writing a text message. If you're telling the audience about a gigantic hill you climbed at the end of your last hike, use your body to give the group a sense of the size of how formidable the hill seemed.

The way in which a speaker uses the platform movement conveys an image to the audience. Your platform movement should look and feel natural, even if you are acting and even if your movement is calculated and purposeful. The best way to accomplish natural platform movement is to move when there is a reason to be in motion, act from time to time when there is a visualization to perform, and remain still when there is neither. You may also want to use platform movement to get closer to the audience to show demonstrate affinity or intimacy, to compensate for audience members who are not paying attention to your message, to emphasize change to a new topic or section of your speech at major transition points, or to create a bit of visual diversity.

YOUR VIEW ─────────────────────────────────

What are two ways you can improve your platform movements?

_____

_____

Appearance

At the unconscious level, *appearance* plays a big role in how your audience perceives you as a credible and professional public speaker. Without even realizing it, your audience may be forming judgments about you based on only seconds of information. Since these judgments are made so quickly, they are quite often based solely on two variables: the first words you say and your appearance. Once this impression of you is formed, the impression tends to stick like glue in the minds of your audience and can be difficult to reverse. This can be daunting for a speaker to overcome and manage.

To make matters worse, often first impressions are completely off-base, based on cursory and limited assumptions derived from how we look. Being judged by our appearance instead of who we are on the inside is maddening and insulting, but it is a truth that cannot be avoided. Even the nicest of people have a propensity to initially evaluate other people based on appearance. It is hardwired into human nature. While the speaker in old jeans and a concert t-shirt may be as competent and credible as the speaker wearing the dark suit or even more so, the audience may assess such attributes based on appearance alone.

Thus, one final delivery key is making sure to look your best on stage. While extreme attractiveness can be distracting to some people, some members of your audience may pay closer attention to moderately nice-looking speakers. This is not to say you can forget about preparing for a presentation and just dress the part and you will then win over your audience. All of the ingredients previously discussed in this text—knowledge, organization, preparation, integrity, and content are also necessary to make a good first impression.

In some contexts but certainly not all, making a good first impression with your appearance is synonymous with dressing professionally. Professional attire is the most formal category of all clothing styles. Dressing professionally means wearing a slightly toned down and modest version of your usual mode of dressing. You do not have to give up your personal style and mute your personality, you just have to keep your individual fashion choices in keeping with current social rules for professionalism and the context of your speech. Tips on how to dress for public speaking success for both men and women are reviewed next.

Men

Men's most formal professional garment encompasses one basic selection: the suit. A dark blue or black suit and tie is the most expected attire for formal contexts. However, in today's business casual world, the traditional business suit is far less common than it used to be. For example, in some hip Silicon Valley high-tech companies in California, a suit would look ridiculously overdressed and out of touch. But just because casual has become the predominant dress code norm in many progressive contexts doesn't mean there are not public speaking occasions when a formal suit would be perceived as more credible. For example, a eulogy at a funeral or toast at a large wedding might demand a suit. How informal or professional you go should be contingent on the speaking environment and your personality.

Regardless of the degree of formality in the context, dress a little better than your audience. It is always a good idea to do some research on your audience and the degree of formality in advance so that you can adhere to it. Whatever you choose to wear, make sure your clothes are cleaned, tailored, and ironed. According to image consultant Aysha Schurman, who wrote an article called "How to Dress Professionally," says that for men, "regardless of the exact garments you wear, your clothes should always fit you perfectly."

Women

Women's most professional garments consists of a dark colored skirt suit or pant suit, a modest dress, or a skirt or dress pants with a conservative blouse or cardigan. Then again, just like with men, women should evaluate the audience, determine the proper dress code for the speaking situation, and stick to the norm. While some contexts are more formal and thus may stipulate more reserved and modest business attire, others strongly support more more relaxed fashion choices. When in doubt, a good rule is to dress one notch above what your audience will be wearing. If you dress several notches above your audience's norm attire, your efforts may backfire and your audience may respond to you unfavorably.

Be it business casual, highly fashionable, or modestly professional, your clothing for your speech should nonetheless always fit well, be professionally cleaned, and be tailored. Make sure your attire is not too tight, too short, and doesn't show too much skin or it might divert your audience's attention. Last, bear in mind that appearance is not just about clothes. You should also be meticulous and subdued regarding your shoes, jewelry, makeup, and hairstyle because they also send a message.

Impression Management

Impression management is controlling the impression you make on your audience.

Impression management can be described as controlling of the impression you make on your audience. How effectively you manage your impression and appearance is another key to effective public speaking. When you pay attention to your impression management, you may find that you receive better treatment and also may be afforded greater respect. This may be true for job interviews and work performance as well. For example, always dress for the job you want, not the job you have. According professional public speaker Alex Coulson in his article "The Dress Code for the Professional Speaker," "People assume that those who dress well have a greater status . . . and will act better." Last, looking your best when you are giving a speech may result in your feeling more confident and secure up on stage.

YOUR VIEW

How will manage your impressions for your next speech?

_____

_____

CHAPTER SUMMARY

This chapter was intended to provide you with practical guidance on how to deliver your presentations withp urpose. The focus of this chapter was primarily on physical and vocal delivery. Physical delivery is defined as nonverbal communication with the body, and it encompasses eye contact, facial expressions, gestures, and platform movement. Vocal delivery, or paralanguage, is best conceptualized via the four Ps: pitch, projection, pauses, and pace. In addition to covering physical and vocal nonverbal delivery elements, this chapter also reviewed the four modes of speech delivery, and the concepts of dynamism, the PREP Model, and impression management. The overall goal of this chapter was to emphasize that engaging speech-givers must attend not just to what they say, but how they say it.

REACHING YOUR GOALS: Evaluating Your Own Speeches

9

As a single footstep will not make a path on the earth, so a single thought will not make a pathway in the mind. To make a deep physical path, we walk again and again. To make a deep mental path, we must think over and over the kind of thoughts we wish to dominate our lives.

—Henry David Thoreau

In this quote, Thoreau suggests that the types of thoughts we think, and how often we repeat these thoughts to ourselves, construct a mental pathway in our minds that influences our reality. So too, how we conceptualize our speech-giving and how we evaluate our progress as a speaker has the potential to influence how good we are at actually giving speeches. Your destiny as a public speaker may well be influenced by how you think about your speaking.

Self-Reflection

Effective communication is created in the mind first and is then transmitted to overt action, such as giving a speech. How do you think about your own speech-giving? Do you berate yourself or praise yourself? Do you obsess on your flaws or rejoice in your accomplishments? How do your thoughts influence your reality?

A sincere examination of our thinking is not an easy task. It requires attention to what has not been attended to. *Self-reflection* is the capacity that we have to exercise introspection. It is the willingness to learn more about ourselves. It is also known as self-contemplation, self-observation, or self-scrutiny.

Self-reflection is the capability that we have to exercise introspection.

The ability to self-reflect makes human beings distinctive from other animals. Only human beings are capable of knowing themselves. We are the only creatures in the universe that can self-reflect and self-assess, observing our own thoughts and feelings as if observing ourselves in a mirror.

This human capacity for self-reflection holds the key to your development. Part of your growth and movement through the four levels of communication competence—that is, from unconscious incompetence to unconscious competence—will be due to feedback from peers, managers, coaches, and instructors. But an additional key ingredient will be your own honest evaluation of yourself as a communicator. This type of introspection, this reporting out, is crucial to enhancing your self-knowledge.

self-knowledge describes the information that an individual draws upon when finding an answer to the question "What am I like?"

Self-knowledge requires ongoing self awareness and self-reflection. *Self-knowledge* is a term used in psychology to describe the information that an individual draws upon when finding an answer to the question "What am I like?" Have you thought about what you are like as a speaker?

The importance of the pursuit of self-knowledge was recognized by the ancient Greek philosopher Socrates. He took as the cornerstone of his philosophy two vital and oft repeated words: "Know thyself." Some would say that no better advice was ever given than this aphorism. However, it takes commitment and courage to truly know yourself. As Benjamin Franklin once wrote, "there are three things extremely hard: steel, a diamond, and to know one's self."

When you are honestly evaluating yourself, you are assessing what you know, what you do not know, and what you would like to know. You are judging the quality of your own work and evaluating your own progress. Think of it like an annual job review, except instead of appraising your performance in your field or in your career, you will be assessing your performance as a public speaker. One benchmark is whether or not you have achieved the goals that you set for yourself at the start of this text.

YOUR VIEW

Revisit the three goals that you set in the first chapter. Evaluate your progress on each of your goals. Are you on track for reaching the goals you set? Have you achieved any of your goals to date? Explain.

_____

_____

_____

_____

Self-Monitoring

Self-monitoring is a necessary component for achieving the goals you set. Mark Snyder coined the term *self-monitoring*, which is defined as your ability and desire to regulate and control communication so that others will perceive you in a favorable manner (Snyder 1974, Snyder 1987). Effectual self-monitors cultivate self-knowledge through self-awareness. This awareness typically assists them in becoming more competent communicators in various contexts, ranging from interpersonal relationships to public speaking because they know how to manage their impressions. Some people self-monitor constantly or even too often, others monitor infrequently if at all. Take the following quiz to determine what kind of self-monitor you are.

Self-monitoring which is defined as the ability and desire to regulate and control communication in public so that others will perceive you in a favorable manner

Self-Monitoring Quiz

Directions: The statements below concern your personal reactions to a number of different situations. No two statements are exactly alike, so consider each statement carefully before answering. If a statement is true or mostly true as applied to you, place a "T" for true next to the question. If a statement is false or not usually true as applied to you, place an "F" for false next to the question.

_____ 1. I find people hard to read and imitate.

_____ 2. At parties and social events, I do not attempt to do or say things just to make other people respond to me in a favorable way.

_____ 3. I am honest to a fault and can only argue for ideas that I already believe.

_____ 4. I can easily make speeches on the spur of the moment, even in front of new audiences or on topics about which I have almost no information.

_____ 5. Sometimes I put on a show to impress or entertain other people.

_____ 6. People tell me that I would probably make a good actor, news anchor, radio commenter, or talk show host.

_____ 7. In a group of people, I stay on the sidelines and am rarely the center of attention.

_____ 8. When appropriate, I sometimes act like a slightly different person and am, therefore, not always whom I appear to be.

_____ 9. I am not particularly good at making other people like me.

_____ 10. I am skilled at reading and responding to messages that people send.

_____ 11. I have difficulty talking in front of a group of people because I never really know how I am coming across.

_____ 12. To be honest, I may deceive people by being friendly when I really do not like them, because I want them to like me.

The answer key is below. Add up your points for all 12 items.

Key:

1. F = 1, T = 0
2. F = 1, T = 0
3. F = 1, T = 0
4. T = 1, F = 0
5. T = 1, F = 0
6. T = 1, F = 0
7. F = 1, T = 0
8. T = 1, F = 0
9. F = 1, T = 0
10. T = 1, F = 0
11. F = 1, T = 0
12. T = 1, F = 0

Your score:_____

According to this quiz, you are likely to be a high self-monitor if your score is 7 or higher. A high self-monitor regulates behavior to fit a particular situation. High self-monitors have a high concern for social appropriateness and positive self-presentation. They are skilled at reading people because of this. High self-monitors tend to carefully attend to feedback from the audience while giving a speech and then make adjustments in behavior as necessary throughout the presentation. If you are a high-self monitor, you may find public speaking to be easier than most, because you understand how your audience perceives you when you are giving a speech. You know how to come across to your audience in a favorable light. Due to these factors, high self-monitoring is considered to be a strength when it comes to public speaking prowess.

Too much of a good thing could have the reverse effect, however. If you are an extremely high self-monitor with a score of 11 or 12, you are probably an extremely pragmatic person who is skilled at meticulously managing your impression so that you receive the response you desire. At times, though, you may be perceived by others as a bit of a chameleon, or even as an actor playing a role. As such, you may have difficulty getting your audience to trust you because they will never know exactly where you stand.

Conversely, low self-monitors do not participate, to the same degree as high self-monitors, in expressive control. They do not share the same concern for situational appropriateness. For them, since they value authenticity, expressing a self-presentation dissimilar from their internal states is undesirable. If you are a lower self-monitor with a score of 6 or below, you are true to your inner wishes and desires. However, at times you may miss out on important cues that your audience sends you when you are giving a speech. Moreover, your may find it difficult to accurately assess how successful you are at getting your message across during a speech. Consequently, it may be challenging for you to gauge your effectiveness on stage.

YOUR VIEW

Is your score an accurate assessment of your self-monitoring skill? How does your level of self-monitoring effect you are as a communicator?

_____

_____

_____

Tools for Self-Assessment

There are several tools in addition to goal-setting and self-monitoring to assist you in the process of reaching your goals on *The Speaker's Path*. Cultivating your public speaking self-knowledge by being self-reflective and by directly self-assessing your speech-giving is vital to your success. The remainder of this chapter will focus on tools for self-assessment. You can self-assess your progress as a public speaker in many ways, such as observing your own speeches on video; completing holistic, quantitative, and qualitative self-evaluation forms; and even through discussions or other alternative assessments that you create such as journaling.

Your instructor, manager, audience, peers, colleagues, or trainer may well be giving you both specific and holistic feedback of your speech-giving. Hopefully these coaches will do this throughout your journey in the form of written or oral evaluations of your speeches after they have seen them. This feedback will most certainly assist you in honing and improving your speaking skills. However, in order for you to become a life-long learner of public speaking, you will need to appreciate the significance that observing and evaluating yourself will have on your progression as a public speaker.

Nitty-Gritty Nine

The first tool to assist you in being self-reflective is to appraise your speech development process holistically using the Nitty-Gritty Nine Speech Appraisal Assessment. Research has found that one of the simplest tools to encourage self-assessment is straightforward evaluative questions such as those found in the Nitty-Gritty Nine.

Nitty-Gritty Nine Post Speech Appraisal

<u>Directions</u>: **After each speech, answer the questions below with a yes or no.**

Yes No 1. I analyzed my audience before choosing a topic and focus.
Yes No 2. I clarified my mission statement before planning my speech.
Yes No 3. I gathered enough quality evidence to support all of my points.
Yes No 4. I completed a Speech Preparation Guide by my deadline.
Yes No 5. I built a comprehensive and cited outline from my Speech Preparation Guide.
Yes No 6. I converted my outline into simple key word speech notes.
Yes No 7. I created quality visual aids that enhanced my mission.
Yes No 8. I rehearsed so that there was a minimum focus on my speech notes.
Yes No 9. I used a credible, professional, and an engaging delivery
          style when delivering my speech.

To score, add up the number of "yes" totals. If you scored 8 or 9, you are in fine shape. If your score is 7 or less, than you may want to make some changes.

Score for first speech: _____ Score for second speech: _____

Score for third speech:_____ Score for fourth speech:_____

YOUR VIEW ———————————————————————————————

Is your score as high as you want it to be? Is there any area where you are lacking? How can your score be improved?

_____

_____

_____

Video Files

In addition to enhancing your self-knowledge by holistically evaluating your speech development process via the Nitty Gritty Nine, it is integral to your growth that you are able to observe your own speech-giving. For that reason, another method of speech examination this chapter will propose is to make video files of your speeches. This section will review creating video files of your speeches as an essential form of self-assessment. A *video file* is a collection of video stream data stored in one unit or file. Video files can be opened, saved, deleted, moved to different folders, transferred across network connections, or uploaded to the Internet. Therefore, whether you give your speeches in front of a live audience or not, you always do have an audience, which is anyone watching your video file.

Video file
A video file is a collection of video stream data stored in one unit or file.

Generating and then viewing video files of your speeches is without question the best way to move through the stages of competence. It does not matter if you do not have access to expensive, state-of-the-art video recording technology. If need be, you can use the technology in your phone to record your speeches. You can even upload your files onto a file-sharing website for friends and family to view. What matters is not the quality of the video file, whether it is in high-definition, or how flawlessly your technology records it. What is most important to your evolution as a public speaker is that you can actually see and hear yourself give your speech after your speech is over.

Our Own Worst Critic

While some people have a great fondness for video-recording themselves and uploading their performances onto file-sharing sites for friends and family to view, most people dislike watching themselves giving public speeches. This is due to two legitimate reasons. In the next paragraphs, these reasonable concerns will be candidly addressed to help you move past them.

To begin with, most of us do not appreciate the image that we see of ourselves as much as our audience does. This is because we judge ourselves based on unrealistic standards set by the media and our culture. We evaluate ourselves from the perspective of a culture that embraces youth, beauty, and slimness. For instance, we are bombarded by images of extremely attractive models who spend hours a day primping and exercising in an effort to look visually enticing. On top of that, whether it is a myth or reality, some say that camera images are unflattering because they may appear to add ten pounds to their subjects. Additionally, we not only are our own worse critics of how we look on video, but also of our words and actions when giving a speech. For example, we measure ourselves against talented actors and who spend weeks, instead of hours, rehearsing specific lines and nonverbal affect behaviors for the movies they star in.

Second, some people complain that their recorded voice sounds funny: wispier, thinner, or with a nasal echo. Their perception of their own pitch and tone is in discord with what they hear. In this case, perception is not reality. When you speak, you hear yourself not only through your ears, but also through the sound waves captured by the tiny bones, membranes, and fluids in your inner ears and also through the bones of your skull. When you are recorded, your voice sounds as it does to others who hear you every day. Try to get used to this reality and look at it as learning something new about yourself.

If your focus is on your distorted appearance or how strange your voice sounds when recorded, instead of on the speech itself, you will be missing the point of video-recording your speech. Do what you can to get over these minor hurdles so that you are better able to effectively critique your speeches.

YOUR VIEW

How can you be your own best critic of your speech-giving? Explain.

_____

_____

_____

Creating a Video File

One tactic for ensuring that you get over the hurdles just described is to make sure that you get the best possible representation of your real self on video. Here are some tips to make the videos of your speeches be a welcomed addition to your video library:

1. First and foremost, make sure your speech can be seen and heard clearly by the camera. If possible, place the camera (ideally on a tripod or stand for stability) between five and eight feet away from you. The more you plan to move around during your speech, the greater the

distance from you the camera should be. Your entire body should be fully within the frame shot, yet the camera should also be close enough that your facial expressions and visual aids can be clearly identified.

2. You will also want to determine a camera location that will allow for an ideal speech context in terms of lighting and background. The background that you speak in must be free of distractions. The lighting should be both natural and bright. However, do not spotlight yourself with a bright light. Instead, strive for even light that makes both you and your visuals clearly visible.

3. Last, once your recording equipment is set up and the camera begins to roll, do your best to forget about the camera and enjoy your speech. Pretend that the camera is not there. Focus on the people in your audience, not the equipment, the microphone, or the camera itself. Do not let the technology make you forget the passion and energy that you have for your topic. In many ways, you will need to get over your anxiety about being recorded in order to fully know yourself as a speaker.

Individual Self-Assessments

To further enhance your self-knowledge and in so doing increase your communication competence, complete detailed individual self-assessments of each of your speeches after watching them on video. John Muir once said, "I only went out for a walk and finally concluded to stay out till sundown, for going out, I found, was really going in." Individual self-assessments will help you to "go in," as John Muir so poetically stated.

There are two types of self-assessments instruments, quantitative and qualitative. *Quantitative Speech Self-Assessments* are methodical self-evaluation tools that produce results that can be expressed as numerical data, statistics, or as an objective quantity that can be numerically measured or analyzed. *Qualitative Speech Self-Assessments* are comprised of subjective, reflective, open-ended questions that encourage greater in-depth analysis and more comprehensive levels of introspection. You can find Basic, Information, Persuasive, and Final types of sample qualitative and quantitative assessments at the end of this chapter.

These in-depth assessments involve reviewing a video of your speech, critiquing it, and summarizing the feedback you received. This course of action is essential to your success as a public speaker. Further, for best results, it is advisable to create videos of three or more consecutive speeches

Qualitative speech self-assessments are comprised of subjective, reflective, open-ended questions that encourage greater in-depth analysis and more comprehensive levels of introspection.

Quantitative speech self-assessments are methodical self-evaluation tools that produce results that can be expressed as numerical data, statistics, or as an objective quantity that can be numerically measured or analyzed.

and then watch each speech multiple times. Yes, this may feel awkward or even agonizing. It may make you really uncomfortable. But your hard work in being self-reflective is well worth the effort.

Public speaking consultant Ken Davis of Dynamic Communications Workshops says in his article "The Painful Process of Speech Evaluation" (2011), "Evaluation is uncomfortable . . . it exposes us, leaving us feeling vulnerable. And precisely because of this discomfort, we grow."

CHAPTER SUMMARY

This chapter discussed why the process of self-assessing your speeches, while excruciating and uncomfortable for some, is essential to growing as a dynamic communicator. To review, there are two main reasons why you must qualitatively and quantitatively evaluate videos of your speeches.

The primary reason is that it facilitates your being more self-reflective because you will become more conscious of what others witness when they see and hear you speak. Thus, you will no longer be a blind spectator to your own speech-giving. Oftentimes we are oblivious to the way we come off to other people, particularly when giving a public speech. This is why self-monitoring is so important to public speaking success.

The second reason that you must prioritize recording, watching, and then honestly assessing videos of your speeches is that doing so will assist you in remembering your speech and the feedback you received. The video files in your video library will serve as recorded memories, not just of your talk and your feelings about the talking, but of the feedback you received from your coach, instructor, manager or your audience members.

Self-Assessment—Basic Quantitative

Watch your speech video twice. Reflect on your speech and feedback, then answer the following questions. Be detailed and thorough in your responses.

1. Did you achieve your specific purpose? Why or why not?

_____

_____

_____

2. Critique your introduction, conclusion, and organizers. What worked? What didn't?

_____

_____

_____

_____

3. Critique your content. Did you support each main point with effective evidence?

_____

_____

_____

4. Critique your delivery. Did you come off as comfortable, confident, and dynamic?

_____

_____

_____

Self-Assessment—Basic Quantitative

Ratings: 1 = very effective, 2 = satisfactory, 3 = needs development

Organization:

				Specific Comments:
Introduction	1	2	3	
Transitions	1	2	3	
Conclusion	1	2	3	

Content:

Evidence	1	2	3
Visual Aids	1	2	3
Language Use	1	2	3

Delivery:

Extemporaneous	1	2	3
Professional/Credible	1	2	3
Eye contact	1	2	3
Facial Expressions	1	2	3
Gestures	1	2	3
Platform movement	1	2	3

Two strengths:

_____

_____

_____

Two growth opportunities:

_____

_____

_____

Self-Assessment—Informative Qualitative

Watch your speech video twice. Reflect on your speech and feedback, then answer the following questions. Be detailed and thorough in your responses.

1. Did you achieve your purpose? Why or why not?

_____

_____

_____

_____

_____

2. Critique your introduction. Did you get the audience's attention? Did you preview your points? Did you relate your speech to your audience?

_____

_____

_____

_____

_____

3. Critique the organization of your main points. How clear were your main points and transition statements? Did you use clear two-part transitions?

_____

_____

_____

_____

5. Turn the volume off. What do you notice about your physical delivery? Eye contact? Posture? Facial expressions? Gestures? Movement? Enthusiasm?

\
\
\
\
\

6. Fast forward your speech. What do you notice about your physical delivery? Eye contact? Posture? Facial expressions? Gestures? Movement? Enthusiasm?

\
\
\
\
\

7. Summarize the positive and constructive feedback from your peers, coach, manager, or instructor. What are the strengths and growth opportunities?

\
\
\
\
\

Self-Assessment—Informative Quantitative

Ratings: 1 = very effective, 2 = satisfactory, 3 = needs development

Introduction: **Specific Comments:**

Attention-getter   1   2   3
Orientation   1   2   3
Point preview   1   2   3

Body:

Evidence   1   2   3
Specific examples   1   2   3
Transitions   1   2   3

Conclusion:

Point review   1   2   3
Closure   1   2   3
Final statement   1   2   3

Content:

Visual Aids   1   2   3
Evidence   1   2   3
Language Use   1   2   3
Source Citations   1   2   3

Delivery:

Extemporaneous   1   2   3
Eye contact   1   2   3
Facial Expressions   1   2   3
Movement/gestures   1   2   3
Dynamism   1   2   3
Confidence   1   2   3
Professionalism   1   2   3

One strength:

One growth opportunity:

Self-Assessment—Advanced Informative Qualitative

Watch videos of all speeches at least twice. Reflect on your speech and feedback, then answer the following questions. Be detailed and thorough.

1. How well did you achieve the purpose of this speech? How did you do it?

_____

_____

_____

_____

_____

2. How clear and effective were your organizers, such as a preview in your introduction, review in your conclusion, and two-part transition statements?

_____

_____

_____

_____

_____

3. Critique your evidence (facts, expert testimony, examples, and visuals). Which main point was most/least developed? Did you cite your sources in each main point?

_____

_____

_____

4. If you had to do it over again, what changes would you make in preparation?

5. Critique your physical and vocal delivery. What changes did you make in this speech? Did your physical and vocal delivery communicate what you wanted?

6. Summarize the positive and constructive feedback from your peers, coach, manager, or instructor.

7. Critique your overall presentation in terms of content, organization, and delivery.

_____

_____

8. What two areas did you improve on between this speech and your first one? Did you meet your last two goals? What are your next two goals for improvement?

_____

_____

_____

_____

_____

_____

_____

_____

_____

Self-Assessment—Persuasive Quantitative

Ratings: 1 = very effective, 2 = satisfactory, 3 = needs development

Organization:

Attention-getter	1	2	3
Orientation	1	2	3
Point preview	1	2	3
Main Point One	1	2	3
Main Point Two	1	2	3
Main Point Three	1	2	3
Transitions	1	2	3
Point review	1	2	3
Closure	1	2	3
Final statement	1	2	3

Content:

Visual Aids	1	2	3
Ethos	1	2	3
Pathos	1	2	3
Logos	1	2	3
Opposing Arguments	1	2	3
Language Use	1	2	3
Source Citations	1	2	3

Specific Comments:

Delivery:

Extemporaneous	1	2	3
Eye contact	1	2	3
Facial Expressions	1	2	3
Movement/gestures	1	2	3
Dynamism	1	2	3
Confidence	1	2	3
Professionalism	1	2	3

How effectively did you persuade your audience?

_____

_____

Self-Assessment—Persuasive Qualitative

Watch videos of all your speeches at least twice. Reflect on your speech and feedback, then answer the following questions. Be detailed and thorough.

1. How well did you achieve the purpose of this speech? How did you do it?

_____

_____

_____

_____

_____

2. How clear and effective were your organizers, such as a preview in your introduction, review in your conclusion, and two-part transition statements?

_____

_____

_____

_____

_____

3. Critique your evidence (ethos, pathos, logos appeals). Which main point was most/least developed? Did you cite your sources in each main point?

_____

_____

_____

_____

_____

4. If you had to do it over again, what changes would you make in preparation?

_____

_____

_____

_____

5. Critique your physical and vocal delivery. What changes did you make in this speech? Did your physical and vocal delivery communicate what you wanted?

_____

_____

_____

_____

_____

6. Summarize the positive and constructive feedback from your peers, instructor, coach, or manager.

_____

_____

_____

_____

_____

7. Critique your overall presentation. What two areas did you improve on? Did you meet your last two goals? What are your next two goals for improvement?

_____

_____

_____

_____

_____

Final Self-Assessment—Qualitative

Watch video of all of your speeches at least twice. Reflect on your speech and feedback, then answer the following questions. Be detailed and thorough in your responses.

1. How well do you think you achieved the purpose or proposition in the final speech?

_____

_____

_____

_____

_____

2. How did your organization (preview, review, and transitions) change and improve?

_____

_____

_____

_____

3. Critique your evidence. What changes did you make? What improvements?

_____

_____

_____

_____

4. How did your physical delivery (i.e., eye contact, facial expressions, gestures, posture, and movement) and vocal delivery (i.e., volume, pitch, rate, emphasis, and ums) change?

_____

_____

_____

_____

_____

5. How have you grown as a communicator?

_____

_____

_____

_____

_____

6. Review the goals you set earlier in the text. How effectively did you achieve the goals you set for yourself at the beginning of *The Speaker's Path*?

_____

_____

_____

ENJOYING THE VIEW
Listening to Others

One thing that you find out when you have been practicing mindfulness for a while is that nothing is quite as simple as it appears. This is as true for walking as it is for anything else. For one thing, we carry our mind around with us when we walk, so we are usually absorbed in our own thoughts to one extent or another. We are hardly ever just walking, even when we are just going out for a walk.

—John Kabat-Zinn

In this quote, Kabat-Zinn encourages practicing mindfulness when walking. You have made it far on *The Speaker's Path* because you have practiced mindfulness when it comes to your own public speaking. You have made a conscientious commitment to complete the steps on speech development, speech organization, and speech delivery. And, you have hopefully achieved some public speaking success as a result of your efforts. Now, it is time to take a step back from your own speech-giving and take pleasure in listening to others give theirs. In other words, it is time to enjoy the view. Chapter Ten is about listening in all its forms, including mindfulness and giving valuable feedback to speakers To be an effective communicator, you must not only be a good speaker, but also a skilled listener or receiver.

Some people conceive of listening as paying attention, as a process of applying meaning to messages, or as simply hearing. Listening is a lot more than these factors; it depends on a cluster of communication skills that you will read about in this chapter. Specifically, we will define *listening* as the active process of hearing, understanding, remembering, interpreting, evaluating, and responding to messages. This chapter will focus on listening as

Listening is the active process of hearing, understanding, remembering, interpreting, evaluating, and responding to messages.

a proactive communication technique that requires the listener to attend to the message, understand what is being communicated and interpret the message accurately, and then feed what he or she hears back to the speaker. The goal is mindful listening, which means giving our thoughtful attention and responses to the messages we receive.

Importance of Listening

If you measured the importance of every activity by the time you spent on that activity, would you rank listening high up on your list of priorities? Ten, fifty, and even one hundred years ago, many people would have. In the classic and once widely confirmed Rankin study at Ohio State in 1926, it was discovered at that time in history close to 45 percent of a person's waking time was spent in the act of listening. According to this study, people spent more time listening than in any other communication skill (Rankin, 1926). Further studies in the 1980s by Barker, Gaines, Gladney & Holley also affirmed that listening was considered the most often used form of communication, followed by speaking, reading and writing. These results were found true for a wide variety of people, from high school and college students to adults from various fields and industries (Barker, Gaines, Gladney & Holley, 1980).

But times have changed, as have our communication habits. These studies are now considered dated by some because they took place before computers and smartphones were invented. In the modern world, writing and reading are more prevalent, as is confirmed by the abundance of blogs and social network sites. A case in point is a 2011 study by journalist Pamela Paul of *The New York Times* called "Don't Call Me, I Won't Call You." She says that in the last five years, people have given up speaking and listening on the phone in favor of writing and reading text messages and emails. She says that in these modern times phone calls are even considered rude and intrusive by some people. She writes that the rule used to be "Don't call anyone after 10:00 p.m. Now the rule is don't call anyone, ever (Paul, 2011)."

Paul's findings have been validated by the Nielsen Company, a company that charts trends. Nielsen in their April through June 2010 research entitled "U.S. Teen Mobile Report: Calling Yesterday, Texting Today, Using Apps Tomorrow" found that people below the age of 24 text more often than they make phone calls that require listening, some as many as 2500 texts a month or more.

Yet even if the intimacy of voice and face-to-face communication has been exchanged by the efficiency of texting, apps, and email, and even if we may not spend 45 percent of our waking time listening anymore, listening continues to be a significant part of most people's daily lives. Other Nielsenwire research conducted later in 2010 found that Americans do still listen to one another on the phone and in person. The study also revealed that the three variables of ethnicity, geography, and gender influenced verbal communication behaviors. For example, they found that Florida ranks high in terms of monthly cell phone voice minutes used and very low for text messaging. However, it is important to note that this finding may have an age correlation as well. This Nielsen study also revealed that on average, women talk on the phone 22 percent more than men, which equates to about 200 more cellphone talk minutes a month.

Further, the research is clear that personal relationships still benefit from phone and face-to-face dialogue. Ron Kincade, in his 2011 article "Why Everyone Should Talk More on the Phone," says there are some great reasons to chat on the phone or face-to-face instead of chatting electronically. He says that when you are actively listening in phone or face-to-face conversation, you can usually recognize misunderstandings when they occur and correct them immediately. With electronic communication however, you may have to send several messages back and forth to clarify the content or clear up the issue. Further, with a thread, you have different people responding at different times, often before reading what someone else has just written. He suggests you can avoid this problem by actually talking and listening (Kincade, 2011).

Professional and business relationships profit from phone and face-to-face discussions as well. In an article by Marina Krakovsky called "The Pitfalls of Email" in *Psychology Today* (2004, 2011), she quoted a study by Janice Nadler of Northwestern University who researched the effects of telephone and email on sales. It was found that when people were attempting to purchase a car, negotiators who first talked by phone were four times more likely to reach an agreement. This was the case because during that initial phone call, people on both sides of the transaction become real people instead of faceless strangers (Krakovsky, 2011). The research further discovered that the missing element in electronic communication is rapport, and it is easier to establish that rapport face-to-face in person or on the phone.

Additionally, professor of Communication at Rochester Institute of Technology Dr. Susan Barnes asserted in a Figure/Ground Communication interview in 2010 that the anonymity of email can lead some people to rudeness because people do not feel accountable if they have never spoken to and listened to the other person (Ralon, 2010). In the interview, Barnes stated that even if we mean well, because emoticons are not a solid replacement for facial expressions, gestures, and tone of voice, oftentimes we perceive the tone of the message we are receiving incorrectly.

Even if listening on the phone or face-to-face are passé to some, we all still need to know how to effectively listen on the phone and in person. In the article "Take the Time to Listen" in 2007, Diane Cole of U.S. News and World Report relays that "The price paid for tuning out can sting: from flubbing a work assignment to broken relationships (Cole, 2007)." But most of us aren't as good of listeners as we can be, not due to lack of effort, but due to lack of listening effectiveness training, according to researchers

Alder & Proctor (2011) in the renown text *Looking Out, Looking In,* and Brownell in her text *Listening: Attitudes, Principles and Skills* (1996) and various other scholars in the field of communications.

This chapter will assist you in honing your listening skills. Imagine what your life would be like if you could get better at retaining directives from your boss, recalling information for exams, and, no doubt most importantly, being present for and understanding the people you care about.

Listening and Childhood

The four categories of verbal communication skills are listening, reading, writing, and speaking (Rankin, 1926). Listening is considered the forgotten verbal communication skill. While listening is the first communication ability babies develop in the womb, it is often the skill for which children and adults have received the least amount of training. Most people learn how to speak, read, and write in elementary and secondary school and some even in preschool. But very few of us were formally trained in school as children or in the workplace as adults to listen effectively. Instead, we gleaned what we know about listening less formally and often without our even realizing it, from family members, teachers, and caregivers during childhood.

Many studies assert that typically girls and boys learn distinct gender-specific communication behaviors starting at very young ages according to leading gender communication researchers Pat Heim (1992) and and Deborah Tannen (2001). This includes what we learned about listening. For example, research has demonstrated that smiling is innate in human beings and that young boys and girls smile equally when listening. Once in adulthood however, some studies found that women smile more than men, especially when there is tension in the air. Women typically learned as girls to smile more to either affirm the speaker or as an approval-seeing behavior. As adults, some women continue to use affirming behaviors when listening more than men, such as "uh-huh" or "really" and nodding, sometimes to their detriment due to misunderstandings. For instance, these affirming gestures do not necessarily mean the woman is in agreement. Rather, it is a way for some women to communicate "I hear you." According to Heim in the book *Hardball for Women,* "when a woman listen and nods, a man may think she is a pushover, when in fact she's merely indicating she heard what he said (Heim, 1992)."

On the other hand, misunderstandings can also occur when a man listens and fails to nod, according to Heim in her film "The Power Dead Even Rule and Other Gender Differences in the Workplace" (1997). A woman may perceive his lack of affirming behaviors as his being inattentive, when in fact he is really listening.

Additionally, Heim asserts that some boys learned to smile less when listening, and in so doing now mask their emotions as men. There are benefits and drawbacks to displaying versus masking emotions when listening as adults. For example, displaying or masking emotions when listening can backfire in personal relationships. However, disguising or masking emotions when listening in business meetings is often considered to be a good strategy because sometimes displaying emotions could be inappropriate or too revealing. Last, Heim suggests that some women in high-power positions are might benefit from coaching on how to camouflage emotions more in this setting.

Many girls and boys not only learned to listen in different ways during childhood, but also may have learned to listen for different reasons. Deborah Tannen, in *You Just Don't Understand: Men and Women in Conversation* (2001), argues that most men are less relational and more factual when it comes to listening. The majority of women, according to Tannen, primarily use listening to build rapport and establish closer relationships, whereas many men predominantly use listening to gather objective nonfictional information and to make plans. Heim, in her film *The Power Dead-Even Rule* echoes Tannen's findings. It is important to note that both agree that while men and women listen for different reasons and in dissimilar ways primarily due to upbringing, they listen equally effectively. Neither listening style is superior as each has their strengths and weaknesses.

YOUR VIEW

What did you learn about listening as a child?

_____

_____

_____

Listening is a skill we were first taught as a child, and we can continue to foster it as adults if we choose to put the energy into doing so. But sometimes adults overestimate how effective they are at listening, sincerely believing that they already listen well. As a result, few people think they actually need to expand their listening skillset.

An example of this phenomenon is a study reported by author William Haney in the text *Communication and Interpersonal Relations* (1992). This study found that of over 8,000 people from businesses, hospitals, universities, and government agencies, virtually all respondents believed that they were as effective, or even more effective, at listening than their co-workers. However, other studies have established that the average person listens at only about 25 percent efficiency. This discrepancy is almost certainly not because listening effectively is incredibly difficult. It is more probable that most people have just never developed the habits to make them proficient listeners. Listening skills development is something that requires effort and practice. To find out how developed your listening skills are, take the Listening Quotient Quiz developed by communication coach Chris Witt (2008) below.

Listening Quotient Quiz

Directions: Answer the following yes/no questions. Be honest so that you can obtain the most accurate results. Circle what is most often true for you.

Yes   No   1.   I anticipate what people will say next as they are speaking.

Yes   No   2.   I discount what other people say if they don't agree with my opinions and values.

Yes   No   3.   I rarely pay attention to people's nonverbal cues (such as body language and facial expressions).

Yes   No   4.   I let my biases and opinions affect my ability or willingness to listen to what some people say.

Yes   No   5.   I prepare what I'm going to say in response while the other person is talking.

Yes   No   6.   I often interrupt people to speed along a conversation.

Yes   No   7.   If I disagree with people, I interrupt them immediately to set the record straight.

Yes   No   8.   Most of the time, I am ready with a response right when the other person stops talking.

Yes   No   9.   If the other person is boring, I stop listening but try to look like I am listening anyway.

Yes   No   10. When I know what people are going to say, I don't wait for them to finish, but answer right away.

Listening Quotient Quiz (www.wittcom.com/listening_quiz.htm). Used with permission

After taking this simple self-assessment quiz, count up your number of "no" responses. Multiply that number by ten to get your listening quotient. Your score should be between 0 and 100 percent.

Write your score here: _____

To interpret your score, review the following. If your listening quotient score is 80 percent or more, you are considered to be an above average listener. You may even have what it takes to be a gifted leader or a counselor. This does not indicate that you do not need to make any improvements in your listening behaviors, but it does imply you are more skilled at listening than other people. If your score is a 40 percent to 70 percent, you are well within the average range. People probably would not call you a bad listener, but they may not call you an extraordinary listener, either. They might just think you are inattentive or too busy or distracted to pay attention all the time, or that you sometimes interrupt more than you should. This score is an indication that you are in decent listening shape but that you may have room for growth. If your listening quotient score is 30 percent or less, you may want to place some of your attention on actively and thoughtfully improving your listening skills.

YOUR VIEW ————————————————————————————

Is your listening quotient as high as you want it to be?

_____

_____

_____

Improving Listening Skills

Although most people would acknowledge that listening is important, few people actually do it well, and most people do not have a listening quotient of 100 percent. This is because it is challenging to actually become a better listener. Your own experience will likely confirm that poor listening is all too common. After all, if everyone listened well, our society would have much less of a need for therapists and bartenders, people who are often paid to listen to others.

Why is it that most of us only listen effectively a percentage of the time? There are several reasons according to researchers Andrew Wolvin & Carolyn Coakley in their text entitled *Listening* (1992). They posit that our culture tends to reward the talker instead of the listener and encourage the cultivation of the skill of expression more than the skills of understanding and retention. They add that it is also difficult for us to focus on messages, even ones that we know are important, because we are so bombarded by information on an hourly basis. Additionally, they assert that we are also often wrapped up in our own personal concerns, and it is challenging to pay attention to someone when we are worried, anxious, or preoccupied. But the most common reason, according to Wolvin & Coakley is that we are hampered with a lack of training in listening.

We know the act of listening to others provides a foundation for all aspects of language, cognitive, and relational development, and it plays a lifelong role in the processes of learning. Yet most of us have some poor listening habits, many of which we are not consciously aware of. What poor listening habits do you have?

Poor Listening Habits

Do you "turn off" to a speaker if you think:

- ◆ the topic is dull, repetitive, or boring?
- ◆ the topic is too technical, detailed, or difficult?
- ◆ the speaker uses words or language that you do not like?

Do you find yourself distracted by:

- ◆ things in the environment (noises, temperature, etc.)?
- ◆ the speaker's appearance (clothing, attractiveness, etc.)?
- ◆ the speaker's delivery or mannerisms (ums, stuttering, etc.)?
- ◆ the speaker's accent?

Do you find you tend to:

- ◆ get so into the topic that you simply think about it on your own instead of learning about what the speaker thinks?
- ◆ prepare rebuttals of questions during the speech?
- ◆ listen only for the facts and details?
- ◆ fool the speaker by faking attention?

If you answered "yes" to some of the above, you have developed some of the most common poor habits. The first step in eradicating some of these tendencies is to become aware that you have them to begin with.

YOUR VIEW ───

What poor listening habits do you have that you would like to change?

_____

_____

_____

Listening Model

The *HURIER Model* is a detailed six-component listening model which serves as a framework for building your listening skills theorized in the text *Listening: Attitudes, Principles and Skills* by Cornell University researcher Judi Brownell (1985, 1996, 2005). The model starts with how to improve mindfulness, attentiveness, and awareness. Competence in each component can be developed by acquiring and demonstrating appropriate attitudes and behaviors and learning relevant concepts and principles.

The letters in HURIER represent the skills of (H) hearing, (U) understanding, (R) remembering, (I) interpreting, (E) evaluating, and (R) responding to messages.

The *HURIER Model* is a detailed six-component listening model that can serve as a framework for building your listening skills.

The HURIER MODEL

H   HEARING

U   UNDERSTANDING

R   REMEMBERING

I   INTERPRETING

E   EVALUATING

R   RESPONDING

Hearing

Researcher Brownell (2005) states that hearing is the first skill in the HURIER Model. *Hearing* is the process, function, or power of perceiving aural and other stimuli from our environment. Hearing has to do with mindfulness and what we focus our attention on. Mindfulness means being attentive and aware. When you are listening to a speech, a sermon, or a lecture, do you choose to attend to your friend shuffling her feet, the ticking of the clock, your smartphone vibrating in your pocket, or the speech itself? Most of us find it difficult to stay focused and to not get distracted by some type of noise. When we get distracted, our minds shift from attending to the message to focusing on the competing stimuli, and we miss out on important information.

Hearing is the process, function, or power of perceiving sound and other stimuli from our environment.

Thought-Speech Differential and Interest

Since we can only focus on a few stimuli at any given time, focusing on what we are supposed to be hearing can be challenging. One reason why

Thought-speech differential
means we can process and understand and process about 400 to 600 words a minute, yet people only speak at a rate of 150 to 250 words a minute.

we find focusing to be bewildering is the *thought-speech differential*. This means that we can think much more rapidly than a speaker can talk. We can process and understand about 400 to 600 words a minute, yet people only speak at a rate of 150 to 250 words a minute (Brownell, 1996). Our minds are processing much faster than people can speak, leading our focus to wander because we have extra time. This is known as mind-wandering. Mind-wandering is a result of the thought-speech differential and is defined as the experience of thoughts not remaining on a single topic for a long period of time. Although mind-wandering is considered to be common and normal, it is a major hindrance to effective listening.

One method to keep your mind from wandering is through vigilance. Modern psychology defines vigilance as sustained attention and alertness over a period of time. One way to increase vigilance is to boost your *interest* in the subject or the speaker. Interest in what the other person is trying to say is a key factor in attending to messages we hear. It is your ability to arouse your attention, curiosity, or excitement. This isn't always easy. It is challenging to listen to something that is not interesting, but once you become genuinely engaged, listening takes less effort. However, if you do not develop that interest, listening can require a great deal of energy in order for your attention to be sustained.

Interest
is a feeling that accompanies or causes special attention.

Hearing is something you can consciously work on improving by first removing distractions and then by focusing your attention and interest on the speaker, being vigilant, and concentrating.

YOUR VIEW

How do you hope to remove distractions and improve your focus and concentration?

_____

_____

_____

Understanding

Understanding
the ability to accurately grasp what you are listening to

Understanding, the second component of the HURIER Model according to Brownell (2005) is the ability to accurately grasp what you are listening to and, in so doing, open up to new levels of comprehension. We often do so by referring to past experiences or attitudes about the topic, but this can often lead to misunderstanding. To improve this skill, you need to be aware of your self-talk and semantic reactions—in other words, your filters.

Filters: Self-Talk, Semantic Reactions

Self-talk, or inner speech, is a cognitive, inner-directed filter in which your energy is focused on identifying past associations with what you are hearing. You apply meaning to words based on your cognitive schema, a categorization system in your mind. For example, if your previous experience of love was affirming and blissful, when a speaker talks of love in a speech, you will likely have positive impressions due to your schema. However, if your last romantic relationship ended in heartache or abuse, your love schema will likely be negative instead of positive. Your accumulated experiences on love provide a frame of reference that you use to make sense of what you hear. Schema are constructed through specific incidents and vivid experiences, according to University of Rhode Island professor Dr. Charles Schmidt in his research entitled "Social Cognition and Cognitive Schema" (2002). They start as a simple network and can develop into more complex structures over time. A person's various types of schema can range between being relatively flexible to being rather rigid. Good listeners are aware of their schema and how they impact message comprehension.

Semantic reactions are associations that people have toward particular verbal or nonverbal triggers. For example, perhaps there is particular word or gesture that generates strong emotional reactions in you, coupled with intense mental images. You might respond to the word or gesture with irritation, perhaps even jumping to false conclusions about the sender's intent. Each of us reacts to verbal and nonverbal stimuli in different ways, based on our perceptions of the meaning. Oftentimes, we are not consciously aware of the triggers we are reacting to. Semantic reactions are usually reduced by recognizing them. Semantic reactions will have less power in your life and will impact your listening less if you are able to determine what semantic reactions you possess and where they came from.

> *Self-talk,*
> or inner speech, is a cognitive, inner-directed filter

> *Semantic reactions*
> are associations that people have toward particular words.

YOUR VIEW

What is an example of when your self-talk or semantic reactions influenced your understanding of a speaker's message?

_____

_____

_____

Remembering

Remembering, the third component of the model (Brownell, 2005) is skill of encoding, processing, and recalling messages. One prominent view on remembering conceives of memory as the flow of information through the mind. In a number of statements about this view, three broad stages of information processing can be distinguished, known as memory banks. First, there is the sensory register, a very short-term sensory memory of the event. The second memory bank is a short-term or working memory, which is a system for temporarily storing and managing information required to carry out complex cognitive tasks such as reasoning. The last memory bank is long-term memory. Information in the long-term memory bank can lasts from days to even years. From long-term memory you can recall general information about the world that you learned on previous occasions, or memory for specific past experiences.

Memory Banks

The *sensory register* is associated with your five senses: visual, auditory, kinesthetic, tactile, and olfactory. Messages float in and out of this memory bank in milliseconds, unless you immediately focus your attention on the messages. Most of the information that enters into your sensory register is not processed further; it leaves your mind as quickly as it came in. When you do focus your attention on a particular message, the information you focused on moves further into your short- or long-term memory banks.

Our short-term memory or working memory is thought to hold from five to nine individual bits of unrelated information, or roughly the amount of digits in a phone number. *Short-term memory* is memory that involves recall of information for a relatively short time. Short-term memory is often used for last-minute studying for exams, job interviews or speech-giving and is considered to be a temporary storage of information. The information can be held there indefinitely as long as the information is rehearsed. If it isn't rehearsed, the information disappears.

Long-term memory has an infinite capacity and is permanent, but the obstacle with this bank is not in how much it holds, but in retrieving the information once it is in there. When information we once obtained cannot be retrieved, it is called forgetting. Some research says that we forget about 50 percent of what we hear two weeks after we hear it. Think about how much valuable information you may be forgetting because you cannot figure out how to recall it from your long-term memory bank. To combat forgetfulness, information that you attend to needs to be stored in this long-term bank and then retrieved at will. For information to get into the long-term memory bank and then be retrieved when you need it, interest, concentration, and attention on the message and speaker are required. Otherwise, the information drifts away just as quickly as it drifted in.

Remembering
the skill of encoding, processing, and recalling messages

Memory Banks

Sensory Register, Short-Term Memory, Long-Term Memory.

The *sensory register* is associated with your five senses: visual, auditory, kinesthetic, tactile, and olfactory. Messages float in and out in milliseconds, unless you immediately focus your attention

Short-term memory is memory that involves recall of information for a relatively short time.

Long-term memory has an infinite capacity and is permanent.

YOUR VIEW

What is one strategy you can you to assist you in remembering what you hear?

_____

_____

_____

Interpretation

Interpretation, the fourth aspect of the HURIER Model (Brownell, 1996, 2005), is primarily about empathy. Developing empathy for others is a key listening skill, relates researcher Mark Davis in his text *Empathy: A Social Psychological Approach* (1994). *Empathy* as defined in Merriam Webster's Dictionary is "the action of understanding, being aware of, being sensitive to, and vicariously experiencing the feelings, thoughts, and experience of another without having the feelings, thoughts, and experience fully communicated in an objectively explicit manner." The three general uses of empathy are cognitive, perceptive, and behavioral (Brownell, 1996).

Cognitive empathy, or perspective-taking is when you figuratively place yourself in another person's shoes and view the world through his or her eyes. It is the capacity and capability to receive physical, social, or emotional situations from a point of view other than your own. This ability to intuit another person's thoughts, feelings, and mental states requires the ability to know that other person's perceptions will be relatively distinct from your own. This talent can help in a negotiation or when motivating people. According to Daniel Goleman author of the best-selling books *Emotional Intelligence* and *Social Intelligence* in his article "Hot to Help: When Empathy Can Move Us to Action" on Greater Good (2008), a study at the University of Birmingham found, for example, that managers who are good at perspective-taking were able to move workers to give their best efforts. Knowing how the other person feels and what she might be thinking is considered by some social scientists to be among the most impressive of human abilities (Goleman, 2008).

Perceptive empathy is your ability to perceive another person's underlying feelings, by reading in-between the lines, attending to nuance and emotional tone. Perceptive empathy also takes into account situational factors and nonverbal cues, and as such, is responsive to sensory stimuli (Brownell, 1996). It is the skill of having or showing keenness of insight, understanding, sympathy, or intuition. There is research that a communicator's personality tendencies may impact perceptive empathy. For example, high-context communicators are often effective at perceptive empathy because they have the ability to observe subtle cues that may otherwise go

> **Three Different Types of Empathy**
>
> Cognitive, Perceptive, Behavioral

Interpretation is developing cognitive, perceptive and behavioral empathy

Empathy is the action of understanding, being aware of, being sensitive to, and vicariously experiencing the feelings, thoughts, and experience of another.

unnoticed. Research has found that those who rate high in "feeling" on the Myers-Briggs Type Indicator, a psychometric questionnairre designed to measure personality preferences, are also associated with appropriate empathic responses.

Behavioral empathy is your ability to demonstrate with your verbal and nonverbal feedback behaviors that you are actively listening to and care about what the other person says, without attempting to evaluate the content of the message being transmitted (Brownell, 1996). Behavioral empathy is about what you do in reaction to stimuli, how you act, and how you react. It is how well you communicate with your behaviors that you validate and affirm the other person. These affirming feedback cues can communicate that you want to understand the speaker's ideas and feelings in a nonjudgmental and open-minded manner. Listeners who are skilled at behavioral empathy strive to accurately understand the speaker without imposing their own opinions. In other words, they promote engaged communication by exhibiting other-centered, and not self-centered, behaviors.

YOUR VIEW

How developed are your empathy skills? How can you improve how you interpret the messages you hear?

_____

_____

_____

Evaluation

Evaluation
the process of critically analyzing the information that you receive

Evaluation is the process of critically analyzing the information that you receive. It is difficult to remain objective and remove yourself from emotional involvement when you hear a speech, and even more challenging to resist putting your energy into defending your own viewpoint instead of analyzing the other person's view.

According to Brownell (1996), "One of the first tests a critical listener applies is to ask whether the information presented is a fact, or whether it is an opinion." Evaluation of evidence and the difference between fact and opinion will overviewed next.

Facts
can only be made after direct observation and can be verified externally.

Facts can only be made after direct observation or by actual experience. A fact is something that is in existence or is an objective reality. Facts can be verified externally, proven, and checked for accuracy. Facts are objective, undisputable, concrete bits of information that can be found in official government and legal records and historical documents, in the physical sciences, and in reference books and some scholarly publications. Objective facts are what researchers seek in laboratories or through controlled studies. Facts are usually expressed by precise numbers or quantities, in weights and measures, and in concrete language. Concrete language is use of specific and tangible words that refer to objects or events that we can see or hear or feel or taste or smell.

An *opinion* can be concrete or abstract. It is a belief that someone holds without complete proof or positive knowledge that the view is correct. Although often based on facts, opinions can be made at any time and are subject to continuing modification and dispute, even by experts. While facts are objective and concrete, opinions are subjective interpretations based on individual or cultural values and beliefs. This means that opinions are often based on prejudiced bias or personal attitudes rather than on information that can be verified. Opinions commonly involve abstract concepts such as right or wrong, good or bad, just or unjust. Opinions are frequently expressed as comparisons such as more, strongest, less, or most, or as evaluations such as best or worst.

Opinion
is a belief that
someone holds
without complete
proof or positive
knowledge that it
is correct.

The difference between fact and opinion is that a fact is something that is empirically true and can be supported by evidence, while an opinion is a belief or interpretation of fact that may or may not be backed up with some type of evidence. An opinion is normally a subjective statement that can be the result of an emotion or an individual interpretation of a fact. Much of what we hear from others in speeches, in the news media, and in life is asserted as fact but is actually opinion.

YOUR VIEW

If you used a recently concluded or upcoming political campaign as an example, what are two facts and what are two opinions? How can you tell the difference?

_____

_____

_____

_____

Two good questions to ask yourself when listening to an evidence-based speech are: Where did the speaker conduct his or her research? Did the speaker prove that what he or she is asserting as objective, factual evidence can be externally verified by a qualified source? Evaluating a speech in this way relates directly to speaker and source credibility. Credibility is judged on both the character and competence of the speaker and on the accuracy and trustworthiness of the speaker's information and research.

Responding
is your enlarging or diminishing response to a message

Enlarging means to lift a person up, enhance a person's self-esteem, and look at a person with compassion and empathy.

Diminishing is showing the person that what he or she says is not important or valued.

Responding

The final component of the HURIER Model is *responding*. You have likely developed habits in the way that you respond to others, many of which you are unaware.

According to author, educator, and public speaker Randy Fujishin (2008) in his book *The Natural Speaker,* some of your habits enlarge the speaker, whereas other habits diminish the speaker. *Enlarging* means to lift a person up, enhance a person's self-esteem, and look at a person with compassion and empathy instead of judgment. To enlarge a speaker is to affirm a speaker or to raise him or her to a higher degree. Examples of enlarging responses when listening are warm eye contact, a genuine smile, leaning the trunk of your body toward the speaker, keeping your arms uncrossed, nodding appropriately, and displaying attentive facial expressions (Fujishin, 2008).

To diminish is the opposite of enlarge. Diminishing makes the speaker feel small or even invisible. *Diminishing* a speaker, even when accidental or unintended, communicates to the speaker that what he or she says is not important, worthwhile, or valued (Fujishin, 2008). Most of us do not aim to diminish someone. Instead, this type of this response tends to happen because we are unaware of the messages we are sending. For example, perhaps we are just plain but the speaker perceives us a bored. Other examples of diminishing responses that many of us unintentionally communicate are verbal interruption, creating physical or emotional distance, crossing our arms, facing away from the speaker, avoiding eye contact, or negative body language such as looking agitated or disengaged.

What do you do when you are listening? To find out, ask a couple of people who know you well about your listening habits. Choose people who will be honest with you. Listen to what they have to say. Based on their feedback, in what ways do you enlarge and diminish the people around you when you listen?

YOUR VIEW

Identify an individual whose communication behaviors have an enlarging impact on your life. List one specific behavior that this individual does that makes you feel enlarged. Do you enlarge this individual in the same way?

_____

_____

_____

Good Listening Habits

One way to improve your listening skills is to become more aware of negative habits such as diminishing others, and positive habits such as affirming others. In addition to enlarging behaviors, there are several other good listening habits that you can develop if you put some effort into it. Fortunately, with the right combination of attitude, willingness, and skill, you can improve your active listening abilities. You can meet the challenge and become a more effective listener. Following are ten tips for success that will assist you in being more effective at listening to speeches.

1. Anticipate the mood and occasion. Look forward to the speech you are about to hear.
2. Arrive at the speech early and with an open, relaxed attitude.
3. Clear your desk or table, putting newspapers, smart phones, and other work away.
4. Reserve your judgment of the speaker until you have heard all that he or she has to say. Be open-minded to new ideas.
5. Concentrate on the message, not the mannerisms, by listening for main ideas, principles, concepts, and connections.
6. Maintain eye contact and attentive facial expressions throughout the speech.
7. Position your body so that your legs and the trunk of your body are facing the speaker.
8. Connect what the speaker is discussing with broader ideas and personal experiences to assist you in retaining the information.
9. Make quick notes of questions that you want to ask the speaker.
10. Review the main ideas and key points that the speaker discussed.

YOUR VIEW

What are two goals you have for improving your listening skills?

_____

_____

_____

Peer Feedback

This chapter ends with the inclusion of peer feedback forms for you to use to evaluate other's presentations. There are three different types of peer feedback forms on the following pages: Basic, Informative, and Persuasive.

Photocopying of these feedback forms is permitted and encouraged. Completing feedback forms after you listen to your peers give speeches will help you to develop more mindful and attentive listening habits. You will learn from others, and they will learn from you.

CHAPTER SUMMARY

Actively listening to speakers, analyzing what is being said, and then giving supportive feedback to your peers is a significant component of *The Speaker's Path*. This chapter overviewed The HURIER Model as a detailed six-component listening model that can serve as a framework for building your listening skills, starting with how to improve attentiveness, and ending with how to respond appropriately. Competence in each component of the HURIER Model can be developed by acquiring and demonstrating appropriate attitudes and behaviors, and learning relevant concepts and principles.

This is how we complete the journey and come full circle. We began our walk on *The Speaker's Path* creating a desire to be successful, and we now end our walk helping others be successful via the Peer Feedback Forms on the following pages. Giving back completes the cycle, and in that sense, brings you back home.

Peer Feedback—Basic

Speaker's Name: _____ Speaker's Topic: _____

Your Name: _____ Date: _____

The following evaluation will be given to the speaker following his or her presentation. Please give accurate, enlarging, and detailed feedback to assist the speaker in both improving his or her speaking and developing confidence. Circle your responses using the key below and add personal comments to the right. Phrase your comments in specific terms and in "I" language. For example: "I had a hard time hearing you in the back of the room," or "I found that your orientation really pulled me in."

Ratings: 1 = very effective, 2 = satisfactory, 3 = needs development

Organization:

Introduction	1	2	3
Transitions	1	2	3
Conclusion	1	2	3

Content:

Evidence	1	2	3
Visual Aids	1	2	3
Language Use	1	2	3

Delivery:

Extemporaneous	1	2	3
Professional/Credible	1	2	3
Eye Contact	1	2	3
Facial Expressions	1	2	3
Movement/Gestures	1	2	3
Posture/Stance	1	2	3

Specific Comments:

Two strengths:

_____

_____

_____

One growth opportunity:

_____

_____

_____

Peer Feedback—Basic

Speaker's Name: _____ Speaker's Topic: _____

Your Name: _____ Date: _____

The following evaluation will be given to the speaker following his or her presentation. Please give accurate, enlarging, and detailed feedback to assist the speaker in both improving his or her speaking and developing confidence. Circle your responses using the key below and add personal comments to the right. Phrase your comments in specific terms and in "I" language. For example: "I had a hard time hearing you in the back of the room," or "I found that your orientation really pulled me in."

Ratings: 1 = very effective, 2 = satisfactory, 3 = needs development

Organization: **Specific Comments:**

Introduction	1	2	3
Transitions	1	2	3
Conclusion	1	2	3

Content:

Evidence	1	2	3
Visual Aids	1	2	3
Language Use	1	2	3

Delivery:

Extemporaneous	1	2	3
Professional/Credible	1	2	3
Eye Contact	1	2	3
Facial Expressions	1	2	3
Movement/Gestures	1	2	3
Posture/Stance	1	2	3

Two strengths:

_____

_____

_____

One growth opportunity:

_____

_____

_____

Peer Feedback—Informative

Speaker's Name: _____ Speaker's Topic: _____

Your Name: _____ Date: _____

The following evaluation will be given to the speaker following his or her presentation. Please give accurate, enlarging, and detailed feedback to assist the speaker in both improving his or her speaking and developing confidence. Circle your responses using the key below and add personal comments to the right. Phrase your comments in specific terms and in "I" language.

Ratings: 1 = very effective, 2 = satisfactory, 3 = needs development

Introduction: **Specific Comments:**

Attention-getter	1	2	3
Orientation	1	2	3
Point Preview	1	2	3

Body:

Evidence	1	2	3
Specific Examples	1	2	3
Transitions	1	2	3

Conclusion:

Point Review	1	2	3
Closure	1	2	3
Final Statement	1	2	3

Content:

Visual Aids	1	2	3
Evidence	1	2	3
Language Use	1	2	3
Source Citations	1	2	3

Delivery:

Extemporaneous	1	2	3
Eye Contact	1	2	3
Facial Expressions	1	2	3
Movement/Gestures	1	2	3
Dynamism	1	2	3
Confidence	1	2	3
Professionalism	1	2	3

Two strengths:

_____

_____

_____

One growth opportunity:

_____

_____

_____

Peer Feedback—Informative

Speaker's Name: _____ Speaker's Topic: _____

Your Name: _____ Date: _____

The following evaluation will be given to the speaker following his or her presentation. Please give accurate, enlarging, and detailed feedback to assist the speaker in both improving his or her speaking and developing confidence. Circle your responses using the key below and add personal comments to the right. Phrase your comments in specific terms and in "I" language.

Ratings: 1 = very effective, 2 = satisfactory, 3 = needs development

Introduction: **Specific Comments:**

Attention-getter   1   2   3
Orientation   1   2   3
Point Preview   1   2   3

Body:

Evidence   1   2   3
Specific Examples   1   2   3
Transitions   1   2   3

Conclusion:

Point Review   1   2   3
Closure   1   2   3
Clincher   1   2   3

Content:

Visual Aids   1   2   3
Evidence   1   2   3
Language Use   1   2   3
Source Citations   1   2   3

Delivery:

Extemporaneous	1	2	3
Eye Contact	1	2	3
Facial Expressions	1	2	3
Movement/Gestures	1	2	3
Dynamism	1	2	3
Confidence	1	2	3
Professionalism	1	2	3

Two strengths:

_____

_____

_____

One growth opportunity:

_____

_____

_____

Peer Feedback—Persuasive

Speaker's Name: _____ Speaker's Topic: _____

Your Name: _____ Date: _____

The following evaluation will be given to the speaker following his or her presentation. Please give accurate, enlarging, and detailed feedback to assist the speaker in both improving his or her speaking and developing confidence. Circle your responses using the key below and add personal comments to the right. Phrase your comments in specific terms and in "I" language.

Ratings: 1 = very effective, 2 = satisfactory, 3 = needs development

Organization: **Specific Comments:**

Attention-getter	1	2	3
Orientation	1	2	3
Point Preview	1	2	3
Main Point One	1	2	3
Main Point Two	1	2	3
Main Point Three	1	2	3
Transitions	1	2	3
Point Review	1	2	3
Closure	1	2	3
Final Statement	1	2	3

Content:

Visual Aids	1	2	3
Ethos	1	2	3
Pathos	1	2	3
Logos	1	2	3
Opposing Arguments	1	2	3
Language Use	1	2	3
Source Citations	1	2	3

Delivery:

Extemporaneous	1	2	3
Eye Contact	1	2	3
Facial Expressions	1	2	3
Movement/Gestures	1	2	3
Dynamism	1	2	3
Confidence	1	2	3
Professionalism	1	2	3

How effectively did this speaker persuade you?

_____

_____

_____

How did this speaker improve?

_____

_____

_____

Peer Feedback—Persuasive

Speaker's Name: _____ Speaker's Topic: _____

Your Name: _____ Date: _____

The following evaluation will be given to the speaker following his or her presentation. Please give accurate, enlarging, and detailed feedback to assist the speaker in both improving his or her speaking and developing confidence. Circle your responses using the key below and add personal comments to the right. Phrase your comments in specific terms and in "I" language.

Ratings: 1 = very effective, 2 = satisfactory, 3 = needs development

Organization: **Specific Comments:**

Attention-getter	1	2	3
Orientation	1	2	3
Point Preview	1	2	3
Main Point One	1	2	3
Main Point Two	1	2	3
Main Point Three	1	2	3
Transitions	1	2	3
Point Review	1	2	3
Closure	1	2	3
Clincher	1	2	3

Content:

Visual Aids	1	2	3
Ethos	1	2	3
Pathos	1	2	3
Logos	1	2	3
Opposing Arguments	1	2	3
Language Use	1	2	3
Source Citations	1	2	3

Delivery:

Extemporaneous	1	2	3
Eye Contact	1	2	3
Facial Expressions	1	2	3
Movement/Gestures	1	2	3
Dynamism	1	2	3
Confidence	1	2	3
Professionalism	1	2	3

How effectively did this speaker persuade you?

_____

_____

_____

How did this speaker improve?

_____

_____

_____

Bibliography

Adams, D. (1995). Health issues for women of color. Newbury Park, CA: Sage.

Adler, R., & Proctor, R. (2011). *Looking out, looking in* (13th ed.). Boston: Wadsworth Publishing.

Alexander, P., Ryan, R., & Deci, E. (January 01, 2000). Intrinsic and Extrinsic Motivations: Classic Definitions and New Directions. Contemporary Educational Psychology, 25, 1.

Ameen, E., Jackson, C., & Malgwi, C. (2007). Student perceptions of oral communications requirements in the accounting profession. *Global Perspectives on Accounting Education Journal,* 7. Bryant University, Rhode Island.

American Library Association. (2000). *Information literacy standards for higher education.* Chicago: Association of College and Research Libraries. www.ala.org/acrl/sites/ala.org.acrl/files/content/standards/standards.pdf

American Library Association. www.ala.org/acrl/undwebev.html

Armstrong, T. (1994). *Multiple intelligences in the classroom.* Alexandria, VA: Association for Supervision and Curriculum Development.

Association of College and Research Libraries. (1989). Presidential committee on information literacy. Washington, D.C. www.ala.org/acrl/publications/whitepapers/presidential

Balpataky, K. (2004). *Quiz: How organized are you?* Chatelaine.com. www.chatelaine.com/en/article/4673--quiz-how-organized-are-you

Bandura, A. (1977). *Social learning theory.* New York: General Learning Press.

Barker, L., Edwards, R., Gaines, C., Gladney, K., & Holley, F. (1980). An investigation of proportional time spent in various communication activities by college students. *Journal of Applied Communication Research, 8,* 101–109.

Barnlund, D. C. (2008). A transactional model of communication. In C. D. Mortensen (Eds.), *Communication theory* (2nd ed., pp. 47–57). New Brunswick, NJ: Transaction.

Beck, A. (1970). Cognitive therapy: Nature and relation to behavior therapy. *Behavior Therapy, 1*(2), 184–200.

Beebe, S., & Beebe, S. (2005). *Public speaking handbook.* Boston: Allyn and Bacon.

Beyer, B. (1995). *Critical thinking.* Bloomington, IN: Phi Delta Kappa Educational Foundation.

Birdwhistell, R. (1975). *Introduction to kinesics: An annotation system for analysis of body motion and gesture.* Louisville, KY: University of Louisville.

Boyd, S. *Using humor in your speech.* The Sideroad. Practical advice. Straight from the experts. Stevenboyd.com. www.sideroad.com/Public_Speaking /humor-in-speech.html

Braden, N. (1994). *The six pillars of self-esteem: The definitive work on self-esteem by the leading pioneer in the field.* New York: Batam.

Brockman, B. (2012). *Some same but different: Unlearning the concept of disability.* Dubuque, IA: Kendall Hunt.

Brownell, J. (1985). A model for listening instruction: Management applications. *Journal of the Association for Business Communication, 48*(3), 39–44.

Brownell, J. (1986). *Building active listening skills.* Englewood Cliffs, NJ: Prentice Hall.

Brownell, J. (1990). Perceptions of good listeners: A management *study. Journal of Business Communication, 27*(4), 401–416.

Brownell, J. (1996). *Listening: Attitudes, principles and skills.* Boston: Allyn and Bacon.

Brownell, J. (2005). *Listening: Attitudes, principles and skills* (3rd ed.). Boston: Allyn and Bacon.

Burleson, B,. & Greene, J. (2003). *Handbook of communication and social interaction skills.* Mahwah, NJ: Lawrence Erlbaum Associates.

Burleson, B. (2006). *Constructivism: A general theory of communication skill.* www.wikiway.net/images/a/a7/Whaley_%26_Samter_Constructivism _Chapter-Page_Proofs.pdf

Burns, D. (1989). *The feeling good handbook.* Penguin, New York.

California State University. Website CSU Mentor, *General education requirements* www.csumentor.edu

Center for Critical Thinking. www.criticalthinking.org Tomales, California

Changingminds.org. *Similarity principle.* http://changingminds.org/principles/similarity.htm

Chapman, G. (1995). *The five love languages: How to express heartfelt commitment to your mate.* Chicago: Northfield Publishing.

Cherry, K. (2010). *The everything psychology book.* Fort Collins, CO: F & W Media.

Cherry, K. *Hierarchy of needs: The five levels of Maslow's hierarchy of needs*. About. com Psychology. http://psychology.about.com/od/theoriesofpersonality/a /hierarchyneeds.htm

Chopra, D. (1998). *The path to love: Spiritual strategies for healing.* New York: Three Rivers Press.

Cohen, R. *Persuasive speech is evident: For it is measured in how you regulate the…* First Level Leadership Group. www.first-level-leadership.com /Menu/Persuasive-Speech/17

Cole, D. (2007). Take the time to listen. U.S. News and World Report. www. usnews.com/articles/news/50-ways-to-improve-your-life/2007/12/20/ take-the-time-to-listen.html.

Coulson, A. The dress code for the professional speaker. Ezine articles. http://ezinearticles.com/?The-Dress-Code-For-the-Professional-Speaker&id=2782060

Daniels, N. A simple exercise for overcoming a monotone voice. Ezine articles. http://ezinearticles.com/?A-Simple-Exercise-for-Overcoming-a-Monotone-Voice&id=6878864

Davis, K. (2011). *The painful process of speech evaluation.* Dynamic Communications Workshop: http://www.dynamiccommunicators.com/blog/ the-painful-process-of-speech-evaluation/

Davis, M. H. (1994). *Empathy: A social psychological approach.* Madison, WI: Brown and Benchmark.

DeFinis, A. (2009). 4 *methods to deliver a great speech.* www.definiscommunications.com/blog/4-methods-to-deliver-a-great-speech

Dement, W. (2010). The sleep well. www.stanford.edu/~dement

DeVito, J. (2005). *Messages: Building interpersonal communication skills* (6th ed.). New York: Pearson Education.

Devito, J.(2008) Human Communication: the basic course. 11th edition. Allyn & Bacon. Massachusets.

Dlugan, A. (2008). *Speech preparation 101: How to prepare a presentation.* Six Minutes Speech and Presentation Skills. http://sixminutes.dlugan.com /speech-preparation-1-how-to-prepare-presentation

Dlugan, A. (2009). *Toastmasters speech 6: Vocal variety.* Six Minutes Speaking and Presentation Skills. http://sixminutes.dlugan.com/ toastmasters-speech-6-vocal-variety

Dlugan, A. (2010). *What is logos and why is it critical for speakers?* Six Minutes Speech and Presentation Skills. http://sixminutes.dlugan.com /logos-definition

Dlugan, A. (2011). *How to stop saying um and other filler words.* Six Minutes Speaking and Presentation Skills. http://sixminutes.dlugan.com/stop-um-uh-filler-words

Downey, S. (1994). Interpersonal communication workshop. Burgess International Group, Inc. Minnesota

Durrell, L. (2009). *We are the children of our landscape.* Importance of place.com www.importanceofplace.com/2009/02/we-are-children-of-our-landscape.html

Eckman, P. (1971). Universals and cultural differences in facial expressions of emotion. *Journal of Symposiums on Motivation, 19.*

Ekman, P. (1999). Basic emotions.In T. Dalgleish & M. Power (Eds.), *Handbook of cognition and emotion.* Sussex, UK: John Wiley & Sons.

Ellis, A. (1957). Rational psychotherapy and individual psychology. *Journal of Individual Psychology, 13,* 38–44.

Emanuel, R. (2005*). The case for fundamentals of oral communication* Community College Journal of Research and Practice 29, 152-153 Tailor and Frances, Inc. Philadelphia

Erard, M. (2008). *Um. . .: Slips, Stumbles, and Verbal Blunders, and What They Mean.* Anchor Publishing.

Fletcher, C. (2012). *Skills needed in business.* eHow. www.ehow.com/way_5280068_skills-needed-business.html

French, D. (2010). *Essential Skills: Communication, 7 Barriers to Communication that can Cause Divorce,* EZine Articles. http://ezinearticles.com/?Essential-Skills—Communication—7-Barriers-to-Communication-That-Can-Cause-Divorce&id=3756177

Fujishin, R. (2006). *The natural speaker* (5th ed.). Boston: Pearson Education

Fujishin, R. (2011). *The natural speaker* (7th ed.). Boston: Pearson Education.

Gaddes, W., & Edgell D. (1994). *Learning disabilities and brain function: A neuropsychological approach* (3rd ed.). New York: Springer.

Gardner, H. (1993). *Multiple intelligences: The theory in practice.* New York: Basic Books.

Gardner, H. (1999). *Intelligence reframed: Multiple intelligences for the 21st century.* New York: Basic Books.

Goleman, D. (2008). *How to help: When can empathy move us to action?* Greater Good. University of California Berkeley.Haney, W. (1992). *Communication and interpersonal relations: Text and cases (6th ed.).* Homewood, IL:

Graham, R. *The windows to the soul: Mastering the art of eye contact.* About.com. http://socialanxietydisorder.about.com/gi/o.htm?zi=1/XJ&zTi=1&sdn=socialanxietydisorder&cdn=health&tm=418&f=20&tt=13&bt=1&bts=1&zu=http%3A//www.grahamcomm.net/articles_05.html

Hagen, S. (2002). *Logical fallacies.* Kennesaw State University, Atlanta Georgia. http://ksuweb.kennesaw.edu/~shagin/logicalfallacies.htm

Halderman, J. (2005). *Top 5 ways to stay calm and reduce stress.* www.solvey-ourproblem.com/artman/publish/article_712.shtml

Hall, E. (1976). *Beyond culture.* New York: Anchor Books.

Harvard Women's Health Watch. (2006). The importance of sleep: Six reasons not to scrimp on sleep. www.health.harvard.edu/press_releases/importance_of_sleep_and_health

Heim, P. (1992). *Hardball for women: Winning at the game of business.* New York: Lowell House.

Heim, P. (1997). *The power dead-even rule and other gender differences in the workplace.* Cambridge, MA: Enterprise Media.

Hope, D. A., Burns, J. A., Hyes, S. A., Herbert, J. D., & Warner, M. D. (2010). Automatic thoughts and cognitive restructuring in cognitive behavioral group therapy for social anxiety disorder. *Cognitive Therapy Research, 34,* 1–12.

Irwin, Richard D., Hasman, R. C., Lahiff, J .M. & Penrose, J. M. (1988). *Business communication: Strategies and skills.* Chicago: Dryden Press.

Joesting, L. (1995). Communicate! A workbook for interpersonal communication. 5th edition. Kendall Hunt Publishing Company. Dubuque, Iowa

Kennedy, G. (Ed.). (1991). *Aristotle: On rhetoric: A theory of civil discourse.* Oxford, UK: Oxford University Press.

Kincade, R. (2011). *Why everyone should talk more on the phone.* eVoice: A Radically Better Phone Number. http://blog.evoice.com/blog/using-virtual-phone-numbers/why-everyone-should-talk-more-on-the-phone

Krakovsky, M. (2004, 2011). The pitfalls of email. *Psychology Today.* www.psychologytoday.com/articles/200403/the-pitfalls-e-mail

Leigh, A. (2007). The power of observation. Pathways Life Direction Coaching. http://www.pathwayscoaching.co.uk/article/23/the-power-of-observation-/

Lorenz, K. (2007). *Do pretty people earn more?* Careerbuilder.com. www.career-builder.com/Article/CB-312-The-Workplace-Do-Pretty-People-Earn-More

Macke, M. (2009) *NACE's Job Outlook 2009 Survey.* National Association of Colleges and Employers. www.naceweb.org/home.aspx

Martin, J., & Nakayama, T. (2011). Experiencing intercultural communication (4th ed.). New York: McGraw-Hill.

Maslow, A. H. (1943). *Motivation and personality.* New York: Harper.

Mayo Clinic. (2011). *Exercise: 7 benefits of regular physical activity.* Mayo Foundation for Medical Education and Research (MFMER). www.mayoclinic.com/health/exercise/HQ01676

Mayo Clinic. (2010). Spirituality and stress relief: make the connection. Mayo Clinic Foundation for Medical Education and Research (MFMER). www.mayoclinic.com/health/stress-relief/SR00035

McCroskey, J. (1970). Measures of communication-bound anxiety. *Speech Monographs, 37,* 269–277.

Mehrabian, A. (1981). *Silent messages: Implicit communication of emotions and attitudes* (2nd ed.). Belmont, CA: Wadsworth. Schramm, W. (1954). How communication works. In W. Schramm (Ed.), *The process and effects of communication* (pp. 3–26). Urbana: University of Illinois Press.

Meyer, P. (2008, September 3). Increase your desire to succeed. *SUCCESS Magazine,* www.success.com/articles/369-increase-your-desire-to-succeed

Mindtools, Essential Skills for an Excellent Career. *The conscious competence ladder: Making learning a happier experience.* www.mindtools.com /pages/article/newISS_96.htm

Mireles, S. *How to measure outcomes and evaluations.* http://www.ehow. com/how_6578817_measure-outcomes-evaluations.html

Muir, J. (1901). Our national parks (p. 56). Boston: Houghton, Mifflin and Company.

Nayala, H. (1997). *Point last seen: A woman tracker's story.* New York: Pocket Books.

Nielsenwire. (2010, August 24). *African-Americans, Women, and Southerners talk and text the most in the U.S.* Nielsen.com. http://blog.nielsen.com/ nielsenwire/online_mobile/african-americans-women-and-southerners-talk-and-text-the-most-in-the-u-s/

NSA code of ethics. (2007). National Speaker's Association. www.mynsa. org/INSIDENSA/Policies/CodeofEthics.aspx

Parker-Pope, T. (2011, February 28). Go easy on yourself: A new wave of research urges. *The New York Times.* http://well.blogs.nytimes. com/2011/02/28/go-easy-on-yourself-a-new-wave-of-research-urges/

Patzer, G. *Physical attractiveness phenomenon.* Gordonpatzer.com. www. gordonpatzer.com/aboutgordon.html

Paul, P. (2011, March 18). Don't call me, I won't call you. *New York Times.*

Prather, H. (2000). *The little book of letting go.* Berkeley, CA: Conari Press.

Ralon, L. (2010) *Susan b. barnes.* Figure/Ground Communication. http:// figureground.ca/interviews/susan-b-barnes/

Rankin, P. (1926). The measurement of the ability to understand spoken language. *Dissertation Aspects, 12.* University of Michigan.

Roberts, W. & Aristotle (2012). On rhetoric. Indoeuropeanpublishing.com

Roberts, W. (Ed.).*Aristotle: On rhetoric.* Indoeuropeanpublishing.com

Robinson, R. *Lectern etiquette.* InstantProSpeaker.com. http://www.instantprospeaker.com/lecternetiquette.htm

Rogers, C. & Freiberg, H. (1994). *The freedom to learn.* Prentice Hall

Rohn, J. official website www.jimrohn.com

Ryan, R. (2010). *Spending time in nature makes people feel more alive, study shows.* University of Rochester, www.rochester.edu/news/show.php?id=3639

Ryan, R. M., Weinstein, N., Bernstein, J., Brown, K. W., Mistretta, L., &Gagné, M. (2010). Vitalizing effects of being outdoors and in nature. *Journal of Environmental Psychology, 30*(2), 159. DOI: 10.1016/j.jenvp.2009.10.009.

Samovar, L., & Porter, R. (2003). *Communication between cultures* (5th ed.). Wadsworth Publishing.

Sandoval, R. (2009). *Information literacy.* Saratoga, CA: West Valley College Library.

Schleter, I. (2007). *Impromptu speaking tips.* Siglap Toastmaster's Club. http://siglaptoastmasters.wordpress.com/2007/11/07/impromptu-speaking-tips/

Schmidt, C. *Social cognition and cognitive schema.* The University of Rhode Island. www.uri.edu/research/lrc/scholl/webnotes/Dispositions_Cognitive-Schema.htm

Schurman, A. *How to dress professionally.* Life123. Answers at the speed of life. www.life123.com/beauty/style/womens-clothing/how-to-dress-professionally.shtml

Scott, E. (2007). *Cognitive restructuring for stress relief: A little cognitive restructuring can bring significant change.* About.com Guide. http://stress.about.com/od/professionalhelp/a/Restructuring.htm

Shannon, C., & Weaver, W. (1949). *The mathematical theory of communication.* Urbana: University of Illinois Press.

Sleep Aid Tips. *Relaxation with herbal aroma therapy.* www.sleep-aid-tips.com/sleep-aid-relaxation-aromatherapy.html

Snyder, M. (1987). *Public appearances/private realities* (adapted). New York: Freeman.

Sousa, D. (2005). How the brain learns. Corwin Press. (October 14, 2010) *U.S. Teen Mobile Report: Calling Yesterday, Texting Today, Using Apps Tomorrow.* Nielson Wire. http://blog.nielsen.com/nielsenwire/online_mobile/u-s-teen-mobile-report-calling-yesterday-texting-today-using-apps-tomorrow/

Statewide Parent Advocacy Network. *Multiple intelligence worksheets.* www.spannj.org/BasicRights/appendix_b.htm#test

Steele, J. (2010). Ethics in public speaking. Speechmastery.com. www.speechmastery.com/ethics-in-public-speaking.html

Stevens, B. (2005). What communication skills do employers want? Silicon valley recruiters respond. Journal of Employment Counseling. v42 n1 p2 Mar 2005 National Employment Counseling Association. Alexandria, Virginia

Stuart, D., & Sprague, J. (1984). *The speaker's handbook.* Boston: Wadsworth

Sousa, D. (2005). How the brain learns. (3rd edition).thousand Oaks, California: Corwin Press

Supple, J., Gruber, A., & Reid, R. (2010). Connecting with your audience: making public speaking matter. Dubuque: Kendall Hunt

Swinton, L. (2005). *7 Tips for giving positive feedback.* www.mftrou.com /management-articles.html

Tannen, D. (2001). *You just don't understand: Men and women in conversation.* New York: William Morrow Paperbacks. Witt, C. (2008). *Listening Quotient Quiz.* www.wittcom.com/listening_quiz.htm

Tessina, T. (2005*). Letting go of anxiety.* www.tinatessina.com

The case for fundamentals of oral communication. (2005). *Community College Journal of Research and Practice, 29,* 152–153.

The Telegraph. (2010). *Men with monotone voices are irresistible, audiences say.* www.telegraph.co.uk/science/science-news/7603548/Men-with-monotonous-voices-are-irresistible-scientists-say.html

Toastmasters International. (2011). *Training club leaders.* Mission Viejo, CA. www.toastmasters.org/217training.aspx

U.S. Department of Labor. (1992). *Secretary's Commission on Achieving Necessary Skills* http://wdr.doleta.gov/SCANS

UC Berkeley Library. www.lib.berkeley.edu/TeachingLib/Guides/Internet/Evaluate.html

UCLA College Library. www.library.ucla.edu/libraries/college/help/critical University of Maryland Library. www.lib.umd.edu/guides/evaluate.html

Vankooten, J. (2010). *The importance of communication in success Ezine rticles,* http://ezinearticles.com/?The-Importance-of-Communication-in-Success&id=5433430

Wares, B. (1998). *The importance of setting goals* My Success Company http://www.bluinc.com/news/theimportance.html

Watzlawick, P., Beavin-Bavelas, J., Jackson, D. (1967). *Some Tentative Axioms of Communication. In Pragmatics of Human Communication - A Study of Interactional Patterns, Pathologies and Paradoxes.* W. W. Norton, New York.

White, P. D. (1994). *Dictionary of American biography, Supplement 9: 1971–1975.* New York: Charles Scribner's Sons.

Wolvin, A,. & Coakley, C. (1992). *Listening* (4th ed.). Dubuque, IA: William C. Brown.

Yager, J. (1999). *Friendshifts: The power of friendship and how it shapes our lives* (2nd ed.) Stamford, CT: Hannacroix Creek Books.

Youngs, B. (n.d.). *Success and the goal-setter.* http://bettieyoungs.com/index .html

Zigler, Z. *Positive thinking.* www.evancarmichael.com/Entrepreneur-Advice/448/Positive-Thinking.html

GLOSSARY

Academic dishonesty is when a speaker attempts to show a possession of a level of knowledge or skill that he or she does not possess by cheating or plagiarizing.

Accuracy is a criteria for evaluating evidence that means the evidence is an exact and precise conformity to an established fact

Action verb is something that a person, an animal, a force of nature, or thing can *do.*

Acts of service is a love language that consists of doing things for other people, or serving others.

Adapters are gestures that convey emotions

Adjectives is the part of speech that modifies a noun or other substantive by limiting, qualifying, or specifying.

Adverbs are a word or group of words that serves to modify a feedback sentence.

Advocacy is speaking up, pleading the case of another, or fighting a cause.

Advocate is someone who speaks on behalf of a person or cause.

Analogical examples is an example that illustrates a point or illuminate a connection by comparing the point to a known or more easily understood point.

Apathetic audience types are an indifferent or detached audience, an audience who does not have strong emotions about you or your topic.

Argument is identifying, evaluating and constructing logical arguments.

Argumentation is the act or process of forming reasons, justifying beliefs, and of drawing conclusions and applying them to a case in discussion.

Assertion of fact speeches argue whether something is true or is not true, whether something happened or did not, or whether something exists or does not exist

Assertion of policy speeches argue for a specific course of action that others should take, or how things should or should not proceed

Assertion of value or belief speeches argue whether something is good or bad, right or wrong, just or unjust, fair or unfair, or worthy or not worthy.

Assumptive adverb uses an adverb to make something appear true and uses words such as obviously, naturally, evidently, or clearly.

Attention-getter is a component of the introduction and seeks to gain the attention and interest of your audience right at the start of the speech.

Attitudinal profile is a type of audience analysis that analyzes your audience's attitudes toward and about your topic and/or proposition

Audience adaptation is the process of ethically using the information you have gathered when analyzing your audience to help your audience clearly understand your message and to achieve your persuasive objective.

Audience analysis is choosing and focusing your topic based on the needs, desires, and values of your audience.

Audience Type Matrix will assist you in gathering the evidence that will best persuade your audience to respond to your proposition

Auditory/Linguistic channel is learning through listening to words and how the words are spoken

Authority is a criteria for evaluating evidence and involves whether the evidence has an authoritative voice

Being style communicators are more flexible and relationship focused, and is less worried about time constraints.

Belongingness needs in Maslow's Hierarchy of Needs are also known as love, affection, or social needs

Cause-and-effect reasoning is a type of reasoning that assumes that one thing is caused by something else and that every cause has an effect

Channels are the bridges that connect the sender to the receiver

Cheating is the act of obtaining or attempting to obtain credit for work through the use of dishonest, deceptive, or fraudulent means

Chronological pattern is a method of informative speech organization in which the main points follow a time pattern.

Closure is the part of your conclusion that lets your audience know that your speech is coming to an end

Cognitive restructuring is the process of identifying and challenging irrational self-talk so that you can think more productive thoughts

Communication apprehension is the level of fear or anxiety associated with either real or anticipated communication

Communication competence is the degree to which a speaker's goals are achieved through effective and appropriate interaction with the audience

Communication is the sending and receiving of messages

Communication style is the method by which you communicate, largely based on your culture, personality, gender, and experiences

Compliance gaining is the act of intentionally trying to alter behavior.

Computer-generated speech notes use a computer-based presentation program such as PowerPoint, Keynote, or other multimedia notes as a guide

Concrete language identifies things perceived through the senses, such as touch, smell, sight, hearing, and taste, not just by our intellect

Context is a component of orientation that involves the circumstances that surround the situation where your public speaking address occurs. It is also defined more broadly as the situation, climate, environment, or the place where communication occurs

Credibility is a component of orientation that involves the trustworthiness, competence, goodwill, and integrity of the speaker.

Criteria are defined as being able to apply different criteria based on credible sources that are free from logical fallacies in reasoning.

Critical listening is a rational process of evaluating arguments and statements put forward by others.

Critical thinking is higher order thinking that questions assumptions, or thinking about thinking.

Cultural awareness is developing an understanding of a cultural group that is different than your own.

Cultural competence is a person's ability to know the social rules that govern the appropriate use of verbal and nonverbal language patterns and apply these rules to their communications with particular cultures

Cultural competence is the ability to effectively communicate in different cultural contexts.

Cultural dimension consists of the rules, norms, and beliefs of a group of people that is passed along from one generation to another

Cultural identity is the identity of a group or culture, or of an individual that has been influenced by belonging to a group or culture

Cultural knowledge is familiarization with selected cultural characteristics, history, values, beliefs systems and behaviors

Cultural sensitivity is being aware that differences as well as similarities exist, without assigning judgments on the similarities and differences.

Culture is the behaviors and beliefs that are characteristic of a particular group.

Currency is a criteria for evaluating evidence that examines if the evidence is up-to-date or recent

Debate is the formal discussion of a motion before a deliberative body according to the rules of parliamentary procedure.

Decoding is when the receiver assigns meaning to a message that was transmitted.

Deductive reasoning is a kind of reasoning that moves from the general to the specific and attempts to show that a conclusion necessarily follows from a series of premises

Delivery is all of the nonverbal components to your speech-giving

Demographic profile is a type of audience analysis that analyzes the audience's demographic makeup

Dialect is a regional or social variety of language distinguished by pronunciation, grammar, or vocabulary

Diminishing is showing the person that what he or she says is not important or valued

Direct style speakers will speak directly and honestly, even if what is being spoken is offensive or hurtful

Discrimination is the overt action to exclude or avoid all people within the group or culture

Dispositions means having healthy skepticism, being open-minded, and respecting evidence.

Doing-style speakers pay closer attention to deadlines and the timing of the speech

Dynamism refers to the energy of a speaker, the ability of a speaker to engage and audience, the rapport a speaker has in front of a group, and the power a speaker has at the podium.

Editorial review is a tool to access the quality of the evidence you use in your speech

Elaborate style speakers use rich, expressive, emotive language to communicate messages.

Emblems are gestures that have specific verbal translations

Emotional effects of speech anxiety are the emotional reactions or feelings in response to stress.

Empathy is the action of understanding, being aware of, being sensitive to, and vicariously experiencing the feelings, thoughts, and experience of another.

Encoding is converting ideas or emotions into a verbal or nonverbal language pattern or code

Energetic is part of the PREP Model and is possessing or exhibiting enthusiasm or vigor in abundance.

Enlarging means to lift a person up, enhance a person's self-esteem, and look at a person with compassion and empathy

Esteem needs in Maslow's Hierarchy of Needs reflect our personal worth

Ethics is having a moral compass and a code of conduct

Ethnocentrism is when a person has the belief that his or other own cultural group is superior to all other groups.

Ethos is the strategy of using your credibility or ethical appeals to persuade

Evaluative feedback is defined as making an evaluation about the speech and then conscientiously phrasing positive feedback and constructive growth opportunities.

Evidence is the supporting material for the main points in your speech, and includes facts, examples, and expert testimony.

Examples are specific cases that clarify and reinforce your topic, including analogy, personal experience, and narratives.

Expert testimony is a statement of opinion or inference from an expert in the field.

Expertise is what you know about your topic.

Extemporaneous method is a mode of delivering speeches that is prepared beforehand, with the exact words chosen at delivery

External noise is when bright lights, equipment, an attractive person, vivid clothing, or any other external or physical stimulus provides a potential distraction.

Extrinsic motivations are external motivations that come from outside the individual.

Eye contact is meeting your audience with your eyes

Facial expressions are gestures executed with facial muscles

Facts are not in dispute and are verifiable by objective measures.

Favorable audience types considers you to be credible and to some extent approves of both you and your proposition.

Feedback is an immediate or delayed response to a message

Final Statement gives a sense of finality at the very end of your speech conclusion.

Frame of reference is your individual worldview based on your culture, gender, beliefs, experiences, and values.

Fujishin Three-Step process is a three step method for citing sources during your speech

General purpose is the overall desired effect you want to have on your audience

Gestures are arm and hand movements that communicate nonverbally to express a meaning

Glossophobia is the fear of public speaking

Hearing is the process, function, or power of perceiving sound and other stimuli from our environment.

High-context style communicators attend to, and highly value, contextual and nonverbal cues

Highly favorable audience types views you as exceedingly credible or fully supports you proposition and may even already be acting on it.

Hostile audience types openly opposes you and/or strongly resists your proposal

HURIER Model is a detailed six-component listening model that can serve as a framework for building your listening skills.

Hypothetical situation is an attention-getting technique that is an example that describes an imaginary or fictitious situation or event.

Illustrators are gestures that go along with speaking

Imagery language is using words to create dramatic visual images in the mind of the audience with it.

Impression management is controlling the impression you make on your audience.

Impromptu method is mode of delivering speeches that is unrehearsed or rehearsed just a little and is spontaneous and improvised

Incentive Theory is the influence of rewards on behavior.

Indirect style communicators emphasize politeness and maintaining harmony above being truthful

Inductive reasoning is a kind of reasoning that constructs or evaluates observations of individual instances

Inferences are conclusions or interpretations that follow our observations.

Information literacy is a set of abilities requiring a speaker to recognize when evidence is needed, then have the ability to locate, evaluate, and use the evidence effectively

Intensifier adverb amplifies the effect of a verb by using an adverb that intensifies the meaning and particularly the emotional content.

Interaction model is a linear model of communication that focuses on the back-and-forth nature of communication,

Interest is a feeling that accompanies or causes special attention.

Internal noise is a barrier to communication when you focus on yourself, how you feel, your stresses, or choosing your responses to a message, rather than on the other person speaking.

Interpersonal is communication between people.

In-text cites are source citations that occur within the context of your outline or paper.

Intrapersonal is communication with ourselves, in our minds.

Intrinsic motivations are less tangible as the rewards come from within the individual.

I-statements is a method of giving feedback with a statement that begins with the word "I."

Language is the communication of messages through a system of arbitrary verbal and nonverbal symbols

Learning styles are various approaches to ways of learning

Level One: Superficial communication is a simplistic type of communication that is on the surface

Level Three: Validation communication is the most sincere and heartfelt type of communication

Level Two: Personal communication is a more intimate and personal type of communication

Linear model is a model of communication that views the transfer of information as an act being done to the receiver by the sender.

Linguistics is the study of verbal messages

Listening is the active process of hearing, understanding, remembering, interpreting, evaluating, and responding to messages

Logical fallacy is a fallacy or error in logical argumentation

Logical/Mathematic channel is learning through reason, logic, and numbers.

Logos is using logical appeals, sound reasoning, and factual data to persuade

Long-term memory is memory that has an infinite capacity and is permanent.

Low-context style speakers place the most emphasis on the explicit written or spoken word rather than in the more implicit nonverbal.

Main points are sentences that support, develop, and explain your specific purpose.

Manuscript method is mode of delivering speeches where the speech is read word-for-word

Maslow's Hierarchy of Needs is a psychological theory that suggests that people can be motivated to fulfill needs in a specific order, from basic safety and health needs to personal actualization.

Memorization method is a mode of delivering speeches with a written manuscript that is memorized word-for-word

Message is meaning or content; can be verbal or nonverbal

Message noise is a barrier to communication that happens when you focus on and limit yourself to understanding specific facts rather than the underlying idea or message.

Mindfulness means being attentive, being aware.

Monroe's Motivated Sequence is a persuasive organizational pattern that adds a third main point called visualization to the problem-solution pattern

Multiple intelligences are, different ways to demonstrate intellectual ability

Musical/Rhythmic channel is learning by listening to sounds, rhythms, and patterns.

Narratives are short stories or extended examples

Neutral audience types are on the fence; they have mixed feelings about your credibility or your topic.

Noise is a barrier to communication

Nonverbal competence is a communicator's being able to notice nonverbal subtleties in others' messages and "read between the lines

Nonverbal messages are everything but the words

Objectivity is a criteria for evaluating evidence that involves the extent to which the evidence presented displays bias

Observations are based on concrete information that can be seen and/or heard.

Opinion is a belief that someone holds without complete proof or positive knowledge that it is correct

Opposed audience types are in opposition to your proposal and/or is in mild disagreement with you.

Oral communication skills are a set of abilities enabling individuals to become confident and competent speakers by the time they graduate.

Orientation is part of a speech introduction and consists of relevance, context, and credibility.

Outcome measure is the evaluation of the results of a plan, process, action, or program

Pace is the rate or tempo at which you speak

Paralanguage is vocal features that accompany speech, such as projection and pitch

Pathos is when you use psychological appeals to arouse feelings in the audience

Pauses are using silence instead of filler words, un-words, or filler phrases

Perception is to become more aware of through the senses.

Perceptual competence is the ability to effectively gather and utilize information about the social world

Perceptual language is when a speaker uses words to indicate how he is observing or interpreting a situation, event, person, place, or idea.

Perceptual noise is a barrier to communication that occurs when you feel the person is talking too fast, not fluently, is low in status, is unattractive, or does not articulate clearly.

Personal experience is a type of example that presents your ideas in humans terms and provides real-life perspective

Personal pronouns are powerful words such as the singular and plural "you" and "we" that can add significant power to your speech

Persuasion is a thoughtful act of attempting to change, influence, or reinforce thinking, beliefs, attitudes, intentions, motivations, behaviors, or actions

Persuasive plan is the detailed formulation of your motivational strategy.

Phonology is the study of the sound system of language, including how words are pronounced

Physical dimension includes the lighting, temperature, and arrangement of chairs, decor, and the degree of natural light in the room.

Physical effects of speech anxiety are what the body does in reaction to stress symptoms.

Physical needs in Maslow's Hierarchy of Needs include the most biological, instinctive, and intrinsic needs that are vital to survival.

Physical noise is a barrier to communication that occurs when your body is calling for you to attend to it instead of the message or speaker, often due to hunger, stress, illness, sleep deprivation, or excessive anxiety.

Physical touch is a power vehicle of love language nonverbal expression and includes hugs, holding hands, massages, or sex.

Pitch is the rate of vibration of the vocal folds

Pithy language refers to words that are precisely meaningful, forceful, and brief

Place is an area with definite or indefinite boundaries, or a portion of space.

Plagiarism is representing the work of someone else as your own

Platform movements are movements that a speaker makes that involve the entire body

Point of View is the ability to view phenomena by different points of view in the search for understanding

Polished is part of the PREP Model and means to be refined, cultured, and graceful.

Possibility language cultivates imagination and communicates that anything is possible

Pragmatics is the study of the practical use of language.

Prejudice is a negative attitude toward a cultural group based on little experience

Preview is a part of the introduction and lists each main point in sequential order at the end of the introduction.

Primacy-recent effect is a cognitive bias that results in a listener to most effectively recall primary information or the most recent information

Primary strategy is the persuasive appeal that you will use more than the others based on your audience analysis

Principle of Balance is an organizational principle that means that the three major parts of the speech (Introduction, Body, and Conclusion) should be in proportion to each other

Principle of Coherence is an organizational principle means that the relationships among the three main points of a speech should be logical and clear to the audience

Principle of Emphasis is an organizational principle means that in persuasion, the most important ideas should be stressed

Principle of Unity is an organizational principle means that everything you include in your speech should relate to the proposition

Pro/con pattern is a method of informative speech organization that presents both sides of an issue

Probing feedback is attempting to gain additional information or clarify a point the speaker has made by asking a question at the end of the speech

Problem/cause/solution pattern is a persuasive organizational pattern that extends the problem/solution pattern by adding a main point on what causes the problem to occur

Problem/solution pattern is a persuasive organizational pattern that argues that a widespread problem exists and then proves that a particular solution will solve the problem

Professional is exhibiting the standing, practice, character, spirit, or methods of a professional, as distinguished from an amateur.

Proposition is the desired effect you want to achieve, the action you want your audience to take, your proposal or assertion, the change you hope to create, or the outcome of your speech

PRPSA is a survey developed by James McCroskey (1970) that focuses on accessing public speaking anxiety

Psychological effects of speech anxiety are what the mind does in reaction to stress.

Qualitative Speech Self-Assessments are comprised of subjective, reflective, open-ended questions that encourage greater in-depth analysis and more comprehensive levels of introspection.

Quality time is a love language that consists of giving someone your undivided attention.

Quantitative Speech Self-Assessments are methodical self-evaluation tools that produce results that can be expressed as numerical data, statistics, or as an objective quantity that can be numerically measured or analyzed.

Reasoning is the ability to infer a conclusion by examining relationships among data.

Reasoning is the process of drawing inferences or conclusions from evidence

Reasons pattern is a persuasive framework that explains either the three reasons to justify why you should support the proposition, or the three reasons to refute why the audience should not be against your proposal

Receiver is the listener, the recipient of the message.

Receiving gifts is a love language symbol, something you can hold in your hand, that does not necessarily cost money.

Receptive is part of the PREP Model and is being open and positive

Recipient phenomenon phenomena is the belief that in order for communication to have occurred, the message must be received

References are a list of your sources at the end of your speech or outline.

Regulators are gestures that regulate the flow of a conversation

Relational channel is learning by relating to and understanding self and others

Relational satisfaction is how content you are in your relationships.

Relevance is a component of orientation that shows your intended audience how your speech relates to them

Repetition is the act of repeating key phrases or words for dramatic effect or to add emphasis

Reputation is what your audience knows about what you know about your topic.

Review is the first component of the conclusion that recaps each main points

Rhetoric is the art of persuasive speaking or the use of persuasive language

Rhetorical appeals are the persuasive strategies or proofs of ethos, pathos, and logos

Rhetorical questions are questions that invite the audience to pause and reflect without the expectation of a response

Rhythm is the pattern of the sounds you produce

Second level of editorial review is when your evidence has been verified by a scholarly or highly reputable published source

Security needs in Maslow's Hierarchy of Needs are also known as safety needs and include our need to feel safe and secure.

Self-actualization is the summit of Maslow's motivation theory

Self-esteem is having a favorable opinion of yourself

Self-knowledge describes the information that an individual draws upon when finding an answer to the question "What am I like?"

Self-monitoring is the ability and desire to regulate and control communication in public so that others will perceive you in a favorable manner

Self-reflection is the capability that we have to exercise introspection.

Self-reflection is the capacity that we have to exercise introspection and the willingness to learn more about ourselves

Self-talk is a cognitive, inner-directed filter or inner speech.

Semantic noise occurs when a word is used differently than you prefer and may cause you to focus on the word and not the entire message.

Semantic reactions are associations that people have toward particular words.

Semantics is the study of the meaning of specific words and phrases and how words and phrases communicate the meaning we are trying to get across.

Sender is the speaker, the originator or creator of the message

Sender phenomenon is the belief that if the sender attempted to send the message, it is communication

Sensory register is an aspect of memory that is associated with your five senses: visual, auditory, kinesthetic, tactile, and olfactory.

Short-term memory is memory that involves recall of information for a relatively short time.

Simple language is being modest or free from vanity

Situational dimension deals with audience size, audience demographics, or the occasion of your speech.

Situational profile is a type of audience analysis that analyzes the surroundings of your speech or the context, including your audience and the room

Social learning theory is a theory proposed by psychologist Albert Bandura that focuses on the learning that occurs within a social context.

Social-psychological dimension can include personality characteristics and social factors like status, relationships, power, formality, friendliness, or competitiveness.

Spatial pattern is a method of informative speech organization in which the main points follow a directional pattern

Specific purpose illuminates the mission of your speech and provides it with focus

Speech anxiety is a fear of speech-giving that manifests with physical, emotional, and psychological effects.

Speech is the faculty or act of expressing or describing thoughts, feelings, and perceptions by the articulation of words. Speech refers to the actual grammar, the spoken utterance, the pronunciation of sounds

Stereotypes are widely held beliefs about a group of people

Sub-points are examples used to develop the main points of a speech

Supportive feedback is when you attempt to bolster or enlarge the speaker by fully attending to the speech as it is being given, providing authentic praise after the speech

Syllogism is when one or more major premises, one or more minor premises, and a conclusion are all stated

Syntactics is the study of the structure of language, the rules for combining words into meaningful sentences

Tactile/Kinesthetic channel is learning by doing, moving, and touching.

Talking is delivering or expressing in speech to exchange ideas via the spoken word

Target audience is the segment of your audience that you most want to influence and that you should target your persuasive appeals toward

Teleprompter is an electronic device that, unseen by the audience, scrolls a prepared speech line by line as a prompting aid to the speaker

Temporal dimension has to do with where a particular message fits into a time sequence

Thought-speech differential means we can process and understand and process about 400 to 600 words a minute, yet people only speak at a rate of 150 to 250 words a minute.

Topical pattern is a method of informative speech organization in which the main points divide the topic into logical and consistent sub-topics

Traditional paper speech notes use a keyword outline or note cards as a guide

Transaction Model is a nonlinear model of communication that views communication as dynamic and continuous

Two-part transitions are between each of your main points and tell your audience where you have been and where you are going.

Understated style communicators discourages emotional displays and values restraint and simplicity

Uninformed audience types does not have enough knowledge about your credibility or your topic to make a determination.

Verbal competence is a communicator's skill in using language effectively

Verbal messages are spoken and/or written words

Video file is a collection of video stream data stored in one unit or file.

Visual aids are objects, charts/graphs, computer-generated materials, or audio/visual clips that enhance your speech visually

Visual/Spatial channel is learning through seeing

Visualization is an attention-getting technique that paints a picture of something in the minds of audience members, and is also a step in Monroe's Motivated Sequence

Vocal range is the measure of the breadth of pitch, the span from highest notes to the lowest notes

Voice projection is the strength of speaking whereby the voice is used with volume and with power

Walk and plant is a delivery method when you deliberately walk two to four steps to your left or right, and then pause and stop

Words of affirmation is a love language that consists of verbal compliments or words of appreciation.